THE HARMS OF WORK

Studies in Social Harm

Series editors: Christina Pantazis, University of Bristol, UK
Simon Pemberton, University of Birmingham, UK
Steve Tombs, The Open University, UK

Environmental harm: An eco-justice perspective
by Rob White (2013)

Harmful societies: Understanding social harm
by Simon Pemberton (2015)

Labour exploitation and work-based harm
by Sam Scott (2017)

A sociology of harm
by Lynne Copson (2019)

*Global kitchens and super highways: Social harm and the
political economy of food*
by Reece Walters (2019)

Pharmaceuticals and social harm
by Sarah Payne (2019)

Deviant leisure and social harm
by Oliver Smith and Thomas Raymen (2019)

New perspectives on Islamophobia and social harm
by Chris Allen (2020)

See more at
https://policy.bristoluniversitypress.co.uk/studies-in-social-harm

THE HARMS OF WORK

An ultra-realist account of the service economy

Anthony Lloyd

First published in Great Britain in 2019 by

Bristol University Press
1-9 Old Park Hill
Bristol
BS2 8BB
UK
t: +44 (0)117 954 5940
www.bristoluniversitypress.co.uk

North America office:
Bristol University Press
c/o The University of Chicago Press
1427 East 60th Street
Chicago, IL 60637, USA
t: +1 773 702 7700
f: +1 773-702-9756
sales@press.uchicago.edu
www.press.uchicago.edu

British Library Cataloguing in Publication Data
A catalogue record for this book is available from the British Library

Library of Congress Cataloging-in-Publication Data
A catalog record for this book has been requested

ISBN 978-1-5292-0403-2 paperback
ISBN 978-1-5292-0401-8 hardcover
ISBN 978-1-5292-0404-9 ePub
ISBN 978-1-5292-0405-6 Mobi
ISBN 978-1-5292-0402-5 ePDF

Contents

About the author

Anthony Lloyd is Senior Lecturer in Criminology and Sociology at Teesside University. His research has investigated reconfigured labour markets under neoliberal global capital and has thus far focused on call centres and the service economy. The connection between the workplace, subjectivity and the fields of critical criminology and social harm form the basis for his current research. His first research monograph, *Labour Markets and Identity on the Post-Industrial Assembly Line* was published in 2013 by Ashgate.

Acknowledgements

In writing this book, I have again recognised the truth that books may contain a single author's name but are in fact the result of a much wider number of influences. Colleagues at Teesside University and within the Teesside Centre for Realist Criminology deserve special mention for their support, advice and discussions over the years. Avi Boukli and Justin Kotzé invited me to contribute a chapter to their edited collection *Zemiology: Reconnecting Crime and Social Harm* that forced me to think carefully about the connections between social harm and the workplace so I thank them for that. Jo Large, Alex Hall, Mark Horsley, Louise Wattis, Victoria Bell, Pauline Ramshaw, Rob MacDonald, Georgios Papanicolaou and Georgios Antonopoulos have provided ideas, inspiration and support for which I am extremely grateful. Colleagues beyond Teesside University are too numerous to mention but your work and determination to make sense of what is going on in our communities continuously motivates me to be better at what I do.

My largest academic debt is reserved for Simon Winlow, Steve Hall and Philip Whitehead. Their impact upon my personal, professional and intellectual development is immeasurable and their support has been unwavering. Their contribution to this book through discussion of ideas, moral support, and generously reading through proposals or drafts has helped shape my thinking and writing considerably and has never been taken for granted or gone unnoticed. Of course, the errors are my own.

A big thank-you must go to everyone who gave up their time to speak with me. Their words provide the heart and emotional context to my academic argument and without them this book would be impossible. I sincerely wish the best for each of you in the future. I would also like to thank Bristol University Press and the Studies in Social Harm series for providing this work with a home. The support and advice from Rebecca Tomlinson, Victoria Pittman and Laura Greaves have been particularly important and appreciated.

Finally, Nietzsche said 'if you wish to strive for peace of soul and happiness, then believe; if you wish to be a disciple of truth, then inquire'. In my commitment to inquiry I incur considerable debts to my family who put up with a lot. My love and thanks go to Gabriel, Elizabeth and Briony for taking me on and to my Joey for everything.

Foreword

The book series Studies in Social Harm seeks to advance the disciplinary agenda of zemiology by encouraging innovative approaches that can produce accurate and systematic analyses of injury in late capitalist societies. It encourages theoretical and methodological approaches that seek to build a more sophisticated picture of the lived reality of injury, focusing for example on the interrelated nature of harm, its social patterning, and how harms accumulate across the life course from the 'cradle to the grave'. One of the principal motivations driving this work is to foreground structural harms within social science analysis, to understand the varied ways that the organisation of societies serves to injuriously compromise human flourishing.

In this, the latest contribution to the series, a further aspect of harm production in contemporary capitalist societies is explored, this time in relation to the shifting nature of the labour market. Over the last 65 years, the UK like many wealthy industrialised nations has seen a marked shift from the manufacturing to the services sector. In the UK, this has been more dramatic than many G7 countries with the service industry now constituting approximately 80% of economic output, with more than four of every five UK jobs being an occupation with a service focus. The sector provides goods and services that have an impact on many aspects of our lives ranging from our financial security, health and well-being through to leisure and consumption. However, following the Sports Direct and Amazon scandals in 2016, which revealed workers to be employed on zero-hour contracts, paid under the minimum wage, undertaking 55-hour working weeks and working under severe surveillance and disciplinary regimens, the sector came to be questioned in political and policy debates. Indeed the very practices that appear to ensure savings and convenience demanded by the consumer (as well as the profits required by the shareholders), inflict untold injury on the workers in this sector.

Anthony Lloyd's *The Harms of Work* meticulously documents the lived experience of the service sector through a detailed ethnographic study of the service sector in the North East of England, that draws on the testimonies of both low-paid workers and their line managers across call centres, shops and retail, fast-food establishments, bars, pubs, takeaways, restaurants, and shopping centres. Through this data, Lloyd is ideally placed to importantly map the injurious practices that take place in these settings, but the text also makes a broader contribution to the social harm literature, in respect of three significant points.

First, much of the academic effort expended on the social harm approach to date has focused on the definition of harm, and in particular the boundaries of the concept. Various approaches have been pursued to define harm, but ultimately they result in the adoption of broad categories. In studies, empirical instances of injury have come to be mapped onto these harm categories. This can often result in fairly static approaches to the documentation of the lived experience of harm. Lloyd's analysis demonstrates the interconnected and related nature of harm – harm is layered, multi-dimensional and the interplay of combined harm produces further harm. For many of the low-paid workers, whose testimonies constitute the empirical basis of the book, the harmful states of insecurity, powerlessness and alienation coalesce to stunt flourishing in numerous ways. Ultimately, the lived experience of harm is dynamic and Lloyd offers us a way into understanding the realities of harm as a fluid phenomenon.

Second, the emerging work on social harm tends to ground explanations of harm production within a political economy approach. However, the emphasis within these aetiological frames tends to be on the macro at the expense of understanding the role of agency within the production of capitalist harms. Lloyd skilfully combines recent work in ultra-realist criminology and, drawing on the ontological tools offered by Žižek and the transcendental materialist subject, a framework is offered that grounds motivation and opportunity within the depth structures of ideology and political economy of capitalist society. Through the empirical analysis offered in the book, a persuasive case is made that locates harm production within the repertoires and practices of individuals (for example, line managers) that are shaped by the dominant cultural imperatives towards individualism, competition and status, signifiers of the deep structures of neoliberal capitalism. Lloyd prompts questions of the aetiological frame that has emerged from the social harm literature and arguably offers a means to fill this lacuna that warrants consideration.

Third, as the disciplinary agenda of zemiology evolves, a distinguishing feature of this approach seeks to connect specific harms to the features of social organisation from which injuries arise. *The Harms of Work*, offers a quintessential social harm analysis, insofar as it does not simply descriptively map the injuries of the service sector, but systematically connects these to the practices of the sector. Through the analytical excavation of such practices, we are able to begin to ask more uncomfortable, yet critical, questions in relation to the interests that are invested in these social arrangements. Put more simply, who stands to benefit from the continued production of these harms? The asymmetry of harm production within contemporary societies, means that many of us who benefit from the arrangements that Lloyd describes fail instinctively to connect the low cost or convenience of these goods and services to the injuries that are documented in this book. More social harm analyses are required like this one, that articulate these connections and prompt a collective sense of responsibility for these harms, and ultimately calls to address these injurious practices.

Christina Pantazis, Centre for the Study of Poverty and Social Justice,
School for Policy Studies, University of Bristol
Simon Pemberton, School of Social Policy, University of Birmingham
Steve Tombs, Faculty of Arts & Social Sciences, The Open University
September 2018

Introduction

As the media spotlight on Sports Direct grew more intense, its owner, Mike Ashley, played the pantomime villain. His brand targeted bargain sportswear at the lower end of the consumer market. He was notoriously media-averse. As the owner of Newcastle United Football Club, he had recently been embroiled in controversy over the decision to rename its stadium after his company. Plans were abandoned after considerable pressure from supporters, horrified at the cynical commercialism. Now conditions at his Shirebrook distribution centre were under scrutiny. Undercover reporters characterised it as the 'gulag' (Goodley and Ashby, 2015). Security and surveillance of workers included: finger-print scans to enter the building and searches by security personnel; public address systems implored harried workers to speed up and work faster; 'crimes' against the company included excessive toilet breaks and were punishable by a 'six strikes and you're out' system; agency workers employed on zero-hour contracts; compulsory security searches forcing workers to remain behind at the end of a shift, unpaid, for up to 15 minutes; minimum wage for hard, physical labour in often oppressive conditions; pressure to perform under fear of dismissal; 'estimated finishing times' for tasks echoing the scientific management of industrial labour; the routine use of performance management (Goodley and Ashby, 2015; Hutchison, 2016).

After the initial furore came the legal battle. The trade union Unite challenged employment practices at Sports Direct, particularly the insistence on compulsory staff searches before employees could leave. This unpaid extension to the working day pulled employees below the minimum wage, in contravention of government legislation, and indicated an alarming lack of trust between employer and employee. Ashley fulfilled his role as the villain of the piece and demanded MPs visit him rather than appear before a House of Commons Select Committee, as summoned. As he attacked press and politicians for unfair publicity, he acknowledged some problems within his organisation but insisted intransigent unions, not his own management, were at fault. Unite eventually forced Sports Direct to reimburse workers affected by security measures.

Ashley reorganised his senior management team and acknowledged failures at management level. His belligerence in the face of government scrutiny and union pressure continued until a report by the House of Commons Business Select Committee reported 'Victorian' working conditions at Sports Direct (Armstrong, 2016a) which raised questions from shareholders as well as parliament. In November 2016, a surprise inspection by the Select Committee ended with a clumsy attempt to bug the committee members during their complimentary lunch (Armstrong, 2016b). A 2017 report into executive pay indicated a chief executive-to-average-employee pay ratio of 400:1, something denounced as 'fake news' by the company who insisted the true ratio was closer to 9:1 (BBC, 2017).

Sports Direct and Mike Ashley had become synonymous with brutal working conditions, zero-hour contracts, and insecure agency work. The company eventually admitted it failed to pay the minimum wage and promised to scrap zero-hour contracts and the 'six strikes' policy. Then reports that other sectors utilised the 'Sports Direct model' emerged, including the use of zero-hour and temporary contracts within the university sector (Chakrabortty and Weale, 2016). This is the crucial point and central to the argument presented within these pages. Sports Direct does not represent an anomaly, a single rogue operator in an otherwise unproblematic labour market. The practices at Sports Direct reflect the *normal functioning of the service economy in late modern capitalism*. Furthermore, the practices within the service economy raise questions about direct and indirect harms to its employees.

Service economy

Western capitalist states, primarily the UK and the US, have enacted significant labour market restructure over the last four decades (Harvey, 2005; Lloyd, 2013; Streeck, 2016). Deindustrialisation, financial liberalisation, and marketisation precipitated a shift from production and manufacturing in favour of consumer markets and services. Job security, previously backed by healthy trade unions, suffered as repeated government adjustment to employment legislation favoured job flexibility. Western economies today rely, to a considerable degree, on providing and servicing outlets for consumer spending (Winlow and Hall, 2013). The composition of labour markets reflects this.

The UK employment figures for spring 2018 (ONS, 2018) showed approximately 75% of working age adults in employment, 4% unemployed and 21% economically inactive. Public sector employment was at its lowest level since 1999, down to 16.6%. The 'services industries' reflect a broad range of occupations, not all of which are pertinent to this study. However, this is illustrative of the trend in labour market composition at the heart of this book. As of April 2018, the proportion of jobs accounted for by the service sector increased to 83.3%, whereas manufacturing, mining and quarrying fell to 7.8%

(ONS, 2018). More than four of every five jobs in the UK can be characterised as an occupation with a service focus.

The US data broadly reflects a similar pattern (Bureau of Labor Statistics, 2018). Around 4% of the labour force is unemployed, approximately 6.6 million people. In terms of labour market composition, services dominate. The broadest employment category in US labour market statistics is 'non-farm jobs'; this includes service work but does not count certain occupations such as government employees, those employed in private households, non-profit organisations or farm work. As of December 2017, fewer than 145 million were in employment in non-farm occupations (Bureau of Labor Statistics, 2018). Twenty-five million were employed in manufacturing and almost 30 million in construction, whereas 91 million were employed in 'private service-providing' occupations. As with the UK, the US service sector is a problematically broad category, and comprises retail trade, transportation and warehousing, publishing, finance and insurance, real estate, commercial banking, advertising, and business support services. However, the shift from production and manufacturing to service and customer-facing functions is clear, despite recent trends through 2017 that indicated a drop in service work and a rise in manufacturing and construction (Bureau of Labor Statistics, 2018).

We live in a service economy. When we do our food shopping, we rely on the efficient transportation and distribution of goods to the supermarket, shelf-stackers to display the goods, cashiers to process our sale. When we relax at the end of the week with a drink after work, we rely on the same distribution networks to ensure the pub or wine bar is fully stocked. We rely on cleaners to make our destination fresh and welcoming. We rely on bar staff to provide us with drinks, on security teams to ensure we can enjoy our evening in peace. When we buy a new smartphone, we rely on delivery drivers to bring our online purchase to the door. When something goes wrong, we rely on call centre operatives to fix it immediately. When we go on holiday, we rely on taxi and train drivers to get us to the airport, personnel to check us in, flight attendants to cater to our needs, hotel staff to make our holiday experience pass without incident or complaint. As consumers in a consumer society, we navigate the circuits of commodified leisure with a particular set of culturally prescribed expectations. The employees within the service economy lubricate this journey. Without them, our consumer lives simply would not function, our attempts to satiate consumer desires would be thwarted.

Low economic growth characterises post-crash neoliberalism and has implications for wage levels, underemployment and the heavy reliance on the low-paid sectors of the labour market to generate employment opportunities (Streeck, 2016). In light of the sheer size and number of service economy jobs in advanced Western capitalist nations, it is imperative to examine the conditions of employment. As an indication of its size and importance, the service economy is a significant area of interest among social scientists (see Leidner, 1993; Taylor and Bain, 1999; Sherman, 2007; Warhurst and Nickson, 2007; McDowell, 2009; Gould, 2010; Korcyznski and Evans, 2013; Woodcock, 2016). Most studies identify problematic facets of service work: employment relations, particularly with regards to job security and levels of remuneration; the employment of cognitive skill within the labour process; bullying at work; lack of control and autonomy; problematic customer encounters. The assemblage of sociological literature on workplace relations paints a predominantly negative picture, often redeemed only by relations with co-workers or a belief that this job, this life, is temporary. Despite the accumulation of negative portrayals, sociology has yet to adequately connect the service economy with the emergent field of social harm or zemiology.

Harm and ultra-realist criminology

In light of considerable evidence which accentuates problematic aspects of service work, it becomes apposite to find a coherent explanation for the complexion of employment relations, working conditions, and the relationship between employer, employee and customer. Much of the sociological literature focuses on the nature of employment relations or the mechanics of labour process but often rarely considers the integration of macro-level political economy and ideology with meso-level organisational culture and micro-level individual experiences (Lloyd, 2013). This book attempts to rectify this absence with a theoretical framework that builds on a critical realist tradition, which examines these tripartite considerations, and a social harm perspective that locates a continuum of legal and illegal yet entirely harmful practices within the context of political economy.

An ultra-realist harm perspective mapped onto the service economy links the 'depth structures' of ideology and political economy (see Collier, 1994; also Tombs and Hillyard, 2004; Hall and Winlow, 2015) with management imperatives and the attendant shift in workplace or organisational culture. Studying the impact of these pressures on the individual subject engaged within such working cultures allows the sociologist to connect daily experience with a theoretical consideration of how the world works. In doing so, ultra-realism provides a context to frame the structural, cultural, and subjective practices which shape working life in Western neoliberal economies (Winlow and Hall, 2016). The connection between individual behaviour, organisational practice and the depth structures of neoliberalism and capitalism leads to the emergence of direct and indirect social harms within the service economy which demands investigation. As Scott (2017) suggests, work-based harm and labour exploitation flourish under capitalist social relations.

Workers are exploited, underpaid, mistreated, and left to negotiate a precarious existence. Surely this is tantamount to a set of harmful arrangements? The theoretical strand of this book aims to provide solid ground to interpret the normal working conditions of the service economy as harmful. Social harm or zemiology has emerged as a profitable avenue of critical theoretical exploration (see Pemberton, 2016; Hillyard and Tombs, 2017). It contends that the normal functions of capitalist political economy generate practices that fall on either side of the legal divide yet both have harmful consequences for communities, individuals and society more broadly. By approaching social harm from an ultra-realist perspective, the negative motivation to harm accounts for the systemic violence of capitalist political economy while the positive motivation to harm fills a crucial gap that elucidates the subject's willingness to inflict harm on others. Society's depth structures of political economy and ideology, tied to subjectivity, *create the conditions within which harms occur*. Political economic change over recent decades has fundamentally reoriented labour markets in favour of flexibility rather than security and stripped employees of protection; from a harm perspective this entirely legal practice has damaging consequences for the individual. Meanwhile, the organisational restructure around profit and targets generates a workplace culture that disavows ethics or moral responsibilities in favour of the bottom line and creates conditions within which competitive co-workers and managers willingly inflict entirely legal harms on each other.

The theoretical framework outlined within these pages puts the service economy and its routine functions, relationships between employers and employees, customer interactions and underlying principles within the context of harm and motivation. To do so requires not only an appreciation of political economy and ideology but also a coherent theory of the subject and motivation. The ultra-realist account of transcendental materialism places structure and agency within dialectical tension. Causative absences within our society are as important as the things we can identify. The absence of graduate labour market opportunities, for example, within specific local contexts has a causative effect on decisions made by new graduates; to accept non-graduate employment, to remain in higher education, to move away. While not necessarily harmful, this example demonstrates the causative role of absence.

We must also ask the question, *harm from what?* The answer to this is a sense of recognition secured by a set of positive rights that promotes human flourishing. The negative ideology of consumer capitalism affects the psyche of the human subject, denies recognition and prevents individual flourishing; the subject is tied libidinally to a system which extracts energy in the form of competitive individualism and tied materially to a system which exploits labour and fosters indeterminacy. To elucidate the complex interplay between capitalist political economy, institutional arrangements within organisations in competitive markets, and individuals who seek meaning and survival within the dominant culture of consumer capitalism and its available labour market opportunities, this book will highlight the *reality* of life in the service economy. This will open up space to discuss realistic ways forward.

Teesside

The data presented within these pages represents a long-term ethnographic study of the service economy of Teesside, in the North-East of England (see Lloyd, 2012, 2013, 2017, 2018). 'Teesside' denotes a large conurbation situated along the River Tees. The local authorities of Redcar & Cleveland, Middlesbrough, Hartlepool, and Stockton-on-Tees (plus Darlington) service a population of over 650,000 and act as the popular boundaries of Teesside and the Tees Valley. Comprising large towns such as Middlesbrough (population 135,000), small seaside resorts, upwardly mobile villages, and areas of severe deprivation, Teesside is a diverse area shaped and moulded by its geographic location and natural resources (see Lloyd, 2013 for a detailed exposition).

The discovery of iron ore beneath the Cleveland Hills in the mid-19th century and the strategic access point to the North Sea via the River Tees appealed to industrialists who located factories and plants along the banks of the river. The workers to create their product followed (Beynon et al, 1994). A population explosion transformed the area from an agricultural base to a bustling centre of industry (Lillie, 1968). Industrial expansion outstripped local amenities while working conditions created hardships of their own (Bell, 1985). Conditions may have been hard but Teesside's emergent economy boosted the Empire;

Teesside steel was exported around the world and played no small part in the prosperity of the nation.

Following 1945, the 'post-war settlement' and state-managed industrial policy ring-fenced iron, steel and petrochemical industries on Teesside, which further bolstered the local economy (Beynon et al, 1994). By the mid-1960s, Cleveland (the local authority) boasted the fourth highest GDP in the country (Lloyd, 2013). The labour market was narrow, focused almost entirely on steel and chemicals but jobs were plentiful and a reasonable standard of living emerged. The shocks of neoliberalism and deindustrialisation eviscerated Teesside's economy; no longer protected from international competition or the private sector, one third of all jobs on Teesside vanished in the last quarter of the 20th century (Lloyd, 2013). The social problems that accompanied deindustrialisation (Charlesworth, 2000; Winlow, 2001) were in evidence on Teesside throughout the 1990s and first decades of the 21st century (Webster et al, 2004; MacDonald and Marsh, 2005; Shildrick et al, 2012). Crime, prostitution, drug dependency, juvenile delinquency, low educational achievement, high unemployment, illness, and high levels of mental ill health are all evident on Teesside, making it an exemplar of the effects of political economic change and labour market restructure (Lloyd, 2013). Between 1971 and 2008, 100,000 jobs in manufacturing and production disappeared, replaced by 92,000 jobs in the service industries (Shildrick et al, 2012). In the forgotten areas of almost permanent recession, inward investment is often unreliable and work opportunities congregate at the lower end of the labour market.

This is representative of change across the labour markets of Western capitalist nations. As the statistics outlined earlier, labour markets are increasingly oriented around service occupations while industry and manufacturing declines, often outsourced and relocated to areas of the global South and East where costs are lower (Streeck, 2016). These issues are not unique to Teesside, although each location will have the imprint of local variation. Deindustrialisation and the shift to a knowledge economy hampered by the post-crash reality of austerity cuts are visible across many areas of the UK, Europe and the US (Stuckler and Basu, 2013; Hochschild, 2016; Vance, 2016). Interdependent economies are marked by imbalances of surpluses and deficits, often experienced spatially. Areas of permanent recession are spaces of deficit frequently left out when the music stops (Varoufakis, 2016). In the face of economic restructure and the dominance of the service economy in the UK and elsewhere, this study asks what working conditions are like in these dominant forms of employment.

As consumers, our daily navigation of the service economy is often unproblematic. What is it like to work in the service economy? What are the characteristics of service economy jobs? What are the conditions of employment? How do service jobs fit with employees' plans for their future? What opportunities exist in local labour markets largely typified by service work?

These questions form the basis of this study and I suggest that Teesside can serve as an exemplar of the geographic impact of political economic change, labour market restructure, and employee experience (Lloyd, 2013). Despite its regional variations, Teesside faces many of the same issues as any number of locales across the UK, Europe and the US; low growth, a dominant service sector, marginal graduate labour market, multiple social problems, underinvestment. My previous studies of Teesside's service economy focused on a single site, a call centre (Lloyd, 2012, 2013, 2017). The conclusions from that study spawned a new set of questions that broadened the scope of study to ascertain whether the call centre experience is unique or reflective of the imperatives of service work more generally. This expanded study has involved observations of workplaces within Teesside's service economy over a number of years as well as semi-structured interviews with employees engaged in a number of forms of service work.

As noted earlier, service work reflects a broad category of occupations. For the purposes of this study, I have focused on occupations with a customer focus and those forms of employment that facilitate engagement within circuits of consumer capitalism. Smith and Raymen's (2016) 'deviant leisure' perspective notes commodified leisure activities embedded within the circuits of consumer capital, entirely legal yet generators of significant harms: the night-time economy, gambling, shopping (particularly Black Friday and other Hobbesian consumer spectacles) and tourism. This study focuses on the workers engaged in occupations which service those forms of leisure and consumerism. The data presented here reflects my observations of call centres, shops and retail, fast-food establishments, bars, pubs, takeaways, restaurants and shopping centres. This is supplemented with semi-structured interviews conducted with employees in many of these forms of employment. Over 30 interviews have been conducted with call centre workers, retail employees, delivery drivers, takeaway workers, fast-food employees, and bar staff to gain insight into their working lives, the conditions under which they labour, and their thoughts on work and life opportunities in a labour market characterised by low-paid, insecure, forms of 'flexible labour'.

Structure of the book

The opening chapters are necessarily expositive. Chapter One sets out the requirement for a reinterpretation of social harm. This chapter offers an overview of the key literature on harm before synthesising the valuable aspects of social harm with an ultra-realist framework that accounts for motivation. This theoretical approach accounts for the systemic harms of capitalism and the subjective harms of individuals willing to damage others in order to advance by presenting both the negative and positive motivation to harm. Finally, this chapter contemplates the causative impact of absences and their impact on individuals, workplaces and communities.

Chapter Two begins to consider the theoretical schema laid out in Chapter One and identifies labour market restructure under the neoliberal dispensation. The logic of market freedom, productivity and efficiency, under the control of globalised financial capital, engendered deindustrialisation across the West and signalled a shift from production to consumption. The 2007–08 financial crisis further deepened neoliberal reform and the control of financial capital, bringing austerity, insecurity and upheaval to the high street and the individual. The emergence of the 'on-demand' or 'gig' economy reflects the latest phase of labour market restructure which fragments workers and instils competitive individualism. Within our social harm perspective, deep level restructure on this level creates absences that will impact on individuals and demonstrates the emergence of a new Symbolic Order that shapes daily reality.

Chapter Three focuses on the impact of restructure on organisational cultures based around profitability, efficiency and targets. This chapter begins the process of drawing from empirical evidence to illustrate the reality of working life within call centres, retail outlets, fast food restaurants, and other service economy occupations. Managers seek profitability and efficiency through the imposition of targets, rigid performance management and just-in-time methods of production which shape the work routines of its employees. This chapter highlights some but not all of the working practices within the service economy; those actions elucidated in Chapter Three return in the subsequent chapters as they create space in which harms can occur.

Chapter Four is the first of three chapters which draws on the ultra-realist demand to investigate absences as well as presences. These chapters will build absence upon absence and demonstrate the negative culture within which harms occur. This chapter explores the consequences of reconfigured labour markets, employment protections and opportunities in relation to the harms which materialise through the absence of job stability and the transformative power this negativity has on the workplace. The service economy is marked by instability and indeterminacy, short-term work, flexible labour, zero-hour contracts, employment agencies, instead of genuine promotion, and frequent redundancy. Finally, this chapter discusses the idea of a transition to adulthood in relation to the service economy; achieving the markers of adulthood becomes difficult when job security and stability are almost non-existent. The platform for a stable life is absent; this chapter explores the implications of this from a harm perspective.

Chapter Five offers a critical discussion of those managers and employees who take advantage of these conditions and appear willing and motivated to inflict harm on co-workers and employees. The chapter offers a critical interpretation of the instruction towards freedom which appears in material and symbolic structures and reflects cultural injunctions towards self-interest, entrepreneurial endeavour and individual achievement. Capitalism, in other words, gets the subjectivity it requires and deserves. This generates, in some, a 'special liberty' (Hall 2012a) whereby individuals believe themselves to be exempt from norms, regulatory frameworks or legal strictures and instead possess the freedom to readily inflict harm on others in pursuit of their own ambitions and goals.

Chapter Six continues the theme of absence and focuses on the absence of protection for individual employees. This absence creates conditions within which the processes that drive the sector, those of profitability and competition, generate illegal and harmful actions on the part of employers seeking a marginal advantage through exploitation. This chapter will tie together the previous discussions of organisational culture, employment protection and management practice to suggest that service economy work can be harmful to employees' physical and mental well-being where the absence of adequate protection continues to put individuals at risk.

The final substantive chapter investigates the failure to address many of the harms outlined by this book. This chapter considers the deficiency of policy makers' and social scientists' incrementalist, 'tinkering at the edges' approach to labour market conditions and employment protections. The violence of ideology reflects the failure to address the fundamental harms of capitalism in favour of piecemeal and incremental change. In some ways, it reflects another causative absence: the absence of a coherent alternative to 'capitalist realism' (Fisher, 2009). Calling on one individual to account for his or her practices at one company disavows the knowledge that the entire service economy operates in a way that is often harmful to employees yet profitable for shareholders and owners. The chapter critically challenges social science and policy makers to address the manifest plethora of harms in the service economy that can be imputed to capitalism.

We live in a consumer society. We can all recount experiences as customers and consumers of the service economy. Many of us have worked within the service economy. It plays a significant role in terms of economy, labour markets, culture and subjective experience. This book will demonstrate significant and lasting harms within the service economy but will first explore the concept of social harm and identify avenues for theoretical advancement.

ONE

Reinterpreting social harm

Introduction

Social harm has emerged as a profitable avenue for social science research (Hillyard and Tombs, 2004, 2007; Davies et al, 2014; Hall, 2015; Pemberton, 2016; Smith and Raymen, 2016). Harm perspectives arose from the limitations and frustrations of a discipline wedded to a conceptual framework, 'crime' and transgressions of criminal law that failed to recognise wider 'harms' within late capitalist society (Tombs and Hillyard, 2004). This chapter will outline the key developments within the social harm perspective. The development of an analytical lens that is able to traverse the boundaries of legality and illegality within the context of structural or systemic forces is crucial for social science. A question emerges about an ontological or philosophical platform for social harm (see Hall, 2012a) and some existing approaches do grapple with this. While Pemberton's (2007, 2016) needs-based perspective and Yar's (2012) quest for recognition have ploughed this particular furrow, this chapter will offer an ultra-realist foundation (Winlow and Hall, 2016). If social harm presents an opportunity to identify the continuum of legal and illegal practice within the context of systemic forces of capital, ultra-realism provides analysis of subjectivity, ideology and causation that can underpin a social harm perspective. This chapter attempts to synthesise the core components of ultra-realism – the transcendental materialist subject, the causative absence, and the relationship between capitalism's depth structures and the subjective motivation to act – with social harm theory and its concern with the legal and illegal systemic harms of capitalism.

Social harm: traversing the legal and illegal

Social harm invites the extension of the criminological gaze beyond the horizon of legality (Hillyard and Tombs, 2004; Pemberton, 2016). While debate continues between social harm as an extension of the criminological discipline and *zemiology* as an independent study of social harm (see Copson, 2016; Hillyard and Tombs, 2017), the concept of harm infuses key topics including environmental damage

(White and Heckenberg, 2014; Hall, 2015), workplace safety (Tombs and Whyte, 2007), leisure (Smith and Raymen, 2016) and poverty (Gordon, 2004). The limitations of crime as a conceptual category raise questions about the ability to place criminal activity and state responses in a wider context (Copson, 2013). Social harm proponents echo the Sutherland–Tappan debate (Slapper and Tombs, 1999; also Sutherland, 1940; Tappan, 1947) and attempt to move beyond the narrow strictures of 'crime' and legal frameworks; the consequences of social action become more important than its legality. This is a crucial step forward and provides a useful insight into an investigation of the service economy.

Criminology's focus on the criminal law has served to ignore a plethora of harmful activities that should fall within the purview of the discipline (Tombs and Whyte, 2011) while many petty events attract the criminological gaze (Hillyard and Tombs, 2017). To suggest that activities, intentional or otherwise, that fall beyond the parameters of criminal intent and the criminal law, can inflict great harms on individuals, communities and cultures is not controversial. The weight of evidence that points towards considerable social damage caused by deindustrialisation (Winlow, 2001; MacDonald and Marsh, 2005; Lloyd, 2013; Winlow et al, 2017) functions as a significant example: the actions of government and corporate entities sit comfortably within the boundaries of legality yet the impact on communities, individuals and families could unquestionably be considered somehow harmful.

For zemiologists, 'crime' is a social construction, a conceptual category without ontological grounding or foundation (Hillyard and Tombs, 2004). There is nothing intrinsic to any event or incident that invites the definition of 'criminal'. The sheer range and number of acknowledged crimes, along with recognition that 'criminals' do not form a distinct sub-population, leads to the conclusion that what we define as a criminal act has no ontological basis. However, Lasslett (2010) suggests that the ontological absence at the heart of 'crime' can be filled. Following Marx and Lukacs, objects take on certain concrete properties in particular historical conditions; crime becomes a concrete entity as a result of the social complex in which it is situated. Exploitative social processes engender class relations and influence specific social audiences with the power to define certain traits as criminal. The hegemonic acceptance of characteristics of social practice induces the historical development of violations and sanctions. Meanwhile, Paoli and Greenfield (2018) suggest that harm should be embedded *within* crime, rather than replace it. However, many harm proponents continue to hold firm on the belief that 'crime' is a social construction and therefore, by extension, so is the criminal. As Reiner (2016) notes, there are morally tenuous, if not arbitrary differences, between harms construed as crime and those hidden in complex chains of causality. Zemiology aims to explode these arbitrary differences in order to contextualise the continuum of legal and illegal practice driven by macro-level structural factors.

Hillyard and Tombs (2004) believe the inherent disciplinary problem is associated with the reproduction of the object of study. Criminology, driven by the desire to explore 'crime', produces and reproduces socially constructed narratives of crime and criminality. If crime has no firm basis in reality and is merely the result of social construction and organisation, then criminology's pursuit of empirical evidence of crime and societal response reinforces the belief in what zemiologists regard as faulty foundations (Ugwudike, 2015). The state's role as the arbiter of justice and punishment increasingly requires social science to provide hard evidence of patterns of crime and the efficacy of judicial and penal intervention (Copson, 2014). This in turn invites the expansion of crime control machinery (Wacquant, 2009) in response to the existence of 'crime'. In this sense, zemiology claims to move 'beyond criminology' to inoculate the discipline from its complicit status with an ontologically unsound and morally bankrupt foundation.

Hillyard and Tombs (2004) acknowledge the ontological absence at the heart of crime but also recognise the potential limitations of social harm at the conceptual level. They provide a useful framework of harm that incorporates physical harms; financial and economic harms; emotional and psychological harms; and cultural safety, what they term a lack of autonomy, development and growth as well as access to cultural, intellectual and informational resources. This provides the scope to incorporate a number of disparate events, experiences and incidents within an overarching schema. This interpretation of social harm moves us beyond intentionality and the content of a particular crime towards a holistic approach to harms across the life course, 'from the cradle to the grave', and accounts for a range of social, economic and cultural factors that may increase or decrease the likelihood of harm. Ultimately, Hillyard and Tombs suggest that harm works better than crime as the focus of analysis as it reflects the approach most likely to produce greater social justice.

This drives at the heart of zemiology: the commitment for social science to change the world, not to merely interpret it. This implicit notion of a 'good society' (Copson, 2013) provides zemiology with the political direction to seek meaningful change to the lives of those who suffer direct and indirect social harms. Achieving this vision of 'good' has proved problematic and, at times, counterproductive. Hillyard and Tombs's initial schema move us forward as it allows us to problematise entirely *legal* processes and events that can result in negative outcomes for individuals, families and communities. However, this is a broad categorisation and Garside (2013) notes that broad typologies of harm run the risk of 'flattening out' the concept. An expansive typology turns the concept of harm into a catch-all without philosophical or ontological underpinning. This is an important point to which we will turn towards ultra-realism for support.

Social harm perspectives necessarily move debate beyond the content of crime and the individual to consider the wider implications of structural and systemic violence. To do this, Tombs and Hillyard (2004) and Pemberton (2016) turn to political economy. Capitalism has always generated harm alongside wealth and innovation (Marx, 1990 [1867]). More specifically, harm theorists identify neoliberalism as an explicitly harmful political-economic model (Dorling, 2004; Tombs and Hillyard, 2004; Pemberton, 2016). The neoliberal economic paradigm features harm on a widespread level, not as an aberration but rather an integral feature of political and economic organisation. This excoriation of neoliberalism as a distinctly harmful form of political economy is a key hallmark of the social harm literature (Tombs and Hillyard, 2004; Pemberton, 2016). For example, at an analytical level, Hillyard and Tombs (2004) identify harms endemic under neoliberal capitalism in relation to the dynamics of the market, growing inequalities, and the production, distribution and consumption of goods and services.

In terms of practical examples, Hillyard and Tombs (2017) point to excess winter deaths, workplace injuries and food poisoning as a reflection of the myriad harms engendered by neoliberalism. Who is responsible for excess winter deaths among frail older people? There is an argument that culpability could be levelled at organisations or actors but ultimately such an event is an unfortunate side-effect of *entirely legal processes*. Meanwhile, Large's (2018) work on counterfeit fashion identifies a continuum of 'safety critical' and 'non-safety critical' that obfuscates the harms inherent within the production, distribution and consumption of counterfeit goods. While the harm inherent in the *consumption* of counterfeit medicine (Hall and Antonopoulos, 2016) may be obvious, the harm associated with the *production* of counterfeit fashion products may be less identifiable and therefore ignored. Both have elements of legality and illegality yet harms are present. Importantly, this forces our attention to the level of political economy.

In Pemberton's (2016) work, neoliberal capitalism is singled out as patently harmful. His work attempts to synthesise the theoretical and empirical in its investigation of *preventable harms* across a number of 'varieties of capitalism' (Hall and Soskice, 2001). The relationship between state, regulatory framework and capitalism differs across various regimes, and in this context, Pemberton collates and analyses data on physical and mental health, autonomy harms and relational harms to determine the level of harm perpetrated by different social systems and the most effective harm reduction strategies. He concludes that neoliberalism constitutes the most harmful mode of social organisation, yet harms appear embedded in all capitalist societies. Although Pemberton acknowledges this critique in his 2016 work, there is a degree of 'capitalist realism' (Fisher, 2009) to his analysis; in highlighting the 'best' and 'worst' forms of harmful capitalism, Pemberton clearly identifies differences in what Harvey (2010) calls the 'state-finance nexus' with significant implications for levels of harm, yet his analysis and critique lives within the confines of the capitalist horizon. There is no acknowledgement of 'alternatives to capitalism', merely analysis of 'varieties of capitalism' (see Garside's 2013 critique). While the journey from here to an as yet undefined future configuration of social relations may indeed be difficult or even inconceivable (see Copson, 2013), tinkering at the edges of the intrinsic harms of capital will simply not rehabilitate capitalism or alleviate the suffering generated by its benign indifference. Pemberton acknowledges the inherently harmful nature of capitalism throughout his work yet seemingly stops short, calling for reform rather than transformation.

Work-based harm

In relation to work and employment, Tombs (2004, 2007) considers the multitude of workplace injuries and deaths within a social harm framework. Historically, health and safety legislation and its subsequent enforcement have been imposed on corporations and undermined wherever possible. Tombs provides statistical detail of the Health and Safety Executive's (HSE) failure to inspect workplaces and the disparity between the numbers of recorded incidents and investigations, which range across sectors and locales. Ultimately, Tombs argues that criminal law is an important tool in workplace harm prevention but the continued incidence of harm and death in the workplace demonstrates a broader failure to afford protection and safety at work. This shortcoming constitutes clear harm to individuals, but often falls beyond the purview of criminal law and the power of regulatory agencies. While Tombs clearly outlines the disjuncture between workplace incidents and the response of the state, there is an emphasis on physical injury here but little on the psychological impact of work. This will be addressed in later chapters.

Scott (2017) also asks important questions in relation to work-based harms. Coercive and exploitative forms of abuse at work span a continuum from 'decent' work to extreme forms of slavery. What is or is not acceptable requires questions of morality or ethics which capitalism fails to address. Indeed, Scott suggests that the capitalist system is largely unable or unwilling to address issues of labour exploitation and work-based harm. Essentially, he addresses the question of control in the labour process. How are workers controlled? What are the negative outcomes of such systems of control? As with Pemberton's (2016) interpretation of harm, Scott asks the policy question which pertains to the reduction of negative outcomes. His work-based harm and labour exploitation perspective encompasses non-coercive forms of control which continue to negatively affect the employee and has been addressed in other workplace literature (Fleming and Sturdy, 2011). Ultimately, Scott travels a similar route to other harm-based theorists in that he offers a clear demonstration of the coercion, control and exploitation at the heart of capitalism yet advocates for reforms that stop at the water's edge. The solution to work-based harm should be to shift capitalism away from its neoliberal variety, evolve corporate structures to focus on the long term and common good, increase the role for trade unions, reduce inequality and protect the right to peaceful protest (see Scott, 2017, pp 232-3). An important text in its call for consideration of work-based exploitation from a harm perspective, Scott's work fails to contemplate something beyond the confines of capitalist realism (Fisher, 2009).

Appraising social harm

The strengths of a social harm perspective are clear. The suggestion that 'crime' serves as an inadequate construct, without basis in reality, affords a starting point to widen our horizons towards activity beyond the parameters of criminal law. Social harm asks us to look at social organisation and reflect on the reality that criminality is a reflection of wider social processes and structures; the 'crimes of the powerful' are minimised, ignored or dealt with via regulation while the crimes of the powerless become the bailiwick of the criminal justice system. This elevation beyond the juridical creates room for appreciation of the structural relationship between processes both *legal and illegal*; at the level of political economy, the deregulation of the financial industry creates legal frameworks that justify sub-prime mortgage lending

(Lewis, 2010), high-frequency trading (Lewis, 2014), and Goldman Sachs' decision to bet against stocks they readily sold to investors (Ferguson, 2012). US bankers' singular concern at the height of the Big Bang and beyond was 'is this legal?', not 'is this the right thing to do?' (Martin, 2017). Regulation permitted harmful behaviour that fell within entirely legal strictures. However, the same deregulation also encouraged wholly illegal practices such as the corporate fraud perpetrated by Enron and Bernie Madoff (Dumenil and Levy, 2011).

What is missing from these interpretations of harm? The key absence here is an account of subjective motivation. Much of the strength behind studies of social harm comes from its appreciation of the structural or systemic factors that contribute to the imposition of entirely legal yet dangerously harmful practices on large swathes of the population. However, there is need for a dynamic social harm perspective that accounts for subjective motivation and causation. We can identify 'top-down' causation in relation to harms against communities and individuals battered by the deleterious effects of neoliberalism but a gap exists in relation to social harm's ability to explain subjective motivation to inflict harm. As Messner and Rosenfeld (2001) indicate, the corporate raider employs daring, energy, intelligence and innovation to succeed, which sometimes results in criminal behaviour. These are not personal traits but elements of a social character rooted in broad value orientations; the values that motivate aggressive, competitive behaviour in the boardroom or trading floor are the same values which motivate aggressive, competitive and acquisitive forms of harmful behaviour on the street (see Hall et al, 2008). The search for an account of motivation may require a shift in emphasis from top-down causation and the implication that inequality causes harm. We still require a foundation that connects the systemic and structural with the subjective. However, some harm theorists have sought firm ontological foundations in order to counter Yar's (2012) prescient insight that, without a philosophical foundation, harm risks the same conceptual trouble that led zemiologists to critique crime.

Harm from what? Finding an ontological grounding

Social harm or zemiology clearly demonstrates the inadequacy of 'crime' as a conceptual framework. The wide range of harms, perpetrated under the cover of legality and along a continuum of legal and illegal practices, emerges from the macro-level imperatives of capital and neoliberal governance. Yet Hillyard and Tombs (2004) acknowledge the need for a typology of harm to focus the analytical lens while Yar

(2012) recognises the need for an ontological foundation to anchor the concept. Fortunately, some of this work has already been undertaken. This section will identify a number of attempts to ground social harm and raise questions that create space for ultra-realist support.

Pemberton (2007, 2016) suggests that social harm reflects those systemic formations which compromise human flourishing. This is a positive start as Aristotelian flourishing indicates the object of harm and directs our gaze towards harm reduction. Pemberton suggests that the compromise of human flourishing is identifiable in relation to harms against physical and mental health, autonomy, and social relations (2016, p 9). His ontological framework is derived from Doyal and Gough's (1991) theory of 'human need'. Harm is 'the relations, processes, flows, practices, discourse, actions and inactions that constitute the fabric of our societies which serve to compromise the fulfilment of human needs and in doing so result in identifiable harms' (Pemberton, 2016, p 24). The theory of human need provides a clear ontological platform; if we are to achieve a degree of self-actualisation and social participation, specific needs must be met. The impediments to human flourishing create harm in relation to physical and mental health, for example, long hours at work or limited access to a healthy diet; autonomy harms linked to a sufficient level of control and personal freedom to generate, for example, the capacity for understanding and learning in order to be able to formulate effective choices; and relational harms, which stem from enforced exclusion and social isolation as well as the harms of misrecognition. For example, Garthwaite's (2016) research on food banks clearly shows the impact of state policy on the achievement of basic human need, that is, food and sustenance, while Desmond's (2017) account of housing and eviction in the US demonstrates a similar harm as basic needs prove elusive.

The needs-based platform provided by Doyal and Gough (1991) is problematic, although Pemberton does engage with these critiques in his 2016 work. Doyal and Gough reject the idea of need as drive or motivational force but do subscribe to the belief that needs are goals and strategies for goal attainment that exist on a universal level. The distinction between wants and needs comes from the implicit understanding that a need is inscribed with an avoidance of harm and exists at a social level because that need is understandable to others (the need for food to avoid starvation – as opposed to the want of a cheeseburger). Needs and wants can coincide but ultimately a need is a goal which once attained prevents a certain harm. There are intrinsic needs at the heart of the human condition that go deeper and farther than culturally specific relative needs or want.

Doyal and Gough (1991) ultimately consider our most basic human needs to be survival and freedom. Stifling individual autonomy or personal agency is harmful to the individual. The more freedom we have, the less harmful our society will become (see Hayek, 2001; Berlin, 1969). This argument is problematic on a number of levels. For example, more individual agency, more autonomy risks opening a Pandora's Box of socially and personally harmful practices and actions *because I am free to pursue them*. Second, a theory of human need that satisfies the right to live and the freedom to pursue one's own ends, enshrined in universal human rights, echoes the 'negative' liberty guaranteeing *freedom from* rather than promoting *freedom to* (Berlin, 1969). Unless freedom is accompanied by a positive set of universal ethics to ground the individual in the social, more freedom will be interpreted in accordance with market principles and the ideological circuits of consumer capitalism. This freedom will continue to manifest as self-interest, asocial relations and competition (Hall et al, 2008; Hall, 2012a).

Ultimately, the right to minimal need–satisfaction within a group, let alone optimal need–satisfaction, rests on the belief that members of a social group regard each other as equals and therefore commit an equal amount of energy into a reciprocal moral relationship. We know from research that these reciprocal moral relationships do not exist within competitive markets underpinned by an ideology of individualism and self-interest (Winlow et al, 2015; Horsley, 2015; Ellis, 2016), primarily because the needs of capital disregard morality or duty and generate subjectivities entirely aligned to the amorality of the market. However, Pemberton's (2007) attempt to underpin a theory of harm with a broader framework of human need demonstrates a positive attempt to provide harm with ontological foundations.

Lasslett (2010) seeks to move beyond ethical assumptions around 'injustice' in order to find an ontological basis for social harm. In his critique of Pemberton's 'needs-based' approach, Lasslett suggests that Doyal and Gough present an essentialist conception of 'man'. Lasslett criticises this approach as an attempt to 'delineate the civilised conditions for social development' (2010: 12), with processes which undermine this as inherently unjust. Instead, Lasslett suggests that ontologically man is a natural being but one in which the organic properties of man are reproduced through socially generated practices. The concrete structures of social being become an essential precondition for the preservation of organic life. Harms arise when socially generated processes, for example, labour market reconfiguration, undermine the organic reproduction of man, for example, through exploitative and physically or emotionally harmful working conditions. The harm rests in an inability to achieve social development, often as a result of forces unevenly distributed across time, space and class.

Majid Yar (2012) attempts to underpin social harm with Axel Honneth's (1996) Hegelian concept of 'recognition'. Yar defines harm on multiple levels as a lack of recognition ('disrespect', for Honneth). At a macro level, our rights are either recognised or not; at the level of esteem, we are recognised (or not) through solidarity, social identity and cultural characteristics; and, interpersonally, through love of family, friends, or partners. As a nuanced and multi-axial concept, harm as the 'struggle for recognition' links a range of phenomena without 'flattening' meaning and difference in situation. Yar's (2012) attempt to provide an ontological grounding for social harm is useful. In this framework, we can see what constitutes 'harm' (lack of recognition) and it furnishes us with the ability to conceptually link various harms on multiple levels without the disappearance of nuance and variation.

Pemberton (2016) criticises Yar's framework on empirical grounds; experience of misrecognition in relation to emotional needs such as love and esteem is too subjective to be operational in an empirical framework. Meanwhile, Hall (2012a) offers a philosophical critique, namely Yar's attempt to operationalise Hegel via Honneth misses an important shift in late capitalist society. Honneth's theory of recognition relies on Hegel's master-slave dialectic; the individual comes to know oneself through the recognition bestowed willingly by another. The 'other' is required for recognition in an intersubjective reality. Hall (2012a) notes that late capitalism in its financial phase is capable of reproduction without the requirement of a massed workforce; in an economically embedded account of the master-slave dialectic, the master no longer needs the slave in order to produce and reproduce capital. The rich can – and do – live lives entirely free from encounters with the rest of society (Atkinson, 2016). However, social recognition as the starting point for a theory of harm is a vital step in the right direction.

Finally, Smith and Raymen's (2016) 'deviant leisure' is a fusion of cultural criminology and ultra-realism. It focuses on the embedded circuits of consumer capitalism, particularly within the fields of leisure, consumerism and tourism. Their investigations take place across the leisure economy including parkour, the night-time economy, shopping, and gambling (see Smith, 2014; Smith and Raymen, 2015; Raymen, 2016; Raymen and Smith, 2016; Smith and Raymen, 2016, Raymen and Smith, 2017). The cultural imperatives to partake in late night drinking, online gambling, and the atavistic shopping experiences of

Black Friday all fall within both legal parameters and normative values associated with consumer capitalism; we are compelled to engage with these activities at a deep, psychosocial level. That such behaviour can lead to significant problems, including violence, addictive behaviours, anti-social activity, and debt represents the indirect social harms associated with normative cultural activity.

As consuming subjects seek to expend the libidinal energy generated by consumer capitalism and to satisfy desire, the subject is firmly embedded within the contours of the dominant ideology and political economy of our time; our motivation to act is fuelled by consumer culture and our subjective desire drives the individual into entirely legal yet significantly problematic behaviours. The grounding behind 'deviant leisure' is the 'moral responsibility for the other' (Smith and Raymen, 2016); an absence of 'pro-social' ethics and duty which creates space for harmful behaviours in the pursuit of satisfaction, competition and status. Capitalism is not made to the measure of humanity and is devoid of an ethical component; in its ideological structures and circuits, consumer capitalism generates harmful subjectivities attuned to the competitive individualism of the market rather than a set of universal ethics or moral responsibility. Each of these concepts orientates around notions of ethics, morality and 'good'. Harm is the absence or prevention of 'good'; to compromise need–satisfaction prevents the subject from achievement of a 'good life' (Pemberton, 2016). The absence of recognition reflects the absence of an ethics or morality grounded in social practice and intersubjective relations (Yar, 2012). The absence of an ethical responsibility for the other (Smith and Raymen, 2016) demonstrates the breakdown of ethics and morality based in social function; the locus of 'good' becomes rooted in subjective feeling rather than social ties and responsibilities (MacIntyre, 2011). Without this, harm prevails. Copson's (2013, 2014, 2016) interpretation of 'utopian criminology' suggests that utopia represents an outline for a 'good' or 'better' society. The application of a utopian method requires the *archaeology* of facts, concepts and data, the *architecture* required to build a model of good, and the *ontology* of a type of people the good or better society wants or needs. However, Copson's work raises questions about the nature of subjectivity; the utopian method may identify the subjectivities required or created by a vision of the future good society but does not explain the way in which subjectivity is constituted. This opens the door to ultra-realism as an alternative conception of harm that accepts the concept of recognition and flourishing afforded by positive rights but provides a lucid account of the way in which the relationship between subject and ideology may have an impact on the realisation of these goals.

Towards an ultra-realist schema

The zemiological approach aligns with critical criminology's willingness to find theoretical schemas that explain the nature of harm and inequality in contemporary society, as opposed to an administrative criminology that seeks pragmatic solutions. While social harm theories clearly move the debate forwards, some limitations and questions remain. For the purposes of this discussion, ultra-realism presents an opportunity to explore social harm from a 'parallax' position (Žižek, 2000) and to maintain dialectical momentum. Ultimately, where social harm theorists suggest that harm is a result of widening inequality, ultra-realism argues that *inequality stems from a willingness to inflict harm on others* (Hall and Winlow, 2015).

If inequality stems from the willingness to inflict harm on others, that we allow harms to take place *because some people benefit from it*, we can contemplate an approach that considers the role of motivation. A state, a corporation and an individual are all motivated to act according to a number of different factors. Those actions have the potential to cause either direct or indirect social harm. The *willingness to act* must be the object of analysis from a harm perspective. The space created by the widening gap between rich and poor (see Dorling, 2015a; Piketty, 2014) reflects a negative motivation to harm. This generates both intentional and unintentional harms to communities and individuals. The positive motivation to harm is what Hall (2012a) terms 'special liberty', the sense of entitlement felt by the subject emboldened to act according to self-interest. To have any explanatory power, social harm must account for motivation at the macro, meso and micro level.

Ultra-realism is venturing to thrust criminological and sociological thought beyond the ascendant empiricism directing the discipline, beyond the administrative and pragmatic wings of a social science seeking efficient governance of the current political economic order, and beyond the flaws within critical realism (Hall and Winlow, 2015). Bhaskar (2010; also Collier, 1994) encourages investigation of the social world on three levels, or domains of reality: first, to establish reality through experiences; second, to explain events, those things which occur beyond experience; and third, to look for underlying mechanisms and structures that influence and shape events and experiences. It is not enough to observe the world and to explain events; one must also look for the underlying structures that shape the world. Human sciences study open systems and are thus different from natural sciences which investigate closed systems in experiments. Open systems such as society require the search for and investigation of underlying structures if we are to understand what we observe. Depth structures have causative effects on individuals and the socio-cultural logic of society (Bhaskar, 2010); empiricism furnishes evidence of what we can see, but fails to contemplate the causal influence of the intransitive realm of deep structures on the quotidian reality of individuals and communities (Winlow and Hall, 2016). In this sense, critical realism offers a positive theoretical route towards grasping the relationship between concrete events, lived experiences and the deep structures of society (Collier, 1994).

Ultra-realism delineates a way to interpret the world that accounts for the depth structures of ideology and political economy, the culture and organisation of institutions, and subjective experience. This corresponds with social harm's wide-angle lens that accounts for the plethora of direct and indirect harms associated with political economy (Tombs and Hillyard, 2004; Pemberton, 2016). In utilising this framework to formulate a harm perspective, it is useful to consider a wider continuum of violence (Žižek, 2008; Ray, 2011). Žižek's (2008) triumvirate of violence (systemic, symbolic and subjective) opens up space for the connection of social harm and ultra-realism. The removal of intent as a definitive characteristic of violence is key to Žižek's interpretation (Ray, 2011); as the social harm theorists have already shown, unintentional harms routinely inflict damage on populations.

Systemic violence reflects the structural conditions of inequality, poverty, suffering, war and a host of other factors. The *normal functioning of political economy* creates objective conditions within which significant acts of violence are dispassionately visited on specific populations, both directly and indirectly (Hillyard and Tombs, 2017). Systemic violence is often invisible; how can we clearly identify the violence of capitalism? In addressing the depth structures of the intransitive realm, those invisible and unidentifiable structures and processes beyond empirical validity, ultra-realism supplies an analytical framework for invoking the violence and harm, both direct and indirect, emanating from the dominant structures of political economy.

Within the context of systemic violence, critical realism serves a crucial purpose in acknowledging the importance of absence as a probabilistic causative effect on social reality (Hall and Winlow, 2015). Social science traditionally investigates what is present, particularly within empirical and positivist traditions. However, absences can also have probabilistic aetiological effects (Winlow and Hall, 2016).

Neoliberal restructure does not mechanically cause harm, but the systemic violence at the heart of capitalism is visible through the subsequent absences of, for example, welfare regimes that forestall material deprivation or job security that furnishes a measure of stability. This negativity omits any form of *positive* transformation in material and social conditions but still retains the transformative potential to reshape interpersonal connections and *cultures*. Change within the intransitive realm, the depth structures which underpin social and cultural configurations, can entail causative effects on the experiences of individual actors. Change within the intransitive realm can also create absences which have probabilistic causal tendencies.

Second, Žižek identifies 'symbolic violence'. Bourdieu's (1989) symbolic violence reflects the imposition of a dominant form of symbolic power (symbolic capital) on a subordinate population who are therefore trapped in a system of domination. In the context of domestic violence, the dominant party imposes a set of norms, values and modes of behaviour on the subordinate party who, powerless to resist, submits to the 'Symbolic Order' they face. Žižek expands this to mean the symbolic violence of language. Control on the limits of language, what we can and cannot articulate or make sense of, is a form of violence in itself. The lack of alternatives to what Fisher (2009) calls 'capitalist realism' is a reflection of this symbolic violence; language and ideology cannot visualise or articulate a clear and coherent alternative to the status quo, Copson's (2013) 'utopia'. This ultimately ensures the continuation of current social relations. An inability to articulate an alternative presents a form of violence and harm on those trapped in objective conditions of precarity, uncertainty and violence. The inability to articulate one's frustration in a coherent manner may manifest in an 'unexplainable' outburst of harmful violence.

Finally, 'subjective violence' consists of the interpersonal violence visible on a daily basis. A fight in the street, domestic abuse, a terrorist attack. People willingly inflict harm on one another and have done for millennia (Whitehead, 2018). The motivation behind these actions can be discerned and preventative measures implemented to avoid future occurrences. This, however, represents only the most visible forms of violence and often masks its more problematic brethren. Identification of the subjective and interpersonal forms of violence compels a course of action and often treats those events as causal rather than symptomatic.

This triumvirate of violence maps onto the social harm framework of political economy and the continuum of legal and illegal practice, as well as the ultra-realist schema of investigating events *and* the depth structures of society. Taking into account the direct and indirect social harms of capitalist political economy, ideology, and intersubjective relations allows us to map the connection between macro, meso and micro levels of society and find causative relations. The final brick in the ultra-realist wall is an account of subjectivity and ontology that elucidates the motivation at the heart of the subject. If absence is causative, if subjective and systemic violence emerges from a willingness to inflict harm on others, we must outline a theory of the subject that adequately accounts for motivation and harmful behaviour.

Ontology and the transcendental materialist subject

Broadly speaking, social sciences at the beginning of the 21st century accept three ontological platforms: the Cartesian *cogito* (Tarnas, 2010); the discursive, multiple subjectivities associated with postmodernism or post-structuralism (Žižek, 2000); and the transcendental materialist subject posited by Johnston (2008) and Hall and Winlow (2015) which builds on the work of Lacan (2007) and Žižek (2000). The Cartesian subject, famously inscribed with the dictum *"I think, therefore I am"*, suggests that human subjectivity emerges at the point of consciousness (Neill, 2014). One's ability to think, to consciously muse on the conditions of one's existence, reflects human subjectivity and sets us apart from the rest of the animal kingdom. Descartes posited that it was possible to question everything in the world with the exception of one's self-awareness; if I can doubt the existence of everything around me, it presupposes that I exist. Human reason establishes the subject as a self-defining entity possessing rational self-awareness; the modern mind was central to the Enlightenment concept of progress and human flourishing through science, reason, epistemological certainty, and mastery over nature (Tarnas, 2010).

This interpretation of subjectivity became the cornerstone of social science from its early origins and presupposes an essential human essence. Along the way, this belief in reason and rational thinking at the heart of the subject prefigures explanatory frameworks for social behaviour such as utilitarianism (Mill, 2002 [1862]). In the field of criminology, the belief that humans possess a *hedonistic calculus* and weigh up the benefits and limitations of intended actions creates a clear political and policy-oriented response (Hall, 2012a). In economic terms, the calculating subject rationalises the efficacy of the free market; individuals in possession of all relevant information weigh up the pros and cons and make an informed decision on investment, trade and consumer spending (Hayek, 1945).

The discursive subject stems from the post-structuralist decimation of the modernist project (Žižek, 2000). Western intellectual thought had posited a particular version of truth and knowledge that reflected power relations and inequalities but was not reflective of the way in which the majority of individuals experience the world. Postmodernist discourse upended the universalism at the heart of modernity in favour of the 'micronarratives of experience' (Lyotard, 1974). Diversity and pluralism dominated thinking among post-modernists and deconstructionists who identified difference and change as a permanent condition rather than a *concrete universal* such as the Marxist class project. Subjectivity was the result of discourses and narratives imposed on individuals through systems of symbolic power and domination; for example, Butler (2006, 2011) posits 'gender performativity' as the embodiment of gender 'performances' reflective of the dominant discourse on masculinity and femininity. Gender is, in this guise, a subjective identity performed by an individual rather than a set of biological or social imperatives. This ontological foundation of subjectivity as the embodiment of discourses, set in relation to power and domination, 'de-centred' sociology and the subject; 'identity politics' suggested that the micro-narratives of experience for minority ethnic groups, LGBTQ communities and women presuppose a reimagined subjective existence. The truth of minority experience is no more or less true or valid than those in more visible and powerful positions within the social hierarchy; subjectivity is the reflection of discourses and power relations. The rejection of universalism at the heart of this ontological foundation has served to fragment social groups along intersectional lines of division which, within a competitive marketplace, compete against each other for the spotlight and resources.

The transcendental materialist subject (Johnston, 2008; Hall and Winlow, 2015) is non-essential, neither good nor evil, yet the possibility of either is inherent (Winlow and Hall, 2016). The human brain is hard-wired for plasticity (Johnston, 2008; Hall, 2012b). Neurologically, the brain's materiality, its neuronal receptors, can break down and reconstitute. This is a vital requirement in order for humans to adapt and survive in multiple environments (Wakeman, 2017; also Johnston and Malabou, 2013; Meloni, 2014). Transcendental materialism suggests that human subjectivity arises from a material starting point, the brain, but exists as more than that material grounding; it transcends its material origins and is therefore no longer reducible to materiality (Johnston, 2008). As the subject acts in the world, interacts with one's surroundings, that external stimulus *feeds back* into the material core. The inherent plasticity of the brain, identified by neuroscientists through work that recognises neuronal receptors as malleable enough to break down and reconstitute, absorbs the external stimuli and reconfigures neuronal patterns in order to adapt and survive in one's surroundings. In his analysis of gendered violence in the US crime drama TV series *Breaking Bad*, Steve Wakeman (2017) suggests that transcendental materialism perhaps offers a theory of *male* violence. If, at its core, transcendental materialism is a theory with biological origins then biological differences between men and women should be considered. The male protagonists *become* violent but the female protagonists do not. The gender implication of transcendental materialism requires further investigation.

Meanwhile, Thomas Raymen (2017) notes that the transcendental materialist subject *reverts* back to a set of behavioural or ethical codes once prevalent in previous forms of social and cultural organisation but long since repressed through a process of pseudo-pacification (Hall, 2012a). Wakeman (2017) is correct to suggest that the *individual subject* undergoes a process of becoming as they interact with the external environment which feeds back onto their neuronal receptors. However, in positioning the transcendental materialist subject within the context of pseudo-pacification, Raymen's (2017) contribution places subjectivity within the stream of history and the relationship between a political-economic generative core and the thymotic energy of a desiring subject (Hall, 2012a).

This non-essential subject is shaped by the material reality of the world in which one lives. Johnston (2008) borrows from Hegel's suggestion that the 'spirit is a bone'; the active solicitation of an external Symbolic Order is grafted onto the corporeal. The inherent plasticity of the brain's neuronal receptors indicates that outside changes can have a material impact on the body and brain function. Carr (2011) notes that neuroscientists have already identified material changes to the brain's synapses and receptors as a result of prolonged and daily use of the internet; the way we think is changed and shaped *at a material level* by the external social organisation of knowledge and information brought about by the internet. However, once our hard-wired brain transcends into mind or subjectification, it is impossible then to reduce the individual to that material origin; we become more-than-material. This is not one-directional; the subject adapts to external circumstance at a material level but also acts in the world. The individual can shape and influence the world with those changes subsequently 'feeding back' into the material composition of the subject. This represents a truly dialectical process.

If the subject is non-essential, neither 'good' nor 'evil', then the organisation of society at a macro and meso level has a fundamental bearing on the subject. The transcendental materialist subject is framed within the Lacanian tripartite register of reality (Lacan, 2007). The Real represents an excess, a powerful experience or feeling for which we cannot find the words. The Real, as opposed to reality, exists beyond symbolisation. That symbolisation is the symbolic; the signs, values, normative codes, representations, language and culture within which we interpret the world. The Imaginary is structured by the symbolic but represents an ideal image of oneself rooted in the external world. The non-essential subject seeks to avoid a confrontation with the Real therefore unconsciously and actively solicits a functionally efficient Symbolic Order. As the subject passes from nature to culture, the codes and representations of the Symbolic Order root the individual in language, norms and values. The symbolic is also limiting; the Real exists beyond the signifying chain of language and symbols, an unnameable excess which has a powerful effect on the subject but of which we struggle to make sense.

The Symbolic Order actively solicited by the subject has considerable impact on the norms, values, dispositions, ethics, codes and language employed by an individual, group or society. A functioning Symbolic Order framed around values of co-operation, mutuality, respect, love and fairness will, over time become hard-wired into the brain; a Symbolic Order framed around competition, envy, status, greed, anxiety and self-interest will, over time, have the same effect. Individual agency and variation exist within this as the subject adapts to the external environment and subsequently influences and shapes that environment. If a Symbolic Order loses its symbolic efficiency, its ability to provide a coherent reality, the subject faces an encounter with the Real and therefore seeks an alternative; the recent popularity of fundamentalist Christianity, New Age mysticism and conspiracy theories reflect this search. Different Symbolic Orders produce different subjectivities (Badiou, 2007).

The transcendental materialist subject is a 'split-subject', torn between being and meaning, between a 'state of nature' and a 'state of culture' (Neill, 2014). The individual is divided by the pre-social bundle of drives represented by the Real and the passage into a 'state of culture' and solicitation of a coherent Symbolic Order which provides the organising logic required to exist in the world. At an unconscious level, the split subject continually seeks unity; at the point of separation a fundamental 'lack' develops as we give up something of ourselves in order to pass into the state of culture. Freud (2002) describes this as the sublimation of drives in order to meet the social contract. The lack at the heart of the subject is essential to living in the social world yet something we continually seek to redress; desire emerges from the unconscious pursuit of lack (Neill, 2014). Unable to face the horror of the Real, we unconsciously desire a substitute object which stands in for our fundamental lack, prevents an encounter with the Real, and motivates our desire. This fantasy, structured at the level of the symbolic, prevents a confrontation with the Real.

Ideology creates symbolic efficiency, the fantasy structure that supports our 'reality' (Žižek, 1989). Ideology is an illusion structuring our social relations, a fantasy-construction enabling us to mask the Real, to offer us an escape from the traumatic kernel of material reality. Instead, ideology works at the level of action: I know this is how things are yet I continue to reproduce the material and social supports and structures buttressing ideology (Fisher, 2009). The fetishistic disavowal at the heart of ideology, knowing something but acting *as if we don't know*, reflects the functional importance of fantasy to mask or prevent a rendezvous with the Real and provide a degree of consistency and 'being-in-the-world' (Žižek, 1989). If that Symbolic Order, that ideological edifice and its material realities, collapses, it forces a return to subjectivity and an encounter with the Real that, for Lacan, signals trauma; we purposely avoid 'madness' by attaching ourselves to structural and symbolic networks that provide meaning. The subject must 'fill the void' by inhabiting a Symbolic Order (Žižek, 2006). This, fundamentally, reflects the motivation to act. At the level of unconscious, the subject is motivated to solicit a functional Symbolic Order to stave off confrontation with the incomprehensible. Within a Symbolic Order shaped by a particular set of values, for example neoliberalism and the values of competition, profit and individual self-interest, the motivation to act will manifest in particular ways. The complex relationship between libidinal desire, the unconscious and the structuring fantasy of the Symbolic Order will determine the willingness to inflict harm.

Within capitalism's consumer phase, for example, an eternal supply of objects and commodities function to channel the energy focused on the search for unity and resolve the lack at the heart of the subject (Hall et al, 2008; Neill, 2014). We are convinced that consumer culture will satisfy our desire, yet in reality it reflects the active adoption of our innermost unconscious drives and desires by the pleasure principle, the continual replacement of objects with another to prevent an encounter with the Real. The split at the heart of the subject generates drives and desires appropriated by the dominant economic logic of society, which channel that libidinal energy in particular directions; for example, the perpetuation of the dominant form of political economy through the absorption of desire within a consumer capitalist framework (Hall and Winlow, 2015). It also has the capacity to generate new and harmful subjectivities (Hall et al, 2008; Ellis, 2016). This continual search for the lost object, satisfaction of the fundamental lack at the core of one's being, accounts for the motivation to act (McGowan, 2016). The absence of something compels us to act. The harmful political economy of neoliberalism identified by the social harm theorists (Tombs and Hillyard, 2004; Pemberton, 2016) represents a Symbolic Order that generates particular subjectivities that we can begin to investigate in relation to the willingness to inflict harm on others.

Towards a new direction?

A synthesis between social harm and ultra-realism presents opportunity for advancement. The focus on political economy, on the processes that generate both legal and illegal practices as well as direct and indirect harms should be integrated with an account of the interrelationship between subjective motivation and ideology. Social harm identifies the continuum of legality and illegality that underpins direct and indirect social harms while ultra-realism accounts for causation and motivation. What motivates the corporation to willingly inflict harm on others? What motivates the individual to willingly inflict harm on others? A harm perspective that accounts for these motivations and addresses the issue of causation provides a significant opportunity to investigate a number of arenas within which harmful activity occurs. Social harm, as it stands, can tell us why harms are inflicted *on* communities, groups and individuals, but an ultra-realist theory of harm and its transcendental materialist explication of subjectivity, develops a powerful base from which to explore the issue of harm perpetrated *by* individuals on others. Harms occur as a result of both legal and illegal practices at macro-, meso- and micro-level processes. The following chapter will begin with a macro-level overview of political economic restructure and labour market shifts that begin to shape current landscape within which absences appear and harms occur on a number of levels.

TWO

Restructuring labour markets

Introduction

Social harm perspectives note that capitalist political economy has harmful consequences (Tombs and Hillyard, 2004; Pemberton, 2016; Scott, 2017). In particular, neoliberal capitalism creates intentional and unintentional harms on a far more problematic basis than other forms of capitalism (Pemberton, 2016). In line with social harm's consideration of structural and systemic factors, this chapter explores the emergence of neoliberalism as the dominant form of political economy. Current labour market conditions did not occur in a vacuum; they reflect a long-standing and systematic 'restoration' (Harvey, 2005; Badiou, 2009) of liberal financial capitalism, updated for our global age. The chapter will discuss the deep structural transformation undertaken as part of the neoliberal project and the emergence of a number of absences, notably the absence of job security within 'flexible' labour markets. This will provide the context for a thoroughgoing investigation of the service economy. If the expanded definition of violence outlined in Chapter One removes intentionality while retaining focus on negative consequences and harm, this chapter will explore social transformation at the level of depth structures. These changes characterise contemporary labour markets and the service economy in particular but also reflect a number of crucial absences that cumulatively create a culture of negativity. These absences constitute a set of harmful conditions; the exacerbation of inequality, the negative motivation to inflict harm through systemic violence and the positive motivation to inflict harm on others.

Shackling the 'animal spirits'

Capitalism did not emerge fully formed with the Industrial Revolution and large-scale manufacturing during the 19th century (Arrighi, 2010). In fact, capitalist social relations had steadily materialised over centuries with social forces systematically pulled into the orbit of market relations and the generative core of what would emerge as a capitalist system of political economy (Whitehead and Hall, forthcoming). A historical process of *pseudo-pacification* (Hall, 2012a) sublimated competitive, aggressive and violent tendencies and channelled such energy into capitalist social relations; markets and trade operate more effectively without the threat of violence. A night-watchman state functioned primarily to enforce laws and suppress discontent on the street but lacked the remit to interfere in the marketplace. The rationality of actors guided by the invisible hand would take care of business, not the state (Smith, 2003 [1776]). However, as Keynes (2008 [1936]) acknowledged (see also Akerlof and Shiller, 2009), capitalism was beset by non-rational 'animal spirits' which by the 1920s had widened inequality across the UK and the US and eventually plunged the system into crisis. The libidinal energy that drove capitalism – the drives and desires of competitive individuals, self-interest, and profitability – created social problems that only the state could remedy. The generative core of capitalism was both non-rational and anti-ethical; in the wake of the Great Depression, a regulatory sleeve located a set of social protections and ethically motivated institutions on the periphery and exterior of capitalism (Whitehead and Hall, forthcoming).

This regulatory sleeve took note of the shocks and causes of the Great Depression and sought to shackle the worst excesses of market forces (see Bew, 2016). A more hands-on state controlled the levers of production and finance, restricted financial speculation, controlled prices, and integrated a more international system of co-operation (Varoufakis, 2013, 2016). The social safety net functioned as a bulwark against personal misfortune. Unemployment benefit, sick pay, old-age pensions and statutory employment rights, backed by activist trade unions, began to improve circumstances for more than just the wealthy (Streeck, 2016). A commitment to full employment, the National Health Service (NHS) in the UK (Pollock, 2004) and Medicare and Medicaid in the US brought health benefits to populations who, pre-war, would have feared the financial and existential precarity associated with illness and the inability to work (Bell, 1985). As the post-war period settled into the new reality of cold war, capitalism's success depended on the acquiescence of the masses (Mason, 2015). Only through the incremental progress of the working and middle classes, the steady improvement in living and working conditions, increased wages, growth in relative affluence, and emergent consumer and leisure lifestyles could capitalism ensure the emotional investment of a generation with living memory of the horrors of untrammelled market forces.

The increasingly interdependent global economy of the post-war period closed the gap between rich and poor to an extent unseen either before or since under capitalism (Piketty, 2014). The destruction of large swathes of surplus capital reserves in wartime, coupled with the regulatory sleeve which imposed a degree of ethical protection over capitalism, shrank levels of inequality considerably. This would prove to be an aberration, a brief interregnum in the history of capitalism (Piketty, 2014) but one that looms large today. Standards of health, and life expectancy, rose (Wilkinson and Pickett, 2009). Stable and secure employment was sufficiently remunerated, often at the insistence of strong and frequently intransigent trade unions; unemployment in the UK failed to rise above 3.1% between 1945 and 1971 (Denham and McDonald, 1996) and remained between 3-5% in the US (US Census Bureau, 1999). The labour movement had shifted from anti-capitalist militancy to fighting for better shares *within* the system (Winlow et al, 2015). The pact between capital and labour was one of continued mutual beneficence; employees would continue to see their pay increase, employers would continue to see high levels of productivity and profit. The post-war period also proved Marx and Engels (1998) [1845] wrong; the workers of the Western world did not want to overthrow capitalism, they sought to share in the spoils (Hall et al, 2008). The symbolic efficiency of social democracy lent comfort to the subject who sought to make sense of their world. A clear sense of stability informed biography, work trajectory and social relations. In an ultra-realist schema, the post-war period represents a functional and efficient Symbolic Order reproduced by the subjects of social democracy.

This 'golden era' was, to some extent, undoubtedly a myth, a tool to demonstrate the vibrancy and strength of a capitalism challenged by obvious ideological alternatives. It overlooks significant problems and harms, including the persistence of Jim Crow laws and racial tension in the American South, ethnic tension in the UK which followed the government's call for former colonial subjects to relieve labour shortages, and the marginalisation of women within public discourse, the workplace and, often, the home. The period that provided full employment, the 'white heat of industry' and the explosion of pop music, also spawned Vietnam, race riots and persistent class inequality. However, a clear sense of progress, stability and security was palpable (Beynon, 1973) as workers found a degree of comfort and solace in steady, well-paid work, increased standards of living for more than the lucky few and the horrors of war and depression faded into the background.

Capital ascendant

By the early 1970s, the post-war social democratic consensus had seen few serious economic fluctuations and a steady increase in the prosperity of the working and middle classes (Harvey, 2005). However, a series of economic shocks in the 1970s revealed the limitations of the post-war settlement (Varoufakis, 2013). The post-war financial mechanism agreed at Bretton Woods to regulate international finance and peg all currencies against the gold-backed US dollar was upended by the Nixon administration in the face of economic forces beyond the reach of the Bretton Woods system (Harvey, 2005; Varoufakis, 2016). Further global shocks such as the OPEC oil embargo and the seemingly contradictory problem of 'stagflation' further revealed the limits of the post-war consensus (Streeck, 2016). Throughout the 1970s, unemployment remained low and while overall earnings began to increase (although this requires further breakdown by sector), so too did the retail price index which climbed dramatically as inflation spiralled (Lindsay, 2003). As the political consensus struggled to meet the challenge of new and emergent threats, the marginal political economic ideology of neoliberalism, under the intellectual sway of Hayek, Friedman and others associated with the Mont Perelin society (Mirowski, 2013) articulated a coherent solution based on monetary policy, free markets, competition and minimal government intervention. The winds of change blew in favour of neoliberals. By the end of the decade, Thatcher and Reagan had brought their avowedly free market policy to the seat of power as an answer to the seemingly intractable force of organised labour and union power brokers holding the country to ransom with the threat of strike action (Mirowski, 2013).

From the early 1980s onwards, deep structural transformations fundamentally recast the political, economic, social and cultural landscape (Winlow and Hall, 2013). Neoliberal attachment to free markets opened nation-states to international competition without the safety previously afforded by protectionist governments; the movement of capital became key to economic success in this new world order. Growth and profit trumped full employment and the newly emboldened financial sector took advantage of reform and deregulation to seek higher profit margins and faster rates of return (Stiglitz, 2010). Industries under public ownership were subject to global market forces, which often hit productivity levels and hastened the decision to move non-performing and bloated assets into private hands (Harvey, 2005). Attachment to an ideology not only underpinned deep structural transformation of Western societies but also reflected the negative motivation to harm; systemic violence, perhaps unintentional but nevertheless problematic and harmful, reorganised society along new lines.

Sensing opportunity for short-term profit, these industries were often stripped, sold or outsourced to foreign markets with cheaper labour and greater margins for profit. The former bastions of secure, stable and well-paid work, manufacturing and heavy industry, had largely vanished within a decade. In the UK, South Wales, Yorkshire, the North East and Scotland suffered heavily from deindustrialisation (Byrne, 1989; Charlesworth, 2000; Winlow, 2001). In the US, the 'rust belt' emerged in former manufacturing and industrial regions of the mid-West and North East (Linkon and Russo, 2002; High, 2003). In areas now devoid of their raison d'être, unemployment soared. The deindustrialised zones of the UK, US and Europe descended into spaces of almost permanent recession in which daylight rarely breaks through the fog of precarity. Fixity was replaced by indeterminacy. As noted below, the absence of stability engenders harmful conditions for many.

Unemployment was accompanied by a cornucopia of interlinked social problems and multiple indices of deprivation which included high crime, an influx of crack cocaine, heroin, and other escapist narcotics, falling educational attainment, rising welfare dependency, a breakdown of traditional social order, teenage pregnancies, anti-social behaviour and harmful and predatory forms of interpersonal violence (Wilson, 1997; Winlow, 2001; MacDonald and Marsh, 2005; Wacquant, 2009). Of course, this was experienced spatially as those areas now devoid of stable and abundant employment descended into a spiral of anomie. To put it in Lacanian terms, the Symbolic Order of social democratic industrial society, with its security and stability rooted in community, class and durable working patterns, was stripped away and left shell-shocked subjects to face the Real of global capital. In the face of such horror and indeterminacy, subjects were left to scramble for an alternative Symbolic Order to make sense of their new existence.

While not entirely a return to classic liberal capitalism, neoliberalism was underpinned by an ideological commitment to free markets, competition, efficiency and the belief that profit-driven private sector organisations could more successfully manage public assets (Harvey, 2005). At an ideological level neoliberalism enacted profound changes on the deep structures of society, economic orthodoxy and the role of the state recalibrated around market forces and competition, previously ring-fenced areas of civic society became subject to market capitalism and new forms of subjectivity emerged which reflected the dominant imperatives of the reconfigured social, political and economic relations

(Hall, 2012a). The neoliberal project systematically punctured the regulatory sleeve which had kept capitalism's generative core in check since the 1940s (Whitehead and Hall, forthcoming).

Harvey (2010) suggests that capitalism requires ways to transcend its limits in order for growth to persist. Neoliberal ideology provided an economic answer to the limits of the post-war consensus; free markets, growth-fuelled capitalism, wage restraint, financialisation and a shift in the balance between capital and labour would restore growth (Streeck, 2016). Competition, productivity, efficiency, and targets became key facets of political and economic rhetoric under neoliberalism. As the political economic landscape changed, the new Symbolic Order of neoliberalism provided a psychic rope for those subjects cut adrift through the economic failure and destruction of social democracy; subjective solicitation of the key tenets of neoliberalism was visible from its earliest days and extensive sociological and criminological research has consistently revealed individual subjects attached to the values of competition, market shares, meritocracy and personal gain (Lloyd, 2013; Winlow and Hall, 2013; Horsley, 2015; Ellis, 2016; Smith and Raymen, 2016; Winlow et al, 2017).

The absence of security and stability reflected both the negative motivation to harm – the unintentional consequences of entirely legal processes of political economic restructure – and the positive motivation to harm as individuals embodied the entrepreneurial spirit of the age to take advantage of uncertainty and commit both legal and illegal acts that resulted in personal gain at the expense of the well-being of others (Winlow, 2001; Hall et al, 2008). Deep restructure according to the principles of neoliberalism saw individualism and competition triumph over the collective and ethical responsibility (Winlow et al, 2017; Whitehead, 2018). Systemic violence visited on institutions and structures was matched by a symbolic violence that closed off the efficiency of social democratic narratives and situated neoliberal ideology as the coherent and logical approach to a new and changing world of globalisation beyond our control; a new world existed and options were limited to adapt and thrive or fall behind and perish. The financial sector would move to the centre of both the UK and US economies but for all of its electronic fortune and technological innovation, it did not create the vast labour markets required to act as a life-raft for those thrown overboard by deindustrialisation. For this group, the rhetoric of knowledge work would induce retraining and skills upgrades while the reality of the service economy beckoned.

Restructured labour markets

The move away from the 'embedded liberalism' of the post-war settlement towards the neoliberal dispensation aroused significant change within labour markets. Industry and manufacturing were outsourced to parts of the global South and East where costs were low. The numbers employed in industry and manufacturing in the West dwindled in both size and significance. By the end of the 20th century industry and manufacturing fell from 28% to 14% of employment while agriculture dropped from 11% to 2% (Lindsay, 2003). By 2017, manufacturing accounted for around 80% of the UK labour market (ONS, 2018). This was not specific to the UK. Across the 20th century, agriculture dropped from around 40% to 3% in Germany and the US and 6% in France (Lindsay, 2003).

Within the UK, a public sector enthused with the ethico-cultural codes associated with the regulatory sleeve of civic society saw total numbers in employment grow but organisations such as education and healthcare reflected a clear shift in organisational philosophy (Hunter, 2008). The implementation of new public management under the Conservative governments (1979–97) and the modernisation project of New Labour (1997–2010) injected business principles into apparently unwieldy and inefficient bureaucracies. Market competition invaded sections of the NHS and education system in the name of choice with non–core functions such as cleaning and catering outsourced entirely (Pollock, 2004; Davis et al, 2015). The austerity agenda imposed after 2010 further reinforced this overhaul of public institutions as the retreat of public investment required and facilitated private solutions to rescue 'failing' schools, hospitals and prisons (Whitehead, 2016). That governments of the left and right have followed the neoliberal agenda in relation to public sector employment demonstrates a prolonged absence of genuine political alternatives to neoliberal orthodoxy with significant impact on employees, 'customers' and institutions. In moving from the left to the centre, the natural opponents of neoliberalism ensured that no genuine alternatives to the free market, competition and global capital would enter political dialogue (Winlow et al, 2017). In this sense, the idea of 'post-politics' gains credence; politicians of all stripes fundamentally agree on the shape of the economy and engage in cosmetic battles over minor points of administration (Ranciere, 2007).

The public sector expanded under New Labour's 'modernisation' agenda (Senior et al, 2007; Barber, 2008). Public sector jobs were decentralised and regional centres absorbed public sector work as a safeguard against the problems of inward capital investment in both manufacturing and services (Lloyd, 2013). The parallel private markets for education, healthcare and criminal justice functions also acted as job creation tools. The development of a knowledge economy and an expanded public sector created opportunities but, for the majority of working-age people, opportunities most likely presented within the burgeoning service sector. Retail, leisure, call centres, food services industry, night-time economy and other customer-reliant roles expanded dramatically in the wake of the political economic shift from production to consumption (Harvey, 2010).

Emergence of consumer capitalism

Service work had grown before the onset of deindustrialisation (Glyn, 2006) but the rise in service industries coincides with a political economic shift towards a consumer society (Winlow and Hall, 2006; Smart, 2010; Hall, 2012a). Consumer culture took a central role in economic growth from the 1970s onwards as global forces began to challenge the hegemony of Fordist, industrial patterns of work (Smart, 2010). While the term 'service industry' is frustratingly ambiguous and can cover a range of occupations, all statistical suggestions show an increase in the service sector; some suggest an increase from 21% to 32% by the end of the 20th century (Mitchell, 1998) with early 21st century estimates as high as 75%' (Lindsay, 2003; McDowell, 2009). France, Germany and the US also saw significant increases in the service economy, from around 10% to 33% (Lindsay, 2003), although the Bureau of Labor Statistics (2017) places the percentage of US jobs within the service economy at 71% of those in 'non-farm' employment.

In the UK the constitution of the 'service sector' depends on the body, institution or individual who wields the term; for example, the Labour Force Survey has separate categories for 'caring, leisure and other service occupations' as well as 'sales and customer service occupations' (ONS, 2018). However, occupations such as 'shelf fillers', security guards, bar staff, waiters and waitresses, and cleaners fall under 'elementary occupations' yet are intrinsic to the service economy. More confusingly, the category 'elementary occupations' cannot be taken as a whole to represent service sector employment due to the inclusion of occupations such as farm workers, forestry workers and construction workers (ONS, 2018). Definitional problems aside, the shift to a consumer economy rapidly expanded opportunities for employment within the burgeoning service sector (Lloyd, 2013).

As the Keynesian consensus unravelled, the limit to growth indicated by stagflation required a solution. Capitalism has always relied on its ability to conduct running repairs on its own fragile system and in this instance it arrested the steady rise in wages in order to tackle the global inflation of the 1970s (Streeck, 2016). This not only aroused unrest but also halted engagement in consumer markets. It also demonstrates the needs of capital come before the welfare of the public; harm can be inflicted in the name of economic growth. Workers are also consumers; the spending power of consumers was central to the consumer economy and a solution to wage freezes was necessary. The expansion of credit to consumers was capitalism's answer to this latest limit. Streeck (2014, 2016) suggests that each running repair conducted by the capitalist system lasts for around 10 years before the sticking plaster falls off and the wound is once again exposed. The expansion of credit raised levels of public debt in the 1980s and private debt in the 1990s (Streeck, 2016). This ensured future problems but at this stage the erosion of manufacturing and industrial production coupled with the expansion of credit to supplement stagnant wages guaranteed that consumer markets and the service economy required to facilitate consumer spending moved to the centre of neoliberal labour markets (Lloyd, 2013).

In the UK and US, the high-tech knowledge economy produced work for those with the education and skills to compete in neoliberalism's meritocratic, socially mobile world (Frank, 2016). However, most new jobs in the UK were at either the top end of the labour market or at the bottom (Judt, 2010). The consumer society was serviced by a labour market which began to reflect certain features and conditions markedly different from the stable, secure and adequately remunerated jobs of industrial and manufacturing work. Neoliberal regulatory upheaval, in the name of productivity and growth, signalled a number of absences in relation to employment conditions. The domestication of organised labour and restructure of employment legislation produced a vital shift in employment characteristics that came to define the contemporary service economy.

From security to flexibility

The transition from employment security to flexibility has far-reaching consequences for late modern society. At the level of depth structures, the shift from Fordism to 'flexible accumulation' (Harvey, 1989) has a profound impact on the daily lives of subjects who attempt to negotiate their place in the world. The certainties and stability of secure, long-term employment under the Keynesian dispensation were systematically removed in order to facilitate the expansion of growth and increase in profitability. At a time when postmodernists concentrated on culture as the site of radical social change, the depth structures of political economy reveal the transition to a 'new spirit of capitalism' (Boltanski and Chiapello, 2005) which significantly restructured labour markets and changed working patterns irrevocably. This restructure also opens up space for a discussion of harm as workers face indeterminate futures as the price for competition and profitability in the marketplace.

This structural adjustment towards flexible accumulation of capital reflects neoliberal belief in freedom for market competition and individual achievement (Gane, 2015). This transformed institutional and organisational logic and practice in the name of profitability and efficiency. Employment conditions radically altered and the security and protections previously accepted as essential, withered. This created a set of absences with causative social consequences (Hall and Winlow, 2015; Lloyd, 2018). Working practices focus on 'just-in-time' service provision, the outsource of key functions to third parties, lean working (Garrahan and Stewart, 1992) and the performance management of staff through quotas, targets and objectives (Taylor and Bain, 1999). The description of Sports Direct's employment practices outlined in the introduction finds its genesis in these reforms.

Within the sociological literature on work and employment, the shift from security to flexibility has been widely acknowledged (Elchardus and Smits, 2008; Gregg, 2011; Kalleberg, 2011; Standing, 2011; Lee and Kofman, 2012; Madrick, 2012; Glavin, 2013; Lloyd, 2013; Chan and Tweedie, 2016). Most of the literature fails to place the empirical evidence identified at the organisational or meso level in the context of society's depth structures or the intransitive realm of political economy or ideology (see Lloyd, 2017). However, the body of evidence collected within the sociology of work and employment presents a significant contribution towards appreciation of the impact of structural adjustment. The flexibility agenda raises the spectre of radical indeterminacy and 'precarity', borrowing from Standing (2011) to objectively delineate the experiences of low-paid, exploited workers.

At the level of employment conditions, flexible work largely incorporates part-time hours, temporary work agencies (TWAs), fixed-term contracts, zero-hour contracts, on-demand work, cash-in-hand work and other aspects of the illicit economy. Pay remains at the level of minimum or living wage, often supplemented by performance-related bonuses which force employees into longer hours, work intensification and greater sacrifices. Income and expenses are covered through bonuses and targets rather than a fixed salary or higher hourly rate. Flexible working arrangements are increasingly common across the knowledge economy (Wheatley, 2016), and while some elements such as working from home are unsuitable for the service economy, others are more keenly felt within the service economy. For example, Wheatley suggests that part-time hours are more likely to be restricted to women within the knowledge economy, yet the service economy does not discriminate; part-time hours are routinely offered to both men and women. That precarious and flexible work appears increasingly ubiquitous and not limited to the service economy (see Gregg, 2011) suggests that objective conditions of employment may generate problematic or harmful outcomes and must be identified.

Within our social harm framework, the negative motivation to succeed in the new economic reality of competition, growth and profit compels managers and owners to implement strategies and policies that will meet their economic drivers. These decisions result in the employment conditions outlined here. This is facilitated by a state apparatus keen to ensure economic viability and growth and therefore willing to regulate and deregulate accordingly (Harvey, 2005). These decisions, by those who have actively solicited the neoliberal orthodoxy and sought ways to ensure their success, create conditions whereby employees are harmed both intentionally and unintentionally by a set of policies that divest them of any sense of security at work and determinacy in their lives. Furthermore, the active solicitation of a negative ideology fuels a positive motivation to harm based on the need to succeed or survive within this environment. The willingness of government and business to strip workers of employment protections and security in the name of efficiency and profitability has harmful consequences for employees and exacerbates levels of inequality.

Much of the institutional data on employment trends and job growth concentrates on the need for 'good quality' jobs without explanation or criteria (OECD, 2015). In what Madrick (2012) calls the 'deliberate low-wage, high-insecurity' model, attachment to economic growth and productivity comes at the expense of labour and the conditions within which service economy employees toil. Some research tries to focus on the positives; Warhurst and Nickson's (2007) work on aesthetic labour identifies a new 'labour aristocracy', an increasingly middle-class set of service occupations where the cultural injunction to 'be yourself' and employ 'attitude' reigns. This contrasts with the traditional servile nature of service work but falls in line with a 'trendy' or 'hip' aesthetic. However, as Misra and Walters (2016) indicate, employment in the 'cool' stores, the use of aesthetic labour and receipt of employee discounts does not compensate for precarious conditions, low-pay and uncertain futures. The need to accentuate the positives in otherwise precarious and flexible work often marginalises the broader context and bigger problems. Flexible, insecure service economy work is, by the weight of evidence presented in academic and popular discussion, problematic and often harmful with very few consolations for employees who increasingly live lives characterised by radical indeterminacy rather than any sense of stability or fixity.

Recognition of the more deleterious effects associated with labour market flexibility and the ostensible absence of security for many workers led to policy discussions that sought to bridge an apparent cleavage between flexibility and security (Auer, 2007). 'Flexicurity' encapsulated a reform agenda seeking to move beyond 'job security' in favour of 'employment security' (Withagen and Tros, 2004; Heyes, 2011). Proponents believed this would allow security for workers as well as flexibility for both organisations and employees (Auer, 2007). Flexibility would improve economic performance, competitiveness and growth, while security would preserve social cohesion (Withagen and Tros, 2004). Advocates of flexicurity argued it reflected a trade-off between competing demands; a degree of social security paid for by the state supported individual workers subject to the vicissitudes of market forces. Welfare support, training and opportunities to move across firms and sectors when downturns and peak periods affected the labour market reflected some of the key components of the flexicurity agenda (Auer, 2007).

Applebaum (2012) questions the ability to support workers during periods of recession when the job market contracts significantly. How can people transition to new jobs when significantly fewer jobs exist? In response to this, Applebaum (2012) advocates further flexibility such as 'short-time working' and reduced hours, complemented by EU studies into new forms of employment which include employee sharing, job sharing, casual work and crowd employment (Eurofound, 2015). While Kalleberg (2011) recommends that the US adopt flexicurity to protect workers without stifling growth, Heyes (2011) notes that the post-crash response across Europe has been to largely move away from the flexicurity agenda. The EU may have encouraged post-crash rebuilding with flexicurity at its heart, but the UK in particular made cuts rather than embrace a balance between security and flexibility. The fact that policy makers promoted 'flexicurity' is indicative of a wider recognition that labour market restructure had shifted markedly from security towards flexibility. While positive for organisations and profitability, it proved problematic for employees who faced the absence of security. Things would get worse when the housing bubble and debt crisis came to a head.

Crash and burn: the limits of debt-fuelled spending

Neoliberalism's deep restructure shifted labour market composition heavily toward service economy work. It also ensured that conditions of employment moved from security to flexibility, which provided a greater degree of latitude for employers to maximise profitability. In general this continues to reflect the reality of labour markets today, albeit compounded by a further crisis of capitalism (Streeck, 2016). The internal contradictions of capitalism created a new predicament which grew from the shift to consumer spending and its attendant service economy (Harvey, 2010). The huge expansion of private debt designed to maintain consumer spending successfully overcame the barriers presented by stagnant wages and high levels of public debt (Streeck, 2016). However, with regulations stripped away in order to facilitate consumer spending and the financial industry focused on short-term return on investment and shareholder demand, opportunities to profit with vast amounts of fictitious capital opened the door to risky investments and predatory lending, particularly in the housing market (Stiglitz, 2010). Neoliberalism in both ideology and practice enabled some operators to profit handsomely. Others follow this path in the hope of similar success and thus a norm emerged that governed sectoral and institutional behaviour. It also demonstrates the absence of ethical responsibility; the bottom line is more important to the financial sector than the welfare and fiscal safety of its customers.

The expansion of the housing market tapped into the consumer dream of home ownership and social mobility in a scenario which substituted a property's use value (that is, a home to live in) for its exchange value (in other words, a way of making short-term profit) (Harvey, 2014). To buy cheap and sell high grew the market, fuelled consumer lifestyles and racked up debt as individuals and banks took on unsustainable loans and lending which would leave them with insurmountable bills if the market failed. Individuals and families were encouraged to take on mortgages which, since the removal of meaningful regulation on credit limits, presented significant risk to the recipients. Mortgages were no longer a tool to get individuals on the property ladder but an instrument used by the financial services to generate quick profit (Harvey, 2010).

Neoliberal ideology celebrates freedom so why can't we have what we want? Neoliberal ideology promotes competition so why should I miss out? Neoliberal ideology invokes status anxiety and envy so why should my neighbour, my co-worker, my friend get holidays, nights out, a new house, car and clothes while I make do with what I've got?

The active solicitation, at an emotional level, of neoliberal ideology and its Symbolic Order of competition, envy and status anxiety propelled millions of people, many engaged in the service economy, into credit card and mortgage debt that was often unsustainable in both the long and short term (Winlow and Hall, 2013; Horsley, 2015). This represents a deep-seated attachment to an ideology pregnant with incipient harms and absent any meaningful protection.

Faith in the efficiency of the market ensured a compulsion towards further accumulation of capital, short-term gains, and a blind-spot in relation to risk within the system (Stiglitz, 2010; Varoufakis, 2013). All meaningful regulation on financial speculation disappeared and most oversight was ignored (Lewis, 2010). Mortgage lenders increasingly sold 'sub-prime' mortgages to customers entirely unsuitable for credit and to individuals who posed a serious risk of default. The securitisation chain, believed to elevate stability within the system by spreading risk around, facilitated sheer greed and naked profiteering without compunction or restraint (Harvey, 2010). The inability to identify risks associated with loans to customers with indeterminate incomes and futures heightened the total amount of risk throughout the financial system exponentially (Horsley, 2015). Once customers began to default on loans, banks were unable to pay their debts and the entire system ground to a halt. Only the intervention of the UK and US governmentss, with unprecedented bailout packages which included the effective nationalisation of sections of the banking sector, prevented the financial system from complete implosion (Harvey, 2010; Varoufakis, 2013; Horsley, 2015).

Consumer debt, which included mortgage debt, forced many to default and lose their property. In the wake of the crisis, the banking industry was fearful of further lending and millions lost their jobs. The Western capitalist economy fell into a deep recession which affected most sectors of the labour market, the service economy included. As much of the social harm literature attests, the normal functioning of the capitalist system generates both direct and indirect social harms with lasting consequences for millions of people (Pemberton, 2016; Hillyard and Tombs, 2017). The victory of markets over morality (Whitehead, 2015) indicated an ethical void at the heart of neoliberalism that ensured intentional and unintentional harms continued to have a significant impact on individuals and communities. The entirely legal procedure of sub-prime lending and securitisation, the illegal fraud perpetrated by Bernie Madoff, and the practices of Goldman Sachs and others that live in the grey areas of regulation but are ethically dubious, all stem from the same imperatives: growth, profit, competition. These practices also inflicted harm and damage on a remarkable scale.

The recession hit the debtor nations of the Eurozone countries, creating a debt crisis in Greece, Ireland and Portugal which had forsaken their central banks in favour of the single currency and were unable to underwrite bad debts or undergo quantitative easing (Varoufakis, 2016). Instead, creditor nations, led by Germany, demanded austerity in exchange for loans. In the UK and US, consumers were no longer spending; jobs had gone, credit was scarce. The growth in inequality precipitated by an economic system perpetuated by competition and free markets had, according to Piketty (2014), returned capitalism to 'business as usual'. The errant 'golden era' of the post-war settlement had reduced inequality but capitalism's long-term tendency has always generated inequality where return on investment outstrips wages. The financial crisis and its aftermath showed this inequality in stark colours; the new gilded age promulgated in the financial centres of Wall Street and the City of London stood in clear contrast to the swathes of foreclosures, job losses and shifts in employment conditions for the rest of the population. In the throes of financial difficulty, demand drops as consumer spending falls (Ford, 2016). As a result economic growth stagnates and requires political solutions.

Rather than acknowledge the root causes of the financial crisis – the progressively risky and under-regulated avenues that were pursued to solve the crisis of 'over-accumulation' (Harvey, 2010) within a capitalist system built on perpetual motion – the target became levels of public spending and 'bloated' welfare budgets (Streeck, 2016). This reflected Streeck's (2014, 2016) assertion that the latest running repair self-administered by capitalism was the shift towards a 'consolidated state' designed to service capital and consolidate public debts through spending cuts and austerity. The Obama administration, the Conservative–Liberal Democrat coalition and the European Union imposed various degrees of austerity and belt-tightening on their respective populaces. Swingeing UK spending cuts created significant problems for local services, welfare recipients and the public sector (O'Hara, 2014). Direct and indirect harms also followed as services vanished and public sector institutions failed to meet their mandates to help in the face of rising levels of inequality.

Labour markets in austerity

Insecurity reigns across the labour market. Figures show almost 7.4 million people employed in the public sector in 2009 reduced to 5.35

million in December 2017, or 16.6% of the labour market (ONS, 2018). This attempt to shore up capitalism through the 'consolidated state', committed to the reduction of public debt, resulted in two million fewer jobs in the public sphere as local authorities and other public sector organisations engaged in severe belt-tightening activities and balance sheet contortions in order to meet revised budgetary demands from central government. The decline in public spending, coupled with hesitant banks uneasy about lending and the economic slump which cast many back into unemployment and underemployment, resulted in slow growth that has yet to improve in any meaningful way (Streeck, 2016). If harm is the absence of recognition of the positive rights needed to flourish then the huge numbers of public sector jobs cut in the name of fiscal responsibility reflects a clear harm, as does the impact of those job losses on the services provided to communities.

Significant reductions in the level of public sector employment are compounded by continual clamour for the neoliberal tenets of efficiency, productivity and value for money (Whitehead, 2015). For example, the Carter report (2016) recommends concerted effort by NHS trusts to realise efficiency and productivity. In a climate of cuts and austerity, the demonstration of efficiency savings has become a prerequisite for government funding, a quid pro quo approach that sees the NHS sell off buildings, outsource functions and rationalise services in order to meet imposed targets (Davis et al, 2015; El Gingihy, 2015). The 'any qualified provider' provision of the 2012 Health and Social Care Act opens the door to private provision of healthcare, and further fuels competition under the rubric of choice as it stimulates profitable opportunities for private providers (Davis et al, 2015). In an atmosphere of fiscal consolidation at state level the market provides an efficient alternative. Meanwhile the culture that dominates public sector organisations, particularly at managerial level, reflects the ideology, language and values of neoliberalism; balance sheets and efficiency suck the life out of public services.

By 2017 the service sector had expanded further, taking up a larger percentage of the UK labour market (ONS, 2018). As of December 2017, the proportion of jobs accounted for by the service sector increased to 83.3% (ONS, 2018). More than four in five jobs in the UK can be identified as occupations with a service focus. The UK unemployment rate fell from over 8% at the height of the financial crisis to 4.2% at the end of 2017, the lowest unemployment rate since 1975 (ONS, 2018). In the US, the unemployment rate at the height of the post-crash recession hit almost 10%, the highest since the Reagan recession of the early 1980s. However, by late 2017 the Trump administration celebrated a reduction in unemployment to 4.1% (Bureau of Labor Statistics, 2017). Politicians celebrate the reduction in unemployment yet, as Streeck (2016) observes, employment has been restored at a much lower rate of pay and inferior conditions; the 'recovery' amounts to switching unemployment with underemployment. The replacement of public sector jobs with service economy jobs reflects a labour market shift but also further ensures that newly created jobs will likely be flexible and almost certainly low paid. The growth of underemployment is masked by the employment statistics. In the UK, the Labour Force Survey defines employment as the completion of one hour of work in the last week. This allows for the inclusion of temporary work agency (TWA) staff and zero-hour contracts where stability and security is absent. Both the UK and US employment figures are drawn from sample surveys which ultimately hide the reality of the labour market.

The systematic retrenchment of neoliberal ideology through the austerity programme affects labour market provision, which further reflects flexibility rather than security. This is visible in employment rights enshrined by the UK government. By 2017, employment law exhibited minimum statutory rights for employees, with notable loopholes that equipped employers with techniques to circumvent formerly statutory obligations. Statutory Sick Pay is a guaranteed employment right across all variety of contracts, but employees must qualify and be absent for four or more consecutive days; workers off sick for one day can still be deducted pay, a regular practice observed in both retail and call centre work. Workers retain the right to request flexible working patterns that, according to the government, 'suit the employee's needs'. The request to work part-time, compressed hours, flexitime, annualised hours or staggered shifts must be made formally and only following 26 weeks' continuous employment with a company. As much of the literature on the service economy illustrates, employee turnover rates suggest that six months' continuous work is often elusive (Shildrick et al, 2012; also Fenton and Dermott, 2006; Southwood, 2011). In the event that the employee is eligible to submit an application, the employer can still reject on the grounds of business need.

The reconfiguration of employment law dispenses freedom and flexibility for employers to navigate the circuits of consumer capitalism unencumbered by vociferous or inconvenient demands from labour. Management practices that preach flexibility for workers guarantee that managers can employ staff on short-term or zero-hour contracts, and with part-time hours. Simultaneously, employees retain skeleton rights and benefits, pay remains minimal, thereby enabling management strategy and institutional practice to focus on 'just-in-time' service delivery or lean staffing models to maximise profit and demand higher productivity from overworked employees. Lewchuk et al (2008) and Wheatley (2016) note the correlation between flexible working, TWAs and non-standard forms of employment with general employee dissatisfaction and higher reported levels of poor health. That TWAs have become a permanent and embedded feature of labour strategies (Knox, 2010; Hatton, 2011), not only in service sector employment but also in other sectors (for example healthcare and education), demonstrates the supremacy of flexibility over security in contemporary labour markets. The absence of security is endemic across post-crash labour markets and this absence represents a clear form of harm visited on workers. The indeterminate nature of flexible forms of employment removes the ability to plan long term, to find a degree of surety and stability in one's life and thus damages the potential to flourish.

The service economy under conditions of spending contraction and austerity reflects further instability and insecurity in relation to business failure. In the three months from Decmeber 2017 to February 2018, 92,000 people reported recent redundancies (ONS, 2018). High-street stalwarts such as Woolworths and British Home Stores disappeared; national chains like Comet, Maplin Electronics, Toys R Us, and others closed too. This demonstrates the difficulty facing businesses that are reliant on customer footfall and expenditure in a period of tightened spending. It also demonstrates the impact of internet shopping; the way consumers shop has changed considerably in recent decades with bricks and mortar retailers now competing more and more with online shopping (Elms et al, 2016). The 'casual dining crisis of 2018' (Butler, 2018) saw a number of high-street branded restaurants including Jamie's Italian and Byron shut stores. Current economic conditions include the uncertainty of Brexit. Each of these closures represents not only precarious businesses in times of uncertainty but also job losses. The service economy may represent the largest form of employment in the UK but it is subject to the vicissitudes of a volatile market unable to demonstrate any significant growth since the financial crisis (Mitchell and Fazi, 2017). This uncertainty and precarity becomes the backdrop for working conditions and the daily lives of low-paid, insecure workers. From a harm perspective, this demonstrates for the absence of protection and flourishing, the insecurity of daily working life but also the conditions within which some are motivated to act in harmful ways.

One area where rising employment figures highlight the ideological attachment to the cultural, political and economic principles of competition, and individual and economic freedom, is self-employment. Fifteen per cent of the UK labour force, some 4.76 million people, are now characterised as self-employed (ONS, 2018). Liberal ideology has always placed a premium on individual freedom. In the wake of the financial crisis and the shift towards fiscal consolidation, labour market precarity escalated (Stiglitz, 2010; Standing, 2011; Lloyd, 2013). Rather than tackle the root causes of instability and insecurity, political rhetoric pivoted back to narratives of freedom. An attempt to convince the beleaguered workers ejected from public and private sector jobs to use this opportunity to grasp the ultimate freedom of self-employment, to work for oneself and to set one's own agenda (Scholz, 2017) clearly found an audience. In the context of welfare reform organised around Universal Credit, fitness to work assessments and punitive sanctions (Garthwaite, 2016; Fletcher and Wright, 2017), the 'low-pay, no-pay cycle' (Shildrick et al, 2012) of oscillation between periods of temporary, insecure and low-paid work and periods of welfare receipt is unappealing. When job searching becomes a full-time activity (Southwood, 2011), many seek to circumvent this pattern by seeking freedom and flexibility.

Nowhere epitomises this more than the growing 'on-demand' or 'gig' economy (Friedman, 2014; Schor, 2014; Berg, 2016; Hall, 2016; Scholz, 2017). The on-demand economy taps into cultural promise of freedom and flexibility, individual empowerment and entrepreneurialism. The push for flexible working has generated an on-demand economy where workers are hired as 'independent contractors' or 'consultants' under flexible arrangements to complete discrete tasks in a defined timeframe (Friedman, 2014). Living on the margins of regulation and backed by venture capital, on-demand platforms such as Uber, Deliveroo and TaskRabbit shifts accountability onto the contractor; they are responsible for upkeep of equipment but are free to set their own working hours. In an economy typified by limited growth, those who are unemployed and more discriminating will not find secure, well-paid opportunities easily. However, they can find the 'liberation' of quasi self-employment. Friedman (2014) notes that many involved in the gig economy extol the virtues of liberation, freedom to set their own conditions and wages, of not being tied to a company for 25 years and being able to set their own time and career paths. While some have always sought flexible labour and can benefit from on-demand work and precarious forms of employment

(Standing, 2011), the majority, given the choice, would still choose stable employment (Friedman, 2014).

The on-demand economy epitomises the latest fragmentation of labour and work. Flexible work is encouraged culturally to be a form of liberation, the embodiment of the entrepreneurial spirit at the heart of liberal individualism, yet it is driven by political economy, capitalism's demand for further growth and neoliberalism's drive for profitability. The extension of precarious employment practices beyond the service economy, including what Hall (2016) calls the 'uberification of the university' and the widespread use of bank and agency staff within healthcare, demonstrates the prevailing wind within UK and US labour markets. Job security and stability have no place in reconfigured labour markets, which demand flexibility in order to provide firms with the maximum opportunity to generate profit. This is an absence with consequences for employees' sense of well-being.

Conclusion

The continued erosion of the regulatory sleeve which once trapped the 'animal spirits' of capitalism's generative core is a key feature of neoliberalism and its retrenchment following the 2007–08 financial crisis. The focus of labour market reform and transformation along neoliberal lines of flexibility, freedom and competition has created potentially harmful agendas for employees. The shift from security to flexibility, exacerbated by the financial crisis and austerity response, radically transformed the experiences of labour markets across the UK, US and elsewhere and increased the instability and indeterminacy in the lives of millions.

The flexible agenda creates numerous absences imbued with probabilistic causal power, reshaping social landscapes, interpersonal relations and labour market conditions. It is no longer controversial to suggest that Western capitalist economies such as the US and UK now operate as plutocracies (Winlow et al, 2017). The systematic transfer of wealth from the commons to the elite (Dorling, 2015a) reflects Harvey's (2005, 2010) assertion that neoliberalism acts as a class project designed to return assets and capital to their 'rightful place'. This 'restoration' (Badiou, 2009) has had far-reaching consequences for inequality but also labour markets.

Economic growth is manageable largely through financial markets and capital flow rather than production. The sluggish nature of the economy represents the inability of vast numbers of individuals to engage in consumer spending, not the vestiges of restrictive regulation and tax rates (Ford, 2016). While the limits of neoliberalism are felt in the everyday experiences of those marginalised in low-paid labour markets, the ship of political economy steadfastly maintains its pro-market course. The deep structural transformation associated with the arrival of neoliberalism, as well as its persistence in the face of its clear limitations, represents systemic violence in the name of ideology. As the values of competition, efficiency, growth and profit became central components of a new Symbolic Order and filtered down from economy to culture, the negative motivation to harm, an unintentional by-product of 'progress', had significant impact on millions of workers now facing indeterminate and precarious working conditions. The positive motivation to harm is also visible in this shift; business and financial leaders have demonstrated a willingness to harm people on a vast scale through calculated and reckless behaviour that demonstrates an absence of ethical responsibility in light of a growing culture of individualism and personal success. What are the implications of these shifts on the lives of those working within the service economy? The following chapters will delve into the detail behind the absence of stability, protection and ethical responsibility. Before that, we will consider the impact of the macro-level changes delineated in this chapter on the meso-level organisational culture of the workplace.

THREE

Profitability, efficiency and targets

Introduction

This chapter is the first of four chapters to put empirical flesh on the contextual skeleton outlined so far. Primary data drawn from a qualitative study of the service economy on Teesside will highlight the relationship between work and harm. Labour market restructure over the last four decades belongs to a clear political economic rationale; the imperative and priority afforded to growth and profitability via the neoliberal dispensation. Pemberton (2016) notes neoliberal capitalism to be more harmful than other 'varieties of capitalism' (Hall and Soskice, 2001) yet acknowledges that capitalism itself generates a particularly problematic set of social relations. The previous chapter identified capitalism unencumbered by its regulatory sleeve, reflected in macro-level shifts towards consumer markets and more recently debt consolidation (Streeck, 2016). In this context, consumer spending is expected to continue as services, jobs and public spending suffering death by a thousand cuts. While the underlying logic of capitalism and its 'coercive laws of competition' (Marx, 1990 [1867]) endure, its neoliberal 'spirit' (Boltanski and Chiapello, 2005) continues to seek growth above all else; released from the regulatory sleeve of post-war 'embedded liberalism', the hegemonic political economic force in contemporary society sustains an emphasis on profitability, competition and freedom of choice. This systemic violence is underpinned by a willingness to inflict harm, directly or indirectly, through often entirely legal processes. We have seen what this means for labour markets at an abstract level: a reconfiguration away from manufacturing and industry in favour of service and consumer markets; a dynamic shift from security to flexibility; the reduction of employee protections; low pay; insecurity; and growth in 'non-standard' forms of work, including on-demand work.

At the meso level, organisations and management structures exist within a competitive market place typified by low-growth. The coercive laws of competition compel firms to seek growth and profit at all costs otherwise rivals will eat up market share and threaten their survival. Transcendental materialism suggests that the subject, in search of fixity in the world, is shaped by the prevailing culture and values of society, and then acts in the world to subsequently shape and influence the attendant Symbolic Order. In this sense, organisational culture shapes and is in turn moulded by those individuals and companies that seek to compete and survive in precarious circumstances. This chapter will demonstrate empirically strategies used by service economy organisations to maximise the goals of profitability and growth, and identify the culture and conditions within which harms can occur.

Work routines and labour process converge around just-in-time methods of production and work intensification strategies with repercussions for the employee. Organisations performance-manage personnel through targets and incentivised bonuses which drive workers to supplement meagre wages through increased performance levels. Employers also meet profitability through the fragmentation of labour and sub-contracting of in-house functions. Finally, the demand for profit within the circuits of consumer capitalism raises questions about the 'social' as interactions are underpinned by the exchange relation and profit motive. All the emotional, affective and aesthetic labour deployed by service personnel rests on a simple premise: whatever money is in the customer's pocket must end up in mine. The aim of this chapter is to link empirically labour market restructure with management demands for efficiency, profitability and targets. The chapter will focus on particular, but by no means all, management practices. The specific attention on some procedures will provide a link to later chapters that will explore the harmful consequences of certain practices.

Management strategies

The central aim of any service economy organisation is to generate profit. In an accelerated culture of immediacy, facilitated by technology that brings us the pleasure and satisfaction of instantaneous and frictionless consumer encounters (Smith and Raymen, 2016), the service economy must keep up. This has undoubted influence on management strategy within retail, leisure and food services industries. The immediate gratification of consumer culture is incongruous with the concept of waiting; the customer must be accommodated now. Proponents of platform capitalism's inherent immateriality often miss this point; online encounters often exchange information or data with no material properties but this is frequently underpinned somewhere along the production cycle by some form of physical labour (Scholz, 2017). Readers who purchased this volume via Amazon paid for the privilege of immediacy; the Kindle offers downloadable instant gratification; Amazon Prime offers next-day or even same-day delivery. The burst of excitement and satisfaction the reader feels is facilitated by Amazon who offer almost instant gratification. In an accelerated culture, this speeds up a psychological process whereby we long for a commodity, gain a short burst of satisfaction on its acquisition, only for the allure to wear off as we unconsciously recognise it to be what Lacan calls *objet petit a*, a stand-in for the 'lost object' at the heart of the subject. Once the novelty wears off, we move on to the next purchase or experience. When technology speeds up this process, we consume at a faster rate.

To facilitate the instant gratification associated with a 24/7 culture (Crary, 2013), platforms such as Amazon employ work intensification and just-in-time production to ensure speed and efficiency. Just-in-time production within a sector based entirely on customer demand is overseen by a permanently temporary and insecure workforce subject to management practices designed to ensure demand is met on time. A small core workforce is supplemented by a larger group of temporary personnel at periods of high demand (Fleming, 2015). Just-in-time gives a firm the flexibility to adjust its workforce to suit predicted peaks and troughs but also shapes working practices and logistics. In the run up to Christmas 2013, Amazon employed 70,000 temporary workers with less than ten per cent offered permanent positions at the end of the peak season (Hsu, 2013); by 2016 120,000 temporary workers were employed at Christmas (Blumenthal, 2016). Stores utilise just-in-time delivery of stock and raw materials which prevents the unnecessary holding of excess goods. When predicted demand rises or customer orders arrive, orders are placed and deliveries received with tight turnaround times which require fast and efficient bursts of work from employees.

Amazon, like Sports Direct, faced criticism for its treatment of employees who, in US distribution centres, endured brutal conditions such as oppressive summer temperatures with no air conditioning and a pace of production out of Taylor's 'scientific management' playbook (Soper, 2011). Employees complained of dizziness and passing out and were treated by paramedics already on site, yet the just-in-time model was not adjusted. Employees face dismissal for failure to maintain the pace of work; those unable to pick items at the required speed are surplus to requirements. This is reminiscent of the call centre 'sacrificial' strategy (Wallace et al, 2000); set the pace of work at a high level and allow for employee burnout and withdrawal. Daniel was 27 and had worked in warehouse distribution. His story will be explored in later chapters but his experience of work intensification strategies for stock pickers left him with physical injuries as colleagues cut corners in order to meet targets. Investigative journalists have exposed working conditions at Amazon's UK distribution centres which consisted of picking and packing items ten and a half hours a day, fifteen-minute breaks which started wherever you happened to be in the warehouse, blisters from walking fifteen miles each shift, and exhaustion (BBC, 2013; Cadwalladr, 2013).

Amazon's boast of cheaper goods and faster delivery – in order to maximise market shares and beat the competition – comes at a price. Warehouses are located in former industrial centres still ravaged by the effects of deindustrialisation. Large pools of available labour clamour for minimum wage jobs and subject themselves to brutal work intensification. The pace of work is set artificially high, maintained by the tyranny of an electronic handset which counts down the seconds while the picker frantically searches for the correct item. Managers pore over performance figures to weed out underperforming personnel who, as agency workers, can be released without fuss. Cadwalladr (2013) notes that each section was set targets; in order to achieve those targets, managers will push pickers harder and faster and employees will silently accept this brutal existence for their slightly higher than minimum wage.

The combination of work intensification and employee surveillance through electronic measures is also visible in call centre operations (Lloyd, 2013). Automated work processes and electronic surveillance, supported by vigilant managers who scrutinise the data, reduces the level of employee autonomy (Taylor and Bain, 1999; Townsend, 2005). Ben, 30, and Jo, 25, both worked in call centres and documented times where work intensification was unmistakeable as managers demanded calls answered, completed, or jobs closed in line with predicted demand or pre-arranged targets. A number of factors including staff levels and internal processes often made this difficult or impossible. The absence of autonomy can be associated with indirect social harm as the management strategies designed to improve productivity and efficiency deprive the employee of control over the work process. This absence of autonomy has been linked to employee exhaustion, withdrawal and heightened stress levels (Deery et al, 2002; Lloyd, 2013).

A company like Amazon, with almost endless demand from a worldwide customer base, can maintain continuously intense work processes on a full-time basis. Other areas of the service economy experience demand-driven fluctuations in the pace of work (Lloyd, 2013). In some cases, quiet periods are punctuated by intervals of intense work, driven by managers eager to satisfy customers who are unwilling or unused to waiting. In fast food retail, customer demand determines the pace of work while the facility to satisfy that demand is based on rationalised work routines, rotas and equipment capacity.

Sophie was 21 and worked on a zero-hour contract in a fast food restaurant. She describes an occupational culture with heightened stress levels; work intensification and increased customer demand is often matched by management pressure. Stressful shifts occur when the atmosphere turns from positive to negative, or "when everybody starts shouting at you". Customer demand in a culture of convenience and speed necessitates intense periods of work but also suitable practices and processes in order to meet requirements. In the call centre, this is an automated 'assembly line in the head' (Taylor and Bain, 1999; Lloyd, 2013). In describing work intensification during predicted busy periods, Sophie explained that drive-through services placed heightened demand on the team,

> 'It doesn't sound like much but we do like £1,500 an hour through the drive-through alone. The average meal now is around £4.10 for a medium meal ... £4.90 for their meal. When you take that into account ... Our record [number of] cars at the minute is sat at about 120 [in an hour] so you can imagine sometimes we do get like ... we get £30–£40 orders ... But yeah you can imagine sometimes it can get rather stressful because like our, what we call the production bin where we store all the burgers and stuff, once that kind of starts getting quite low and if you're in the kitchen you start getting shouted at, "You need to replace blah blah blah," but obviously sometimes we'll have like seven cars waiting at the drive-through in a row waiting on a certain meal and you can only do a run of four at a time [on the grill] so then you've got to do two runs but then by the time you've got all of them out you're waiting on another four so it's just sometimes you're doing the same thing over and over again. Sometimes that can rack up a bit of a queue as well.'

Drive-through services represent an earlier form of convenience and efficiency for the customer who is no longer expected to queue inside or eat in the restaurant. This expectation of convenience and speed raises pressure on staff to ensure the queue subsides and customers leave satisfied. Preparing, packaging and distributing food to 120 customers in an hour requires a standardised work process that can cope with intense periods of demand. However, if a grill can only cook four items at once, employees are limited in their ability to satisfy large orders or high demand. This involves waiting, something incongruous with the accelerated culture of instant gratification. From a management perspective, to successfully satisfy customer demand requires accurate scheduling. Scheduling is based on predicted sales and staff rotas are constructed accordingly. With food services, health and safety requirements result in more frequent staff sickness. If forecasted sales are low and staff sickness reduces the workforce, a sudden rush of unanticipated customers can leave the team short staffed and forced to work incredibly hard to meet demand. The pressure from customers expecting food in a timely fashion and managers wanting a smooth operation filters down to staff.

Contacts also outlined a number of impatient management practices. Managers often expected a higher level of knowledge or skill from new members of staff and showed a significant lack of patience with those who learned their roles 'on the job'. Lee was 18 and worked cash in hand at a local pizza shop. He was regularly berated by one of his managers for 'doing it wrong'. Jessica also 18, felt she was expected to know everything with little guidance or training at her clothing retail job. Jason, 22, worked for another clothing retailer and found his manager's expectations clashed with Jason's inexperience, which resulted in constant reproach. Pressure on service economy operators to provide the best possible service to customers and ensure profitability for the company is often transferred onto poorly paid, overworked staff expected to learn fast and cope with periods of intense work. In these examples we can see the negative motivation to harm, the use of work routines and management pressure to meet economic need. This also demonstrates a positive motivation to harm, a denial of basic respect and a willingness to inflict pressure on employees in order to 'succeed'. One way to ensure employees remain engaged and continue to generate sufficient levels of productivity is to incentivise their work.

Targets, incentives and bonuses

Management strategy within the service economy reflects a wider neoliberal fetish for targets to demonstrate and measure productivity, efficiency and profitability. Targets are the master-signifier of neoliberal society (Barber, 2008). 'Value for money' has always been significant in a competitive capitalist economy but this has been elevated to a position of central importance under neoliberalism. The principles of the market drive public sector management strategy too, with a raft of key performance indicators and targets measure the success or failure of a policy (Barber, 2008). Efficiency, productivity and targets sit at the heart of business ideology and act as a tool to maximise employee output (see Lloyd, forthcoming).

Targets serve several purposes. First, targets are aligned with performance management of personnel (Power, 1999). Auditing employee performance by measurement against key indicators provides employers already in possession of an unbalanced degree of power in the employer–employee relationship with the hard data to discipline their workforce (Power, 1999). Second, employers can use targets as an incentive to supplement low wages. Service economy employees often receive the minimum wage with the promise that incentives to boost earnings are available subject to exemplary achievement: hit your targets and receive a bonus. Finally, targets incentivise employee performance in a way that ensures compliance and effort at work; if pay is based on the ability to make sales or to perform certain functions, self-interested (or precarious) employees will work harder. In each of these three ways, the use of targets and performance management exemplifies working relationships within the service economy.

Targets flow down the corporate hierarchy; regional managers face targets which cascade down to individual stores and eventually to individual employees who are trained and performance managed accordingly. The Symbolic Order of neoliberalism shapes the values of the workplace; as individuals solicit this organisational logic and culture, they further shape the workplace by reinforcing these values in their daily practice. Performance and targets become important. Team briefings were a source of consternation for some contacts who felt that management focus on performance and targets was often manifested in a negative attitude towards the work undertaken by staff.

Leanne was 25 and had worked in retail,

> 'The thing I didn't like was the cheesy management of like rah rah rah, performance meetings, and when they didn't seem to understand that you could do everything you possibly could, that it was always your fault they didn't hit target, it was never their fault, that they were not supporting you in the right way, it was always everybody else's fault but theirs.'

Managers instil a culture whereby responsibility for missed targets rests with the staff on the shop floor rather than wider considerations such as the current economic climate, the weather, the competition or management support and direction itself. Sam was in his late 30s and had spent his working life in retail. He indicated that morning briefings would often focus on targets and what staff had failed to achieve the previous day. He insisted this was counterproductive and left colleagues worried about their perceived failures and concerned about management dissatisfaction. Negative briefings about missed targets would start the day in a pessimistic mood and instil the wrong attitude in employees who would chase sales in order to prevent further opprobrium from dissatisfied managers. This focus on the negatives fuels a culture whereby employees are acutely aware of their limitations or failures rather than any positive recognition of their value or contribution.

Most respondents acknowledged that managers and supervisors were themselves driven by targets imposed by their superiors. The organisational culture of sales, targets and performance management pervades the service economy and shapes relations between co-workers, managers and customers. All respondents indicated that co-workers represented the best thing about their work. 'I love the people I work with' was commonly heard throughout interviews. However, the same respondents also recounted previous occupations rife with bullying, mistreatment and cliques among colleagues or identified self-interested and instrumental behaviour by co-workers driven by targets and incentives. These behaviours are indicative of the organisational culture within many forms of service work and the management practices which underpin and facilitate certain attitudes and actions. Leanne was often effusive in her praise for co-workers. However, she also revealed a more instrumental approach to relations between co-workers, driven by the need to make sales within a commission-based earnings model,

> Leanne: 'What I used to do if I was on the tills and say a customer brought over a product, the sales people I liked, I'd put it on their sales number. If I was doing the online reservations, people [staff] would come over and say, "Oh, put that on my number," but what's in it for me? What's my benefit?'

> Interviewer: 'Did you decide to put sales through on sales people's numbers if you liked the sales person?'

> Leanne: if 'I liked them, if I got on with them, or, it sounds daft but if they bought me my dinner, I could be quite easily bribed. On the sales team, everybody had different people

who you could count on, certain people who could get the benefit from.'

As a cashier, Leanne earned no commission from the sales she processed under her own sales number whereas sales staff did. Although company policy indicated that sales staff could only claim sales they had made, a reciprocal culture emerged based around incentives and targets. James was 32, worked in retail and elaborated on this point,

> 'You scratch my back, I'll scratch yours. But it's like free sales ... If they didn't get anything for it anyway [commission] why not put it on someone else's [sales number]? So they got the benefit from it and then they got paid for ... it made sense didn't it? No one was losing out, apart from the company. The company loses out cos they're paying someone who hadn't done that job. You get paid on commission, that's all you're interested in. Cos you think the company's big enough to swallow the extra fiver they're going to pay me so why not take it off them? You think you clearly work hard enough but you always think you should get more than you get and you try and top it up where you can cos the company can afford it.'

The imposition of targets and commission-based sales fosters an instrumental approach whereby sales colleagues identify incentives to maximise earning potential through the establishment of relationships with co-workers who can provide what James calls 'free sales'. While these relationships were no doubt more complex than an instrumental exchange relation, this is clearly visible in Leanne and James' accounts of their work experiences. As with any culture, workplaces are rife with unwritten rules and rituals, the demonstration of which denotes inclusion within the group. The practices noted above showed a willingness to be part of the team. Management were more than likely cognisant of these strategies but on some level tolerated such behaviours as facilitators of team bonding and a collective effort to hit targets.

Targets were also instrumental in relation to customer satisfaction surveys. Customer surveys are used to elicit information on the level of satisfaction felt by customers with the service rendered by the employee. However, the exchange-relation and profit motive underpins this relationship in a number of ways and serves to remove any substance from the exchange (Baudrillard, 2007). Measuring performance by surveying the customer appears to be a way to ensure high quality customer service and identify training needs for performance-managed staff. However, the employment practice of targets and incentives penetrates this mechanism with consequences for relations between employees and the relationship with customers.

Abbie was 25 and worked in the customer service arm of retail banking. Her bonuses were directly linked to performance management and her achievement of targets. One target was the customer satisfaction survey. Satisfaction surveys are deliberately designed in a way which may lead the customer to believe that they have been generous and positive towards the employee but in reality has the opposite effect. In Abbie's case, questions have options ranging from awful and bad, to good, very good, and excellent; an excellent rating earns 50 points while a very good rating only garners 20. The total survey adds up to 450 points. A customer who answers 'very good' across the board scores Abbie 220 points, under half of the available marks. Abbie recalled an email from her manager which expressed disappointment at a survey awarding her 'very good' service. The customer was obviously pleased yet the survey result counts against Abbie's performance. Should she receive two 'very good' reviews, Abbie's manager must sit in on her customer interviews and monitor her performance. This indicates that performance management and targets have reached the level of absurdity. However, the harm arises when Abbie's performance review and bi-annual bonus is tied, among other things, to the results of her satisfaction survey,

> Abbie: 'They will give you a rating – "under-performing" – which you don't get a pay rise at all, "developing", "good", "strong" and then "top performer" and that's your pay rises, so if you're good you just get the standard 3%, I think it's 1.5 for developing ...'

> Interviewer: 'So you can get quite a sizeable pay rise?'

> Abbie: 'Yes but it's on a correlation so they're only allowed to have one top performer in a branch. And they have to have developing and underperforming so ... it's quite bad really because if you're on that borderline it can very much come down to whether the person likes you, or sees a lot of you, I think the fact that they're looking to put somebody on underperforming is bonkers.'

Abbie and her co-workers are placed in direct competition for bonuses and the customer survey plays a significant part. The outcome of customer surveys is directly linked to her performance review and the chance of securing a bonus. In her organisation, bonuses are a zero-sum game; there can only be one 'top performer'. The organisational culture and management practice within her institution pit co-workers against each other in pursuit of vital and scarce resources such as a bonus or pay rise. Abbie admitted that her salary of £17,000 was low compared to her co-workers and was prohibitive in her long-term plan to buy a house with her fiancé. Her customers may be satisfied and complimentary in their response to the survey but it can result in a considerable financial downside. This makes each of Abbie's customer interactions a precarious event; she must 'perform' (Hochschild, 2003) at the requisite level, ensure a satisfactory outcome, and then pray that the customer is effusive in their praise when surveyed. If harm is related to the quest for recognition (Yar, 2012) then Abbie's requirement to compete with co-workers in a self-interested way ensures her relationships are devoid of mutual recognition or ethical obligation; they are instrumental and anti-ethical, competitive and harmful. The wider political-economic conditions that shape her labour market and organisational culture ensure this; an unintentional harm in pursuit of profit fosters a positive motivation to harm as Abbie struggles to compete for resources.

The idea of meritocracy is endorsed as the key to social mobility. Competitive individualism has become the order of the day and the organisational culture of the workplace actively facilitates this. Moving along one's instrumental journey, maximising opportunities and human capital in order to survive and succeed in an increasingly competitive 'dog-eat-dog' world, the individual must grasp every chance and shoulder the responsibility for success or failure subjectively. This competition is highlighted clearly in the zero-sum approach to Abbie's performance-related bonuses. Co-workers are no longer a source of collective strength, despite the numerous assertions that co-workers represented the best thing about their jobs. Pure competition for bonuses, sales, targets and 'top performer' status has considerable impact on an organisational culture. The greater indignities and iniquities of work within the low-level service economy are exacerbated by management practices which pit co-workers in direct competition.

James, who worked in car sales, described the logical conclusion from an employee's perspective when bonuses are linked to customer satisfaction surveys; he 'coaches' customers to answer the survey in a way that serves to meet his target. Similar to Abbie, only a 'completely satisfied' customer counts towards his bonus. James acknowledged that his *actual* performance was less important than whether or not he ensured the survey came back as 'completely satisfied'. James suggests that the company would be confident in his performance if his surveys came back as consistently 'very satisfied' but they would avoid an obligation to pay a bonus as he failed to reach 'completely satisfied'. However, James also acknowledged that his income and capacity to pay his mortgage was linked to his ability to maximise all available bonuses and incentives. The best way to meet targets linked to satisfaction surveys was to coach his customers,

> 'You're reasonably assured of a "completely satisfied" because you coach the customers. You're not supposed to and the brand don't want you to but that's cos they don't want to pay you the money but equally, you need to say, "Look, they pay me based on this, do you agree that I've done a good job?" "Yes, you've done a good job." ... "Well, if you can pay it forward and show that in the survey I'll really appreciate it." It's a difficult one, the survey should be a reflection of what your experience is but cos we get bonused on it, you're trying to manipulate feedback. You don't want to have to but that's your livelihood. You don't really want to ask for a top score, you kind of think if you can be satisfied you've done a good job then you think you should [get one] but you know from experience, you know you've done everything you should have done but you've had surveys back as "somewhat satisfied", "I should've had a bit more discount" ... I don't know what I'm supposed to have done with that, with people like that you've got to say, "Look we've done the best job we can, if, from where we're sat this is the best job we could've done and we all agree, it needs to be 'completely satisfied'".... It's shit, you'd like to think you can rely on them to do that but if it matters to you then you have to say "This is the crack, this is what it is..."'

In some cases, James even goes as far as to withhold the survey from certain customers if he thinks they are likely to provide negative feedback. Customer satisfaction is incentivised in a way which removes any meaning from the survey, particularly when it leads employees to manipulate the survey or coach the customer. It becomes a substanceless interaction, devoid of any meaning other than the naked exchange relation tied to the employee's bonus. The employee only provides excellent service as there is a further cash reward at the end of it. Employees who face indeterminate futures with serious question marks over income fluctuation that is contingent on bonuses linked to targets will inevitably concentrate on that target. Employers shape the incentives and targets on satisfaction surveys in a way that negatively affects the employee or stacks the deck against them; employees redress the balance and fix the survey to ensure they get paid. The relationships and interactions within this context reflect an instrumental culture whereby the values which underpin these interpersonal exchanges are monetised. When organisational cultures are shaped around profit and targets, it pushes out other forms of exchange and any sense of sociality or mutual recognition; it reflects a simulacra (Baudrillard, 1981), an unreal copy of social exchange. This substanceless exchange is linked to an absence, a culture of negativity devoid of the collective, the social. The ethical obligation is to the self, to maximise one's opportunity from an exchange. The interaction is governed by nothing more than a simple exchange relation.

Maximising profitability

The previous chapter outlined the systematic shift from labour market security and stability towards flexibility. The focus on growth and profitability required the suspension of wage increases and the removal of labour protections (Varoufakis, 2016). As capital ascended and financialisation took grip, labour market flexibility greased the wheels as employers sought to maximise financial output through wage suppression, labour fragmentation and the flexibilisation of temporary and non-standard forms of work (Harvey, 2005; Streeck, 2014).

The growth of non-standard forms of work, temporary work agencies, zero-hours contracts, and on-demand work reflect the fragmentation of the labour market and are the artefacts of the new global capitalist order. Management use temporary, part-time and zero-hours contracts to the organisation's advantage in relation to flexibility and profitability, but these also ensure labour fragmentation. The first form of efficiency in labour practice is an organisation's use of on-demand labour (Friedman, 2014; Scholz, 2017). This fragments the labour force and ensures huge benefits for companies in that they are no longer responsible for potentially unproductive time and activity. Where in-house personnel could find downtime between tasks, on-demand labour pays only for the task itself (Scholz, 2017). If efficiency, just-in-time production and profitability are key features of modern organisations, the eradication of the employer–employee relationship via on-demand contracts serves a signal purpose. Independent contractors who seek discrete tasks for what is often inadequate remuneration compete to earn the right to complete work for companies. The competition within platforms such as Amazon's Mechanical Turk, Uber drivers, and Deliveroo couriers has been highlighted in a range of literature (Friedman, 2014; Schor, 2014; Scholz, 2017). While, ideologically, some are drawn to the sense of freedom and liberation yet significant levels of precarity and indeterminacy are attached to this form of work. For the organisation, it ensures that productivity and profitability remain high; the vast majority of labour costs are no longer their concern.

Further fragmentation takes place within retail in a way that simultaneously lowers labour costs for the organisation and generates significant revenue. Some suppliers seek to ensure a physical presence within large stores in order to maximise potential sales to customers. A manufacturer sells a range of televisions to an electrical retailer but can improve sales if their products are displayed prominently. This comes at a price and has implications for management practice. Sam worked in an electrical retail store but was not employed by that company. He was employed by a manufacturer and was their representative in store. If a customer approached him, it was his responsibility to sell them a particular brand. Many of the larger manufacturers pay retail chains for the right to a certain amount of display space in store as well as the use of their representatives to sell their products. Sam explains,

> 'It's a money-saving exercise because you can get less staff of their own. Initially it wasn't, initially reps were there to help, now reps, in that store, and [they] have actually taken on more reps than there is [store] staff. It's gone the other way; it's probably gone a bit too much the other way. They [the store] gain both ways cos the companies have to pay to have us in there, right, so they actually gain financially, at the same time, they gain because they don't have to pay that staff. Number three, the reps tend to work better than the staff, the reps are more motivated because you're one product, you're one brand, you're no ... cos you've got that much competition it's a dog-eat-dog world in there so you've got to be in there, you've got to be ... I don't know if greedy is the right word but you've got to be motivated, if you're motivated you can be very, very successful as a rep, in comparison to the wages you get as a member of staff [in store], a rep gets a lot more, you're financially motivated to

work harder. Now they have picked up on that and they've cut down on their staff and become more rep-orientated and they're gaining all ways. I've got three stands in there. They [manufacturer] have to pay for that space, so they're renting space out in the store so they're financially gaining. There's a big Samsung area, they'll be gaining a million pound a year, around that figure, from Samsung, just to have them ... Where before ... you bought the products from the manufacturer and then you sold them, now every space on that store has to be paid for by the manufacturer, just to utilise that space. So they gain financially in every way.'

As a cost-benefit exercise, it makes sound fiscal sense. The possession of a commodity, usually land, space or buildings, can be monetised through rental income. The retailer has monetised its physical space in store and generates significant rental income from suppliers who lease stands and displays. The competitive market among manufacturers compels them to play the game and pay the fees otherwise their competitors gain advantage. Marx's coercive law of competition at the heart of capitalism is evident here. Furthermore, the use of manufacturers' own sales representatives rather than in-house staff is of further pecuniary advantage to the retailer. They avoid wage obligations, fringe benefits and overall responsibility for the worker; sick pay, holidays, performance reviews are all conducted by the supplier. In effect, the retailer has outsourced much of its in-store labour supply, a further indication of the flexibilisation of the labour market. The final point to note is that this kind of labour fragmentation prevents employees finding a forum to air collective grievances. They are employed by different companies, in direct competition with one another. From a fiscal perspective, service economy employers can service their bottom line much more efficiently if they invest in physical infrastructure which is rented out, and a small core of employees is supplemented by outsourced staff from the manufacturer. This example is not necessarily harmful but does demonstrate the existence of conditions in which harm occurs; a culture geared around maximising profit at the expense of everything, where everything is measured according to profitability and cost-effectiveness.

'Facilitating the customer experience'

Ultimately, service economy workplaces and management strategies are designed around the need to convince the customer to exchange money for commodities. The customer experience differs in accordance with the look or 'vibe' on offer in each establishment, the aesthetic economy carefully designed to cater for a particular marketable demographic (Chugh and Hancock, 2009). The exchange relation underpins this aesthetic but the layout, display design, music, lighting and staff all work towards a particular customer experience. The importance of the aesthetic is complemented by the use of emotional and affective labour within the workplace. Hochschild (2003, p 7) describes the use of emotional labour as the requirement to 'induce or suppress feeling in order to sustain the outward countenance that produces the proper state of mind in others'. Effectively, employees must draw on their personality, communicative skills and emotion to put the customer at ease and induce them into parting with their money. This section will focus specifically on James and Sam, two salesmen attuned on a visceral level to the requirements of emotional labour but in complete recognition of the cold logic which underpins their industry. James breaks down his role into a simple calculation,

> 'From a selling perspective, whenever somebody walks in, do your best to sell them something. If you can get to that point, well done, however, you've got to also sell them this, sell them that, basically, selling is maximising the opportunity you've got and whether it's a car or a toaster it doesn't really matter cos all you've got to make sure is that whatever money they've got in their pocket ends up in your pocket. The way they go about it might be different but the start and the finish are the same.'

That is the raison d'être behind any service interaction. How the employee ensures 'whatever money they've got in their pocket ends up in your pocket' is established through the use of emotional, affective or cognitive labour. Sam refers to this as 'relationship building' and is worth quoting at length,

> Sam: 'In the sales game, I can have the best product in the world but if I'm not a people person, if I can't sell myself to that person they're not going to buy it. They have got to gain trust from you, as an individual. If I'm just sat there, "Oh yeah, this is the best in the world, that's all I'm going to say," doesn't ... you've got to gain trust off that person. Asking them the questions and not just being about the product, finding out about that person, getting a connection

with that person, asking the right questions, you get a connection, you can then, you don't even necessarily need to ... I've sold products before to people where I haven't even actually talked about the product, I've gained a relationship with that person, they've thought "This guy's all right, he can't be telling us porkies ... he's like a family member to us now, we're having a crack." I've sold to people where I haven't even spoke about the product, I've just gained the trust of the person by just being friendly, just talking about them, their kids, their family life, and then you can gain trust and they'll come back to you. They might not buy there and then but they'll come back and ask for you cos you're not just trying to sell a product, you're building a relationship up with that person.'

Interviewer: 'So a lot of effort on your part?'

Sam: 'Yeah yeah there's a lot ... if you want to be successful I believe you've got to be a people person, you've got to be able to read people, reactions, when I'm talking to people I look, this is not academic, you just look at people's reactions, their eyes, the way their head drops, you know, you can see ... and in the sales environment you've got to be a bit savvy, work out who's pulling the purse strings, you know? There's the family there and there's one person being a bit, "Oh no, you're not having that," you know that person's pulling the purse strings, try and sell to that person, you know, that person's the one who can make the decision, so you speak more to that person. That's not to say you ignore the rest but you know your focus is on that person cos you know that's the one who, at the end of the day, is going to say ... cos at the end of the day it's a results thing, you've got to get results, and it's about trying to read people and pick up who's the person most likely to say "Yes, ok, we'll have it," and make that decision.'

Sam clearly focuses on the need to foster trust and build relationships. He genuinely identifies himself as a people person and takes an active interest in his customers. This was visible in observations of him engaged with customers. However, he also acknowledges that the reason for that interest and the need to build trust is to leverage that relationship in a way that 'gets results' and sells products. The culture in retail and other service occupations is based on profit margins, targets and results, and both James and Sam invest their own personalities into this practice; they employ emotional labour on behalf of the company but also, as target- and commission-based employees, for their own financial advantage. The service economy encounter is a reflection of the capitalist demand for consumer spending; the customer driven by the desired satisfaction derived from a purchase, the employee propelled by targets and the need to make bonus or commission, the employer by the competitive logic of the market and shareholder demand for profit. Within the logic of neoliberal ideology, productivity, profitability and targets shape the management strategy and the organisational culture. In repeated interviews, observations and previous employment, the need to 'hit target' or 'make bonus' was a familiar refrain.

Baudrillard (2007) points to the equivalence of use value within the exchange relation of capital and its negative consequences in relation to the social. The ubiquitous piped-in pop music, the broad aisles filled with products and advertisements, the bright lights beckoning the customer, the clean space inviting us in, the smiling employee ready to offer their assistance. This all brims with use value; each object is used to induce spending and convince us of the necessity of an immediate purchase. The aesthetic and affective have a clear equivalent in the sale of a commodity. The shopping experience and interactions with service economy personnel demonstrate the functional calculation of use value. Sales personnel are not *really* interested in the details of your day so far, they seek to hook you and cultivate a sale through the use of symbolic exchange, emotional and affective labour. A simulacrum of the social exists within the retail outlet, built on exchange and the use value of staff and commodities. Baudrillard (2007) suggests that the social itself retains use value which has far-reaching consequences. The death of the social occurs when it becomes use value, absorbed into capitalist political economy.

As Winlow and Hall (2013) note, a substanceless sociality exists in the anodyne encounters one faces within the service sector. Neither party submits anything *real*. The exchange relation dominates, the accoutrements of aesthetics designed purely to appeal to our libidinal desire for the lost object temporarily replaced by a new purchase, a meal, another glass of wine, and the imperative to 'enjoy'. In both store design and the employment of workers' emotional and aesthetic labour, a simulation of the social greases the wheels of exchange. Management practice within retail, call centres, the leisure economy and the night-time economy (at least until behavioural codes are overturned and the finely balanced dynamics of carnival and safety are disrupted by drunkenness) aims to employ numerous techniques, objects and individuals to convince us to part with our cash.

During observations, in many stores emotional labour was not visible, employees made little or no attempt to engage with customers. Customers ignored staff unless absolutely necessary, employees resolutely concerned themselves with tidying up or maintaining their own conversations rather than engaging with customers. One field note recorded after a day at a retail park noted,

> My abiding memory of this day has been the absence of excitement or fun in the faces of the customers and staff. It is routine, ritual. Employees don't fake interest, customers don't generate enthusiasm. They're shopping out of habit, out of compulsion.

Both customer and employee at times avoid the intrusion of work yet the target-driven culture of service economy work requires it. As Leanne and Sam noted earlier, management briefings focus on targets and benchmarks; management push employees to respond in their own self-interest through incentives. Many, as seen with James and Sam, respond in kind and employ emotional labour to secure sales and bonuses. Others, as with Jessica, Leanne and many of my observations, respond negatively to the pressure to push for sales, and simply appear remote and bored. On some level, recognition of the substanceless and *fake* nature of the service interaction leads the employee or the customer to a 'subjective distance' from the encounter, a psychic withdrawal from a false imitation of social interaction (Fisher, 2009). In doing so, both techniques remove any sense of sociality which makes way for a 'para-social' exchange often experienced as substanceless by one or both parties or a resolute attempt to avoid 'the social' (Baudrillard, 1993; Winlow and Hall, 2013). If harm constitutes the absence of recognition then this subjective distancing represents a failure to recognise the other as something more than a false imitation of sociality predicated on commodified exchange.

Conclusion

This chapter has provided the contexts within which harms occur. Within the service economy, organisational culture and management practice shape the experience of work for the employee and the experience of consumption for the customer in a way that has an impact on both. Management practices are formulated around principles of profitability, productivity, efficiency and emotional labour. Fragmented labour markets and conditions of employment weight flexibility in favour of the employer; outsourced customer support and sales advice to manufacturers keen to boost their market share in store reflects a wider process of profit maximisation and lean working models, most recently exemplified by the on-demand economy. The macro-level demands from a competitive market place drive a set of organisational and management behaviours with significant impacts on workplace culture and staff well-being. Those imperatives are operationalised through a set of practices that encourage efficient working: the production line approach to fast food; call flow monitoring and pressure to 'wrap up' in the call centre; the demand for positive customer experiences in retail. These all lead to stressful and demeaning interactions where staff members are chastised for minor mistakes or face criticism from managers and senior colleagues unwilling to provide additional support.

The use of performance-managed targets and incentives ensure employees exert maximum effort without any guaranteed reward. Daily briefings focus on key performance indicators and targets, particularly those measures not currently achieved. Targets are incentivised which encourages staff to bolster insufficient hourly paid or annual salaries with bonuses based on achievement. While emphasis on targets could discourage some, others enthusiastically instrumentalise the target and enter interactions with customers with this in mind. As James suggested, the aim of the game was to get money from the customer's pocket into his. This is the capitalist system's core function, its undiluted essence – money-making at all costs.

This chapter has identified a number of issues within the management practice and organisational culture of the service economy, which create an environment where instability, precarity and a lack of protection have an impact on the employee. The entirely legal systemic violence of capitalism generates a set of drivers and imperatives for organisations to remain viable in a competitive market place. This creates a workplace culture framed around the need for profit and the immediate satisfaction of customer desire. It empties interactions of any significant meaning and instrumentalises the relationship between customer, employee and management. If this chapter has shown some of the realities of service economy work, the issues identified so far return in chapters four, five and six when investigated in specific contexts and analysed from a harm perspective. Just-in-time production and work intensification affect employee well-being when protection is absent. Targets motivate behaviours that display an absent ethical responsibility for the Other. The wide-angle lens trained on macro-level change in Chapter Two refocused on the meso-level organisational context in this chapter. The following chapters retrain our gaze further onto the particular causative absences created by the systemic violence characterised by deep-level restructuring and organisational culture. Chapter Four will offer evidence to support the belief that the absence of stability has harmful effects on workers.

FOUR

Absence of stability

Introduction

The organisational practice and management culture outlined in Chapter Three reveals realities facing service economy employers and employees. Many of these issues create conditions whereby instability affects workers. Work intensification and just-in-time processes raise stress levels, targets and incentives keep wages low, drive performance management and encourage a particular set of behaviours, while labour fragmentation fosters division and competition. Contemporary labour markets are increasingly characterised as flexible and insecure rather than stable and secure (Walther, 2006; Lee and Kofman, 2012; Glavin, 2013; Wheatley, 2016; Harvey et al, 2017). Precarious conditions emerge through the systematic reconfiguration of labour markets (Standing, 2011) driven by the requirements of neoliberal capitalism. The structural adjustment from job stability towards job flexibility provides necessary opportunities for employers to make efficiency savings and boost profitability (Harvey, 2010) but fundamentally damages the employees' sense of security. The balance of power now weighted entirely in favour of the employer affords a reconfiguration of employment relations, working conditions and organisational culture that serves to heap precarity on the individual and erode a sense of stability.

Absences have a causative impact for both organisations and individuals; this negativity creates a set of conditions in which social relations are affected and harms can emerge. Within this chapter, exploration of the absence of stability in employment and working conditions will begin to reveal some of the more harmful effects of low-level service work and the precarious conditions of work for an increasingly high proportion of people in the UK, US and elsewhere. The systemic violence of neoliberal political economy represents a negative motivation to harm; the willingness to reshape labour markets in favour of efficiency and profit despite the attendant problems and harms this inflicts on workers. The absence of stability creates conditions within which harms occur. This chapter will focus specifically on the absence of stability in terms of employee contracts, the use of overtime and a second income to supplement wages, and the problems of progression up the employment ladder. Part-time, low-hours and zero-hour contracts present significant challenges to a sense of stability at work which, coupled with just-in-time rotas, leave employees in a state of indeterminacy and struggling to plan their lives in advance. This has ramifications for the notion of transitions to adulthood, which will be discussed at the end of the chapter.

Contractual instability

The service economy is characterised by significant use of part-time, temporary, and zero-hour contracts (Friedman, 2014; Eurofound, 2015). The 'flexible accumulation' (Harvey, 1989) of late modern capitalism and neoliberal ideology may promote freedom for the individual yet the fundamental flexibility allows capital to circulate and reproduce unencumbered by onerous or restrictive labour relations (Boltanski and Chiapello, 2005). This represents the systemic violence of macro-level political economy. Organised labour's traditional strongholds were industrial and professional sectors of the labour market; 'new' jobs at the lowest end of the service economy are characterised by 'atypical workers' usually absent from union rolls (Gumbrell-McCormick, 2011). Capital benefits from non-standard work arrangements inadequately covered by organised labour. Workers' rights have been systematically eroded over three decades to the point where non-standard forms of low-paid work become normalised. Although entirely legal, this fundamental shift is nevertheless problematic and harmful for many. The neoliberal subject floats around detached from previous securities and stabilities (Badiou, 2007).

Standing (2011) suggests that the precariat is split between 'grinners' and 'groaners'; those for whom precarity is an accepted choice in order to enjoy flexibility at work, for example, students and pensioners, and those for whom precarity is an existential threat and daily burden. Despite the dominant liberal ideology of freedom, entrepreneurial spirit and liberation from the confines of nine-to-five, Friedman (2014) notes that employers, not workers, drive the on-demand economy; those engaged in temporary forms of 'gig' work would reject their status as 'contingent labour' should permanent and stable positions materialise. However, those for whom contingent status is a positive development become the spokespeople for non-standard forms of work. Of course, students benefit to some degree from flexible hours. When their student job becomes the norm, due to an imbalance between graduate numbers and graduate positions (Brown and Hesketh, 2004), their non-standard, temporary, part-time or zero-hour contract may garner less appeal.

These contractual arrangements were the norm among my contacts. Some held permanent, full time positions but many reported jobs which they characterised as temporary, part-time or precarious. Leanne's retail position was a permanent four-hour contract. Jade, 23, had recently moved from a twelve-hour contract to a sixteen-hour contract. Rachel, also 23, had recently dropped from a twenty-hour contract to an eight-hour contract. Jessica, 18, had been on a four-hour contract at one job and a zero-hour contract at another. Sophie worked on a zero-hour contract. Martin, 30, was now in full-time employment but his previous retail employment had been a permanent, sixteen-hour contract. Lee worked cash-in-hand, one night a week. Jason worked three shifts a week in clothing retail, without a contract. Ben, 30, was now in a permanent, full-time call centre position after a spell with a temporary work agency (TWA). Daniel's job in supermarket distribution posed a potential clash with a new college course so he had asked for flexible hours. His employer offered flexible hours on condition he change job role, from a specialist team of warehouse trouble-shooters to a generic stock picker, a change that resulted in two serious work accidents, considerable time off work and ultimately his dismissal. These are not atypical contractual situations within the service economy and reflect the statistics on growth in part-time, temporary or zero-hour contracts within labour markets.

By late 2017, 1.6 million people, or 6% of the total UK labour force, worked in temporary employment (ONS, 2018), and 1.1 million people had second jobs while 6.9 million worked part-time. Those who identified as being self-employed numbered 4.8 million, of which one-third were classified as part-time self-employed (ONS, 2018). In total, almost one-third of those in employment within the UK were categorised as something other than full-time employed. In the post-Brexit climate, the government celebrated the employment figures as proof that the scaremongering about economic catastrophe was unfounded. As the UK labour market continued to add jobs, this was taken as a sign of improvement. In truth, this reflects a long-standing emphasis on the employment rate as proof of economic growth and stability rather than scrutiny of the *type* of employment available. The rise of part-time work, zero-hour contracts, temporary contracts, independent contractors within the on-demand economy and other non-standard forms of work serves to reclassify people in relation to the employment figures but fails to consider the stability of employment conditions. Streeck (2016) correctly asserts that underemployment replaces unemployment. Furthermore, spatial considerations must be acknowledged as stable opportunities will differ according to the specific and contingent characteristics of local labour markets across the Western world. Places such as Teesside see significant growth of employment opportunities at the low paid, insecure and precarious end of the labour market (Shildrick et al, 2012).

The flexible, part-time hours and uncertain shift patterns create instability for employees who are unable to plan long-term or manage financially without either significant overtime or a second job. Rachel, 23, had recently renegotiated her contract with her employer, a clothing retailer, as her twenty-hour contract was incompatible with her new university course. Despite the decision to reduce her hours, her previous contract resulted in too few hours and required overtime to supplement her income,

> Interviewer: 'Can you manage on your current wages?'
>
> Rachel: 'Only just yeah.'
>
> Interviewer: 'I guess it depends as well how many hours they give you?
>
> Rachel: 'Yeah if there's overtime then yeah I can ... I put £200 into my savings every month, well I try to every month but some months I'll have to dip back into them and bring it back out if I haven't had any overtime. If I haven't had overtime usually I pick up about £600 a month.'
>
> Interviewer: 'Do you find you're just living month to month?'
>
> Rachel: 'Yeah, yeah! Because you never know when they're just going to cut your hours, like recently ... because you've started a new quarter there's been cuts to payroll so everyone's hours have been cut and everyone relies on the overtime there. Everyone is just on the contract but ... it's funny seeing everyone just doing the contracted hours but there's not enough staff at all when you look at it. So everyone relies on the overtime, even they do for staffing.'

Jessica started working in clothing retail aged 16 and recounted similar experiences. She was contracted to four hours a week, a single evening shift, although she often supplemented that with overtime. The overtime was arbitrary so it was not always possible to get extra hours. Jessica disliked this job for several reasons, which included co-workers, managers and the inflexible nature of her shifts. Warhurst and Nickson (2007) suggested the aesthetic labour tied to fashion and clothing retail revealed a 'new labour aristocracy' among service workers; Jessica initially fell into this category as she asserted the positive benefits of working in the 'fashion industry' with her interest in fashion satiated by the steady arrival of latest clothing lines. However, in line with Misra and Walters' (2016) critique, the consolations of staff discount and the fashion aesthetic failed to compensate for precarious conditions, exploitation and hyper-competitive co-workers. When asked what she liked about the job, her response was unambiguous: "I didn't really like working there." Precarious work and exploitative conditions devoid of collegiality and sociality cannot be overcome by staff discount. Rachel also noted this; her staff card provided benefit in the form of generous discount yet her experience of clothing retail was a litany of frustration, injustice and double-standards, as well as accumulated debt.

Jade was 23 and had worked for her retail employer for two years. She recalled a number of previous jobs in a largely negative light with few redeemable characteristics. As a result, she 'loved' her current job and recounted numerous positive features such as her co-workers and customers. However, she also had contractual issues and had recently won an extension to her contract, from twelve hours per week to sixteen,

> Jade: 'What happened was, the company normally works on ... I could be wrong but this is how it's happened in our store ... they employ temporary staff and they'll employ them on a smaller contract so there's a few staff in there that are on twelve and sixteen hours and they work on overtime base so the majority of the time I could be working between, like, twenty to twenty five hours a week, so it is quite good but the company did have quite a lot of cuts, so last Christmas I was stripped back down to my twelve hours a week and I couldn't cope on it, it's just not enough money to live or anything like that ... cos I live at home so I don't really get much student loan or anything like that so I do need the money so that's why I've asked. I've been chewing their ear off that I need these extra ... I know it's only four hours but it does make a lot of difference.'

Interviewer: 'Yeah, it's a little bit of protection isn't it? So if they have to strip everyone back down to contracted hours ...'

Jade: 'I know I've got those sixteen that I can live off, it's absolutely fine, whereas before I was living but I didn't, at the end of the month I didn't have anything left and I was constantly in my overdraft and I didn't want to be like that so those extra four hours I use it as my safety money, type of thing. [At Christmas] the year before that, I actually ... I think I was working forty hours a week so to me that was loads, I had loads of money and when I came back to uni I didn't have to stress out getting loads of overtime which is what I wanted to do last Christmas but it didn't happen so that's why I need these hours, just so I know I can live.'

The company policy of using part-time and short-term contracts provides maximum flexibility to cope with the peaks and troughs associated with service work. Lean or skeleton staff will cover quiet periods while a combination of temporary workers and overtime bolsters core staff at busy times. As Sennett (1999), Hatton (2011), Standing (2011), Harvey et al (2017) and others note, flexible working arrangements provide the greatest freedom for management to maximise profitability without the constraints of a large permanent workforce. This flexibility largely works one way; even those 'grinners' (Standing, 2011) who benefit from flexible working arrangements clearly identify problems and concerns in relation to part-time contracts. The lack of stability posed by flexible employment conditions and contracts ensures a precarious environment and potentially harmful consequences. The absence of stability in contractual and working arrangements is a consequence of the negative motivation to harm, the unintentional damage caused by flexible and insecure conditions.

The consistent practice of core staff levels that largely comprise part-time and low-hours contracts, complemented with overtime to manage fluctuations in demand, provides flexibility for employers to manage quiet periods without maintenance of a bloated workforce. During peak periods, employees benefit from the availability of overtime. However, many respondents experienced the continual use of overtime which ensured that part-time staff became de facto full-time and regularly acquired generous overtime levels to maintain a steady income. However, as Martin, Jade, Phil, Leanne and others identified, the consistent use of overtime had drawbacks with implications for stable working conditions. This was most notable during holiday periods when one's contractual annual leave was calculated and paid in accordance with contracted hours rather than any regular or consistent shift pattern. The financial penalty for employees such as Martin who was contracted to sixteen hours but regularly worked double is evident. His annual leave entitlement, paradoxically, penalises him, as his take home pay is substantially lower than his usual wage. It pays to lose holidays, and work instead.

The absence of stable and settled work routines within low-level service occupations clearly has financial implications for employees. The inability to predict weekly or monthly income is exacerbated by periods of stagnation where the overtime used to bolster minimum income is discontinued. Both Sophie and Jessica acknowledged the insecurity attached to a reliance on overtime. Both worked zero-hour contracts and waited week-by-week for hours that at times failed to materialise. Although both still lived with parents, each acknowledged a set of financial obligations and outgoings, as well as a desire to enjoy the fruits of their labour within the same service and leisure economies that provide their employment. The instability attached to minimal hours and no guaranteed overtime required a supplementary income derived from a second job. Sophie sought a second income from bar work,

> 'I wasn't getting enough hours and I'll be honest I was sick of the place, I was getting treated like shit by one or two of the managers that have now left fortunately. But because of how secure the other job is I couldn't just drop the job. So ... I decided that I was going to do ... until I finished uni and I decided what I wanted to do I was going to do one shift a week at work which meant that when I hit my three years I got my private healthcare as well. I might as well get something out of them. And then I was going to do my two shifts a week at the club which ran my car basically, and paid for any food that I needed.'

Sophie's inability to garner overtime and negative treatment from managers forced her to consider a second job in order to secure additional income. Her mistreatment and lack of sustainable income was not motivation enough to consider complete withdrawal from a job she regarded as 'secure'. She earned minimum wage on a zero-hour contract but it was permanent and almost 'guaranteed' two shifts each week. Coupled with her relative seniority and experience in the workplace, Sophie saw this as a secure income. Her upcoming graduation to a private healthcare plan, 'earned' after three years' service, also informed her thinking. That these employment conditions could be regarded as 'secure' indicates the normalisation of such contractual provisions within neoliberal labour markets. This is simply 'the way it is'; flexible and insecure working conditions are recognised as normal and are accepted as the reality of life in the low-paid service economy. The systemic violence engendered by neoliberal ideology and capitalist political economy, the deep restructure of labour markets in favour of flexibility, removes stability from the lives of service economy employees. The concept of fixity, determinacy or progress diminishes. Within the framework established earlier, this constitutes a set of harmful arrangements.

Rotas

Service economy operators sell products that often cannot be stored (McDowell, 2009). This underpins 'just-in-time' management strategies that require efficient service provision and an adaptable and flexible workforce able to meet demand. Within call centres, managers can predict call flow and schedule staffing levels accordingly but it is not an exact science. Retail can plan for busy periods such as weekends, holidays and sales, as can food services and the night-time economy. Lean staffing models, flexible contracts and just-in-time shift patterns become the dominant management practice. Managers were noted to 'play favourites' among staff (discussed in Chapter five), which affected shift allocation and the levels of flexibility afforded to employees. If your face fits, you will be ok. If not, shifts are allocated with little or no regard for an employee left with the responsibility to change any problematic shifts.

Returning to Jessica, rotas were a big problem, partly because of the necessarily short notice associated with just-in-time staffing models but also through management intransigence. Rotas were published a week in advance and often failed to accommodate Jessica's college obligations and her age; at 16 she could not drive and late shifts were logistically problematic as she travelled from one side of town to the other. Managers allocated shifts based on business need rather than Jessica's availability. When she indicated an inability to work her assigned shifts, Jessica was told to resolve the problem herself,

> Interviewer: 'Did you find it easy swapping with other people?'

Jessica: 'No, because you'd go and say, "This shift, I can't do it, is there any way you could ask someone or tell me who to go to," and they're like "Well, you need to do it yourself," and obviously it's not, everyone's always got plans and obviously you get your rota a week in advance so you organise all your plans around those shifts, so it was always a nightmare trying to find people who didn't have plans or people who could actually do your shift.'

Interviewer: 'And if you couldn't find someone to swap with would you have to do the shift?'

Jessica: 'Yeah, it was "tough luck", sort of thing. A lot of times I got put in and I didn't even know I'd got put in and obviously didn't turn up for my shift so then I'd be getting phone calls like, "Where are you? Where are you?", not knowing, and turn up late and then you'd get docked for your hours, or sometimes I'd literally, there'd be a point where I had no way of getting there at all, and I'd be like "I can't come in," so you'd get put down as an AWOL, and if you get three, you get sacked.'

This came up repeatedly throughout interviews. The rota played a significant part in work life as the tool which organised and structured work patterns. The rota would reveal allocation of overtime. Plans for the week ahead would be determined by the rota. In some cases, temporary staff at the end of a contract would learn their fate through the rota; no shifts next week indicated they were finished, rather than a conversation with a manager. Shift changes were often delegated to the employee; it was no longer management's function or responsibility to accommodate employee need. Flexibility at work is often highlighted as beneficial to the employee. Work when you want and fit work around other responsibilities and obligations; in practice, flexibility was reserved for the employer and any changes to set work patterns had to be negotiated between employees. This reflects the ideological and structural shift in responsibility onto the individual (Cederstrom and Spicer, 2015); management do not provide a safety net or support mechanism. Fix the problem yourself. The way management processes affects employees and their sense of comfort or well-being at work has an impact on the ability of the employee to successfully engage in customer interactions. This also indicates an absence of recognition; managers fail to recognise Jessica as an individual with other priorities, needs and desires. They see her solely as an employee, to be deployed in the service of the company's bottom line. This absence of recognition constitutes harm.

The political economic driver that facilitates the movement of capital and further accumulation allows employers to seek competitive advantage in the market through reliance on temporary workers at peak times, just-in-time staffing models that put 'lean' workforces at risk of overwork, agency workers devoid of employment rights, and the outsource of tasks and functions to third parties (Hatton, 2011; Berg, 2016). The extension of flexible working through the 'on-demand' economy further erodes job stability (Friedman, 2014; Berg, 2016). While flexibility works for capital, the deterioration of job security generates problematic effects for workers who face the indeterminacy of insecure labour markets. The precarious nature of employment within this sector creates instability within a working culture geared towards profitability. If 'getting on' is critical to individual success, the absence of stability places considerable emphasis on progression.

Progression

The literature on low-level service work often identifies flat hierarchies and limited opportunities for advancement (Mulholland, 2002; Lloyd, 2013). However, this is variable; large national or multi-national chains provide greater opportunity to transfer staff to other branches and often have head office, human resources, and distribution centres which offer opportunities for progression. Within individual branches and stores the hierarchy is often limited and difficult to traverse. Smaller and more independent service sector employers have significantly less scope for progression. However, the interviewees in this study all talked about career progression in one way or another, some keen to seek progression with their current employer, others within the service economy, and others determined to move forward in different fields entirely.

Martin, 30, worked in retail and was a sales adviser in a relatively small store. He was also an acting team leader when needed, for which he earned a one-off payment each time he was asked to open or close the store. After two years at this store, Martin had thought about progression but recognised the limitations of employment in a small store,

> Martin: 'It's unlikely in the store where I'm at now because of the size of the store and we already have a sales team leader and there's no reason to have two. Plus I'm one of

the only two full-time sales people there so it'd be pointless having two team leaders and one full-time sales person ... if I was going to get it, it was going to be at a different store, possibly Gateshead ... there's going to be a role opening up.'

Interviewer: 'Would you be happy to go and work in Gateshead?'

Martin: 'Yeah, I think I would. I'd quite like a change of scenery, it's a different place. Sometimes the one thing that gets you down about that sort of job is your surroundings don't change and sometimes it's nice to freshen it up a little bit.'

Martin did not drive and acknowledged that the logistics of a 35-mile journey to work was something he would need to resolve quickly, should this opportunity materialise. The outlay for driving lessons and a car would be considerable, in order to successfully progress to the next rung of the ladder within his current occupation. If an opportunity to progress arose, Martin would consider it but he was not tied to his place of work and had contemplated further education as an alternative. He acknowledged a degree of stability from regular hours which ensured his pay was steady but also recognised that it was just over the minimum wage. He was generally happy with his current work, and was open to consider advancement and progression with his current employer but had given no serious thought to his options beyond that. Two years after this conversation, Martin was still in the same role, with the same employer, in the same store.

Ben, also 30, had transitioned from the building trade to call centres after the housing market downturn which followed the financial crisis but now had no plan to resume his former trade. Instead, his long-term future was with his current employer. His initial foray into call centre work (see Lloyd, 2013) had been a permanent post but one fraught with disagreements and tension with managers and team leaders. This led to his departure and a period with a temporary work agency (TWA) that placed him in a new call centre. Ben left that post and contemplated a return to the building trade but this opportunity did not materialise. Still registered with his TWA, he received an opportunity with his current employer. He regards his call centre career trajectory in favourable terms; from a job he felt was 'laid back', to a position through a temp agency in a 'stricter, more regulated' call centre, and ultimately to a permanent position as a complaints manager with a 'good' employer. This career narrative gave Ben the sense that his recent employment history demonstrated progression. His current employment looked increasingly like his long-term option. After three years with this employer, he was seen as an experienced and knowledgeable member of his team and often called on to monitor calls for more inexperienced colleagues and train new members of staff. This creates a variety of work; call centre management recognises the 'reward' felt by employees who could 'escape' the phones (see Lloyd, 2013). However, he received no extra money for this extra-curricular activity. Although he earned around £20,000 per year and was happy in his job, Ben looked to advance within the company,

> Ben: 'I'm currently getting a level 3 salary but doing level 2 work. The only problem that poses is if I'm going to look to better myself, move up in the business, I'll have to try and skip to level 4 to notice any difference in pay otherwise I'd be sidestepping. I'd be going up a job grade but my pay grade, I'd be sidestepping. The level 4 grades are team managers and they're quite ... I've had a couple of interviews and scored quite highly on them but the other people who got them had already been seconded to them so they got them.'

> Interviewer: 'So you've thought about moving up?'

> Ben: 'Yeah, I've been applying. I like my team but I just want to ... I've worked on phones for six years, I just fancy getting off them, not speaking to people now. There's loads of other jobs available, team manager would be quite cool. I do all the coaching stuff, call monitoring.'

> Interviewer: 'So doing what you're already doing?'

> Ben: 'Yeah, I'd like to have my own team. I'd like to stay on the department but do a TM [team manager] role.'

> Interviewer: 'Are you happy to stay with the company?'

> Ben: 'Yeah definitely. I look at it like, the building trade has pretty much had it and I've been out of it for too long which doesn't help but yeah, it's a good place to be ... you can make a career out of it, earn good money. It's all right

cos you don't need any skills to go for it. I know it sounds like a cop out, sort of thing, I mean, I've got skills but I can't use them anymore so it's an easy job to fall into and succeed.'

Ben saw the expansion of his company as an opportunity for him to find a route up the managerial ladder. He had largely jettisoned his previous career and saw no route back into his skilled trade yet he was happy with his current employer and keen to move up, should a team leader role materialise. The management practice of encouraging willing employees by offering elements of responsibility such as training and monitoring (see Lloyd, 2013) dangles a carrot in front of workers like Ben. He sees opportunities for advancement but as yet has not found a promotion to his desired level. It is not clear how long Ben will hold out for a promotion before he reassesses his future progression.

Jo was 25 and had worked in retail and call centres. Her most recent employment had been in a call centre for an international bank. She was initially employed through a TWA on a six-month contract which eventually became permanent. After two years, she applied for a role in the complaints department and was offered a contract to work directly for the bank. After two years as a permanent employee, Jo left, partly because she planned to move away for family reasons, but also because relations with her co-workers had broken down. Prior to that, Jo had envisaged a long-term future with the company. Her working life to date had been a number of retail positions, none of which had been seriously considered as a long-term career. The decision to apply for a job in the complaints department was a reflection of her desire to further cement her place with the company, become a full-time member of staff, and progress with her employer. Once ensconced in her new role, Jo admitted that she felt this had potential for long-term employment. However, her plans changed and, given the negative atmosphere at work, Jo decided to leave the company.

McGowan (2016) suggests that the fundamental gesture of capitalism, that which ties the subject to a system that to all intents and purposes produces dissatisfaction for many, is the promise. The promise of future satisfaction in every sense; of accumulating wealth, of buying a dream home, of purchasing objects and commodities, of finding the dream job. This wager on the future ties us materially and psychically to the capitalist system. The promise of progress, the belief that one need just work hard enough, get lucky, make the right decisions, prevents the subject from the recognition that a search for something that fundamentally *does not* exist is the ultimate source of dissatisfaction. Those respondents who identified a future career path and set targets for their progression reflected this promise of future happiness. However, the attainment of a promotion or a pay rise will only ever bring temporary satisfaction, immediately replaced by the next object of future satisfaction. Of course, when the present is marked by indeterminacy, the promise of future success, progress and growth is far more attractive than the hard work of finding satisfaction and contentment in one's current conditions. That the promise of future satisfaction appears to be increasingly elusive for so many people within the current configuration of consumer capitalism, demonstrates a declining symbolic efficiency which fuels unrest and disaffection. The steady progress promised by post-war social democracy is no longer an option for a generation who face the future and see little of value or promise.

The absence of stability in relation to future plans is indicative of a capitalist system unable to fulfil its ideological promise. The symbolic violence of capitalism dims horizons and removes the possibility to countenance a coherent alternative to the status quo (Fisher, 2009). Wedded psychically to a system that forecloses alternative means of achieving future or present satisfaction, the subject attached to capitalism's promise sees possibilities for the recognition of positive rights, required for flourishing and contentment, diminish. Within the context of social harm the grip of capitalist ideology has negative consequences for service economy employees who put faith in an indeterminate future.

Transitions

The harms associated with inherent instability extend to successful passage through life-course gateways. Many contacts were aged between 18 and 30. Debate continues around definitions and boundaries between life stages; the traditional trajectory of childhood into adolescence and youth onto adulthood (see Furlong and Cartmel, 2007; Coté, 2014) may be interrupted by the psychologically distinct phase of 'emerging adulthood' (Arnett, 2000), while the complete 'life-stage dissolution' of late modern consumer capitalism (Hayward, 2013) is exemplified by the bi-directional processes of 'infantilisation' (Barber, 2007) and 'adultification' (Hayward, 2013). Meanwhile, the linear progression to adulthood has long been contested as structural conditions of education and employment 'fragment' or fracture transitional paths (Johnston et al, 2000; MacDonald and Marsh, 2005; Tomaszewski and Cebulla, 2014). As noted elsewhere (Brannen and Nilsen, 2002; Lloyd, 2012), some literature suggests that transitions are subjectively ignored in favour of an 'extended present'. Finally, Silva (2014) opines that transitions to adulthood are acknowledged subjectively rather than objectively; the personal victories over subjective obstacles such as parental breakup, criminal behaviour in adolescence, drug addiction, homelessness and other biographical factors, rather than an objective measure of success such as a steady job, marriage, family, or a home of one's own.

In the context of an ultra-realist harm perspective, the transition to adulthood is one measured by the causative absence of stability and the subjective solicitation of the external Symbolic Order of competitive individualism and consumer capitalism. Psychologically distinct phases of the life course (Arnett, 2000) are less important than a psycho-social attachment to, and solicitation of, a set of values and principles, which guide one's subjective actions as the individual seeks to maximise Weberian 'market shares' through negotiation of structural barriers and an individualistic 'winner-take-all' culture (Cook and Frank, 2010). The ideology of social mobility and meritocracy reflects in the narrative of 'progress' and 'progression' noted earlier; there is always a next step to contemplate, the acquisition of qualifications, the next rung on the career ladder, the next job opportunity, the next milestone to achieve (McGowan, 2016). The depth structures and systemic violence of neoliberal capitalism place impediments and barriers in the way of a significant proportion of the population. If meritocracy and social mobility are real, if hard work and endeavour can ultimately result in progression up the slippery slopes of social hierarchy, it is inevitably exclusive; within a capitalist society, there are always 'winners' and 'losers'. The transition to adulthood comes against a backdrop of competition for precious resources and the individualistic journey which embodies neoliberal capitalism.

Within this setting, the neoliberal subject actively solicits the Symbolic Order of neoliberal capitalism (Hall and Winlow, 2015). The dichotomy between structural reality and ideological rhetoric is faced subjectively; negotiated by each individual within his or her own agentic context. There is no recourse to class or community, to politics or protest, in order to redress any imbalance between individual aspiration and material consequences of the depth structures of ideology and political economy. Interviewees either reflect a firm commitment to social mobility and the desire to document transitions to adulthood through successful negotiation and attainment of a 'good' job, house, stable relationship, family and the disposable income to enjoy leisure and holidays, or they focus on the present, maintaining vague notions of 'the future' yet concentrating on managing day-to-day.

Both reflect a 'retreat into subjectivity' (Winlow and Hall, 2013), which represents an acknowledgement that the subject is ultimately responsible, the only one to be counted on, and that opportunities are either there to be grasped or entirely unattainable and therefore to be dismissed. This has implications for the concept of intersubjective recognition as individuals look inward for meaning, solace and value. Capitalist hegemony establishes the sociosymbolic parameters within which to negotiate existence, find meaning and define loss or success. However, it also harms the subject. For many of my respondents, transitions to adulthood were a reflection of a desire to capture some degree of freedom and liberation, either at work or in the ability to stand on one's own feet. The inability to achieve this without a heavy dose of instability or precarity was clear. Within the theoretical schema outlined above, this constitutes a set of harmful conditions.

Martin and Ben both demonstrate transitions described in the literature as 'fragmented' while their housing situation reflects a 'yo-yo' or transient pattern. Martin's housing 'career' has been a repetitive cycle of moving out of the family home to live in rented accommodation with girlfriends or friends, before moving back in with his parents after relationships break down or friends move on. His last move back into his parental home came following redundancy and a period of unemployment. Although he is now in steady work with some thoughts of progression, and earns enough to put some money aside, he has reached 30 and continues to find it hard to maintain independent living arrangements. Sharing with friends becomes common as pooled incomes make rent and bills manageable yet when friends also exist within precarious and unstable labour markets, agreed living arrangements are inevitably precarious and unstable. Ben demonstrates a similar trajectory. He has repeatedly moved from the family home into rental accommodation with girlfriends, work colleagues and old school friends, only to move on again when relationships break down or friends move on. Unlike Martin, Ben no longer has a family home to fall back on but is now in rented accommodation with friends. He at least appears settled, albeit with the complication of travel problems for work as his new home provided a more logistical challenge for someone unable to drive. While Ben's living arrangements do not entirely reflect a 'yo-yo' between independence and the family home, they do present a clear picture of instability and uncertainty.

Both Ben and Martin regard their earnings from retail and call centre work as relatively good. While both acknowledge they could be paid more, they are generally satisfied with their current situation. However, in terms of transitions, instability in housing and living arrangements proves difficult, largely because rent and mortgages are beyond the scope of their single incomes. Ben's fragmented living situation reflects an inability to cover rent and bills on his salary; Martin's yo-yo between rental accommodation and the family home reflect the same situation. The absence of stability in relation to work is something that neither Ben nor Martin would currently recognise; they see their jobs as secure and steady, relatively well paid and with potential progression opportunities in the near-term. However, the absence of stable and adequate remuneration traps both in a fragmented transition as they enter their thirties. The absence of stability is also embedded at the level of practical knowledge; they do not see the harm they suffer. Their integration within the cultural conditions of neoliberalism means they fail to recognise their structural position and their ideological deficit (in terms of the idealised life of stability, wealth and progress) as harmful.

Abbie's story exemplified the competitive individualism required to negotiate her way through the workplace. As outlined in Chapter Three, the competitive environment of bonuses, performance management and targets placed her in a zero-sum game against her co-workers. She insisted that she was worth more than she was paid, worked harder than others and that the significant salary difference between her and more experienced colleagues working at the same level was unfair. At the time of our first conversation, she had applied for the management programme within her company and, at our second conversation, had been successful and was now on a course which exposed her to different aspects of the business. Her upward trajectory was a reflection of her hard work and effort, the naturalised myth of meritocracy.

When it came to the thought of 'growing up' and the transition to adulthood, Abbie began to explain how she had set out a plan when she was very young: "I planned to be married and living in my own house by the time I was 27 so I'm still on track with that!" When asked what would happen if she didn't meet that target, she replied "It's something I worry about. Having had this plan or vision for so long, it'd be a big thing if I didn't do it. But we've started saving for a mortgage now so we've got time to do it." Her long-term plan included all of the traditional markers associated with the transition to adulthood, many of which were difficult to attain in a climate devoid of any sense of stability. That she was now in a job with prospects, recently engaged and in a position to take on a mortgage for her first home, at 25 years of age, was a reflection of her single-mindedness and determination to achieve the traditional markers of adulthood in an economy and culture where such things are harder to come by. However, in moving up the corporate ladder onto a graduate management scheme, Abbie had effectively left the low-level service economy; given her upwardly mobile outlook, she would not have found job satisfaction and a mortgage deposit in her previous role earning £17,000 per year and in direct competition with colleagues for bonuses and good performance reviews.

Abbie also exemplifies McGowan's (2016) belief in capitalism's promise of the future. Her search for stability and the path to adulthood reflects the objectification of home, job and relationship, their embodiment as future satisfaction and accomplishment. The loss at the heart of the split subject seeking Lacan's *objet petit a*, the lost object, fuels the subject to act and desire. We replace the lost object with any number of commodities and objects in the belief that attainment would bring satisfaction. Given that desire and satisfaction are tied to capitalism, any sense of achievement or satisfaction will be temporary as a new goal or target will appear. McGowan's crucial point centres on the role of loss at the heart of the unconscious subject: we unconsciously derive satisfaction from loss rather than acquisition therefore Abbie's focus on objective and subjective markers of attainment as the key to satisfaction misses the point; loss acts as a barrier which protects the subject from the realisation that the original lost object does not exist and no amount of substitute objects will produce lasting satisfaction. Abbie's single-minded focus on the future is an economic necessity in a precarious labour market, necessary for capitalism's survival, and a guarantee that satisfaction will forever be postponed.

Movement through the life course can be marked objectively, through the signposts of work, relationships, living situation and family, or subjectively, through a feeling of responsibility or a personal triumph over adversities such as addiction, broken home, mental or physical ill health. Within a capitalist society, focus on the future is essential; what we will achieve, the path we will take, the signs and markers we can show off to others. The pursuit of future success is motivated by the satisfaction we expect to derive from its attainment but also our relationship to the Other, a symbolic or collective fiction that provides a degree of functional consistency in our intersubjective and social interactions. The relational aspect of transition and progression comes from being able to show the Other our achievement; to parade external signs of success, competence and responsibility. The absence of stability within indeterminate labour markets prevents the successful demonstration of competence over one's circumstances and the attainment of a set of established markers. This harmful outcome is directly linked to an absence of recognition for one's place in the world and inability to demonstrate culturally prescribed markers of success or achievement.

Many respondents found instability at the heart of their living and working arrangements and were unable to transition to adulthood in the way society expects. Their transition experience was much more fragmented and fractured. In this case, the subject can be inclined to look inward for a sense of progression, to mark adulthood through feelings and responsibility rather than objective markers of work, wealth and home. For others, the compact with the future which lies at the heart of capitalism, the belief that satisfaction awaits with the acquisition of desirable markers and objects, shifts from a long-term plan for steady progression in a traditional sense to the satisfaction of desires in an immediate sense, through consumerism, through the night-time economy, through a retreat into online worlds. While the promise of the future is uncertain, satisfaction is at least within reach right now. Of course, for psychoanalysis, if our desire is bound up with an object or commodity, satisfaction will be fleeting while living and working arrangements will continue to be unstable and precarious. This absence of stability impedes and restricts a sense of genuine flourishing under consumer capitalism; dimming horizons, failure to find lasting contentment and indeterminate existence all indicate harmful conditions at the bottom of the labour market.

Conclusion

These issues collectively demonstrate an absence of stability at the heart of service economy work. The post-war period was characterised by stability in employment relations, pay and conditions and a degree of relative prosperity emerged as inequality reduced. Stability at work provides fixity; a platform for families, homes, social relations. The neoliberal shift from security to flexibility offers freedom to employers and capital in order to maximise productivity and profitability. The absence of security, the absence of stability, for employees engaged on zero-hour contracts, fixed-term contracts, minimum wage work, cash-in-hand or low-hours contracts, in companies with flat hierarchies and few opportunities for advancement, has a causative impact on health and well being.

As the balance of power rests with the employer, organisational culture and management routine takes advantage of precarious workers and transfers responsibility for shift changes onto the employee. Indicative of a wider ideological move to place responsibility on the individual rather than activate or harness support mechanisms, this increases pressure on staff to work unsuitable shifts or find their own replacements. As Jessica and Rachel suggest, the exploitation of particularly young staff is easily done and ensures that the company gains and management can concentrate on performance management and profit instead of changing rotas. Just-in-time and lean workforces predominate within the service economy which further heaps precarity on its employees. As Jessica and Rachel demonstrated, rotas published a week or two weeks in advance leave employees little time to prepare or plan their lives. Zero-hour contracts exacerbate this; to keep your week free and clear in the hope of a phone call with the offer of work has an obvious impact on your ability to plan for the week ahead.

Employment conditions no longer afford the employee a degree of security in their work. Contracts do not last, pay is low, shifts are not guaranteed, overtime is essential to making ends meet, responsibility lies with the employee for functions traditionally managed by the employer, and progression is often limited. The instability generated within these conditions is harmful to the employee who is unable to plan for the future, unable to plan for the week ahead, unable to find stable living arrangements. The presence of instability denotes an absence of stability.

Inequality itself does not generate social harms; inequality emerges through a willingness to inflict harm on others (Hall and Winlow, 2015). The evidence presented here demonstrates the neoliberal restructure of labour markets and the attendant shift in organisational practice in accordance with market logic indicates negativity at the heart of the service economy. The absence of stability in the name of growth and profit has harmful consequences for those individuals who seek recognition, fixity and safe ground amid the indeterminate uncertainty and fluidity of contemporary patterns of work and employment. Precarity becomes the operational characteristic of service economy labour; it reflects a willingness, at a political-economic level, to inflict harm on individuals and communities, in the name of efficiency, profitability and growth. When growth and profitability take precedent over well-being and stable employment, inequality increases, workers suffer and shareholders prosper. The willingness of neoliberal capitalism to jettison security in favour of flexibility excavates the ground of stable, secure work; the absence of this stability reflects a set of harmful working conditions for service economy employees. Within such a culture characterised and influenced by an absence of stability, some individuals take advantage of these causal absences and embody a positive motivation to inflict harm. This is outlined in the following chapter.

FIVE

Positive motivation to harm

Introduction

The previous chapters have underlined the reconfiguration of labour markets to facilitate efficiency, flexibility and profit. The evidence presented so far falls within the context of systemic violence and the negative motivation to harm. Unintentionally harmful outcomes are driven by institutional and organisational responses to deep level structural attachment to ideological commitments of competition, efficiency and profitability. The reorientation of management practice and organisational culture to meet these imperatives originates a specific set of normative cultural values, rules and expectations. The absence of stability creates insecure and precarious conditions of employment and working practice. Within this context, these institutional absences hatch a culture imbued with a further absence; the absence of moral or ethical responsibility for the Other (Whitehead, 2015; Smith and Raymen, 2016; Whitehead, 2018). This absence manifests as the *positive motivation to harm* another individual (Winlow and Hall, 2016). This positive motivation reflects a 'subjective distancing' whereby those subjects of 'capitalist realism' (Fisher, 2009) or 'cynical disaffection' (Stiegler, 2013) withdraw from positive social bonds and increasingly view the 'other' as competition; the negative ideology of neoliberalism fosters a negative solidarity (Adorno, 1973) where subjects identify the Other by their differences, not similarities. When co-workers, employees and customers appear higher or lower on the slopes of inequality and hierarchy, they can become obstacles to overcome. Accordingly, some individuals imbue themselves with a 'special liberty' (Hall, 2012a), which grants them the right to act as they wish, unencumbered by the constraints of ethics, morality or duty.

Chapter Two elucidated the core-periphery model at the heart of macro-level analysis of capitalism. The generative core of capitalism, the release of the amoral and non-ethical essence of libidinal and sublimated energy, has systematically eroded the ethical shield and regulatory sleeve constructed at the periphery in the post-war settlement. The locus of morality existed at the periphery; virtue, ethico-cultural norms and shared values of trust, mutuality and solidarity that had been affixed to temper the excess of capitalism's generative core (Whitehead and Hall, forthcoming). The neoliberal project punctured this ethical exterior and expanded the reach of the non-ethical centre; capitalist pursuit of growth, efficiency and productivity reflect a market mechanism driven by pure libidinal energy and not made to the measure of humanity. When meso-level recalibration in line with market value rather than civic value or public good infiltrates social institutions such as the workplace, the absence of ethical responsibility in a culture of competitive individualism foments the conditions within which harms can and do occur. The locus of morality in an Aristotelian sense existed in social function; we understand 'good' by learning and doing (MacIntyre, 2011). However, late modern capitalism signals the ascendance of 'emotivism', an ethical doctrine where 'goodness' is related to how we feel. If social functions increasingly lose their intersubjective ethical core, neoliberal subjects identify 'good' and 'right' subjectively. For some, in this context, the right thing to do is that which benefits the individual.

The transcendental materialist subject actively solicits an external Symbolic Order as a defence mechanism to provide internal meaning to external stimuli (Hall, 2012a). The intrinsic plasticity of the brain ensures neuronal receptors adapt and reconfigure to equip the subject with the values, norms, language, comportment, and symbolic framework necessary to exist in the world (Johnston, 2008; Winlow and Hall, 2013). The Symbolic Order within neoliberal consumer capitalism is one which valorises competitive individualism, individual achievement and the maximisation of one's 'market shares' (Hall and Winlow, 2015; Smith and Raymen, 2016). The subject is shaped by the external environment and then acts on that environment in a dialectical movement that feeds back onto the subject. The more we act as subjects of competitive individualism and consumer capitalism, the more engrained this becomes both within wider culture and individual subjectivity. This underpins the motivation to act and places emphasis on the promise of future satisfaction and desire fulfilment (McGowan, 2016). As a result, status and envy come to the fore as the subject jostles for position and attempts to secure a degree of stability and meaning in a precarious culture. This necessarily involves measurement of distance between oneself and others; to look down on the servants of the service economy for 'only' working at McDonalds, to belittle co-workers or employees in order to reinforce one's sense of superiority and status or to successfully compete for material benefits such as targets, tips or commission, or symbolic benefits such as status and respect.

Desire and satisfaction are inherently linked to the Other; we wish to attract the desire of the Other and therefore we desire what we assume the Other desires (McGowan, 2016). In order to achieve future satisfaction, we must also achieve the object of our desire which ties us, and our motivation to act, with the Other, in this case co-workers, employers and customers. The entire edifice of the consumer-driven service economy relies on convincing customers to spend money on desirable commodities. The employment of flexible pay regimes, exemplified by a basic hourly rate supplemented by sales-based bonuses, fosters competition among employees and is encouraged by managers as it fuels sales-generated income. Within this space of competitive individualism and commodity fetishism, status attainment and envy, precarity looms large which in turn drives anxiety and insecurity. Jobs are scarce and insecure, bonuses are linked to achievement, and customer desires are temporarily satiated through successful negotiation of the consumer experience. Within this insecure and substanceless setting, it is inevitable that some individuals will exercise their perceived right to inflict harm.

This chapter will describe those individuals who take the active solicitation of cultural imperatives towards individualism, competition and status to its harmful extremes. Not all subjects within neoliberal consumer capitalism act on these drives, but those who do often act because they believe they are entitled to do so.

Bullying at work

The literature on workplace bullying reveals its significance (Sloan, 2012; Berlingieri, 2015). Studies often focus on the psychological implications of workplace mistreatment (Einarsen et al, 2011). According to Berlingieri (2015), three interpretations cover workplace bullying: a behaviourist perspective; a dyadic issue between individuals; and those who situate it within a broader context of organisational culture and practice. Often, workplace bullying is reduced to a discussion of power-relations and control within the manager-employee relationship (Chamberlain and Hodson, 2010). Meanwhile, Sloan (2012) investigates the importance of supportive co-worker relationships to mitigate the worst excesses of unfair treatment and subsequent low levels of job satisfaction. Some studies do attempt to place workplace bullying in a broader discussion of management practice and employer behaviour as a response to competitive markets and the economic imperative to survive (Hoel and Salin, 2003). Berlingieri (2015) calls for an expanded theory of violence that places workplace mistreatment and bullying on a continuum reflective of socio-structural, symbolic and interpersonal violence in late modern culture. Beyond this, ultra-realism allows us to explore the *motivation* behind acts of violence in the workplace, as well as the impact of workplace bullying on the victim.

Sam, who we met in Chapter Three, pointed to numerous examples of good management and specific managers who had earned his respect. However, he also highlighted two specific examples of managers who used their position to intimidate staff and bully co-workers. First,

> 'She made people's lives hell in that store, I remember she got rid of girls because they were good looking and they didn't fit, she got rid of people who were confident because she didn't feel confident working with them. I know there's people in there she absolutely annihilated them, she brought their confidence down, some of them left of their own accord and others ... she vindictively got people sacked, that's the sort of woman she was. She got that job through arse-licking, it wasn't on merit, it wasn't on her performance, it was how she was with certain people, she intimidated certain managers as well, even the people above her cos of the way she came across. She should never have been put in that position of management, at best she was a team leader. She was good at certain things so I'm not going to totally ... but she totally ... there was a few girls she annihilated, she mentally tortured them into thinking they were worthless in the business. I remember her saying to a few of the young girls, "You're nothing," maybe I should've stuck up for them a bit more but it's all about self-protection at the time, you tend to want to not rock the boat yourself, but on reflection you think, no I should've dealt with it.'

Sam believed that this manager bullied co-workers and intimidated others due to a lack of personal confidence. Her behaviour reflected her own insecurities, which manifested in a destructive and negative attitude towards her co-workers. The ability to intimidate her own superiors reflects a subjective distancing which acts as a defence mechanism; reflective of a culture devoid of positive value, the manager scorches the earth with negativity and harm as an act of self-preservation to protect against objective and subjective conditions of precarity. On a subjective level, the lack of ontological grounding breeds a diminution of confidence and stability which is reflected back on relations with co-workers. On an objective level, a manager in low-level service work is no less precarious or insecure than the employees beneath her. The preservation of status through intimidation and scare tactics bolsters her position; you have nothing, and I'm indispensible. This induced psychology of competition rather than co-operation has significant consequences.

Alternatively, this manager could display a common cultural form, the competitive incentive to fight for reward and status. If co-workers and employees are seen as competitive and self-interested, she reproduces this position and abandons any social obligation to her co-workers. There is no duty of care, no shame and no sense of responsibility for those under her direction; if they would deprive her of rewards and dignity in order to assert their own position of strength and security, she must fight fire with fire. As a transcendental materialist subject, she reveals her inner core of self-interest, competition and post-social orientation in her willingness to intimidate and deploy negativity to maintain her position. The subject is conceived of lack and insecurity and seeks the stability and coherence of a logical Symbolic Order (Žižek, 2000; Winlow and Hall, 2013).

Sam's post hoc acknowledgement of his own self-preservation reflects conditions highlighted throughout this book. In a culture of competitive individualism and precarious conditions, to stand up for co-workers is to potentially become a target. This is incongruous with self-preservation and the maintenance of one's own fragile position. Managers such as the one described here are aware of this; the apparent unwillingness to challenge certain behaviours grants them the liberty to impose emotional harm on employees and co-workers too scared and precarious to fight back. Second, Sam describes his relationship with a different manager,

> 'To this day, I still feel affected by her, I feel affected more by her because I was intimidated a little bit by her. She was one person who did intimidate me. I didn't know where she was coming from and I couldn't deal with that, she mentally intimidated me and made me feel terrible. In the end she wasn't there for long ... When they'd get you in that office it was to try and get you out, it was literally they wanted you out and you'd have to be mentally strong to be able to ... there were times where I'd come home and cry, I'd break down at home, you couldn't sleep because you had that physically sick feeling in your stomach. You

know where you enjoy going to work? It was the complete opposite. What's going to happen today? Am I going to have a job by the end of today?'

In this example, Sam becomes the object of management intimidation and identifies a significant negative impact. Sam's description of management intimidation and bullying highlights the harmful consequences of a labour market constituted around a particular set of values. Profit and targets come first as the generative core of capitalism seeks to expand and reproduce; this reflects the absence of a set of moral or ethical imperatives towards the Other. Within this context, certain managers enjoy the freedom to intimidate, bully and harm co-workers who suffer significant emotional consequences and face the daily anxiety of a working environment devoid of any meaningful protection.

Daniel was 27 and had worked in call centres, retail and supermarkets. His career in the service economy was a series of jobs infused with management strategies that focused on the achievement of targets. Daniel was paid just above minimum wage but his performance-managed targets could net additional bonuses and income. Although he consistently hit his targets, he felt that the management culture of pressure and demand for more was pervasive and spilled over into outright bullying.

> 'You're always pressured towards targets but the thing is I used to do well. Whenever they used to talk to me [it was] very rarely about my performance. I used to get recognition from the area manager for being the top salesman in the area for selling the most, or whatever. I'd never been aware of any complaints against me. I'd had people praising me and stuff like that and I had good rapport. I do very well with my scores and stuff like that. In terms of did my face fit? Hmm ... Probably not. And I think part of that is because I used to say something [to challenge what was said to me] but after a while it got too much and unreservedly without batting an eyelid I was bullied while I was there and it was awful. It was disgusting some of the stuff that used to go on. Now I know to a certain extent people used to go "Oh, it's just because it's you this week," but it never used to stop.'

The management pressure to hit targets and make sales generated a culture whereby sales staff accepted harsh treatment from managers as routine. As the normal culture of the workplace, it was often rationalised by the suggestion that managers would rotate the object of derision or ire each week; if stats improved, you were left alone. Daniel's experience, as a top salesperson, undermined this belief. He felt he was bullied continually, regardless of his performance, and this treatment went unnoticed because of the wider culture within the workplace. His bullying led to a period of ill health where he was further castigated by superiors for 'letting the team' down. The organisational logic of profit and targets creates a culture that shapes and is in turn shaped by harmful subjectivities that solicit these values in order to survive and succeed.

> 'And this cold, this flu would not go away and I remember I went to the doctor's and uh ... I was sitting at the doctor, I'm really bad ... burst into tears, crying my eyes out, I was like this I can't do this anymore blah-blah-blah. He was like right I think you need some time off. And so ... he diagnosed me with stress induced depression and uh ... it was horrendous. And I remember I used to take my sick note and drive up to work and sit outside and I'd sit outside for 10-15 minutes plucking up the courage to go in. I'd wander in and I'd look white, and I'd just look awful and I remember once I went in there and I stood there for ages trying to catch someone's eye, people would just ... colleagues would say "Dan you don't look so well, are you still off?" Management would walk by, ignored me, ignored me, ignored me, one of them came up to me and was like "Extended sick note? Right!" Took it off me and walked away! I was like what can I do? So I went to the car and like a man I cried about it!'

After he returned to work, Daniel developed, in his words, 'paranoia' about his treatment by managers and began to smoke and over-eat to cope with the stress. Eventually, oppressive management practices and an atmosphere of bullying and intimidation forced Daniel to leave the company. From a business perspective, store managers and team leaders are driven by targets and pressure from above. As noted earlier, this has consequences for the style of management within an organisation. The pressure and target-driven performance management slides down the corporate hierarchy to sales personnel often pushed to extremes by the imperative to make profit. However, Daniel clearly distinguishes between the pressure of work and the outright bullying he suffered at the hands of his managers. A crucial problem lies in the inability of his co-workers to tell the difference and recognise when the regular coercion for performance and targets spills over into bullying. Management pressure and a fundamental focus on the bottom line imbue some managers with the belief that their behaviour is justified as long as targets are met. Their possession of special liberty, the freedom to act autonomously and break rules and norms in order to succeed, is justified in relation to targets and profitability.

Cliques at work: inclusion and exclusion in the workplace

Employees often recognise the naked exploitation at the heart of the low-paid service economy and self-interestedly align themselves to the path of least resistance; in this case, the manager who can make life unbearable or can ease one's passage through the workday. Precarious workers and managers display a certain cynicism; they often reject the conformist agenda behind the injunction to 'be yourself' at work and create a 'fun and vibrant atmosphere' (Fleming and Sturdy, 2011). They instead opt for self-interest and a measure of 'subjective distance' associated with what Stiegler (2013) calls 'cynical disaffection' or Fisher (2009) calls 'capitalist realism'. In the process of inclusion within management cliques, other colleagues are necessarily excluded.

Jade worked briefly for a national coffee chain but left after a few weeks because of the harm perpetrated by a manager-led clique. Her desire to pay for a holiday became the sole motivation to stay. Her first day at work was described as "going back to school with a pack of bullies" and ended with her crying to herself when she got home. She put herself under pressure to succeed but resorted to short-term milestones in order to reach her goal. She narrowed her horizons to "one more week", "stick it out for a bit longer". Once she had the money for her holiday, she left. Cederstrom and Spicer (2015) assert that responsibility for wellness sits with the individual and not the culture or management of the workplace; Jade responded to her treatment subjectively and searched for faults with herself. Only after repeated mistreatment at work did she begin to look at the culture of the workplace in order to explain her experience,

> 'Yeah, I thought the people we worked with ... were all women and it was very bitchy and very cliquey and I thought it was just me, what have I done? Am I horrible? What's wrong with me? But it wasn't just me, there was another girl they did it to and then they employed another

girl while I was there and they loved her, and it was because she was friends with one of the girls who already worked there so she was instantly in, whereas me and these other two girls were a bit like, right we're the outsiders. And I'm happy to be the outsider cos you're always going to be when you first start but it wasn't welcoming with open arms which is why I put the pressure on, come on, just try and make the best impression you possibly can and that still wasn't enough. It was more of a 'no, don't like you, don't like the other girl either, don't want you to work here', so they made your life hell until you leave.'

In Jade's case, the manager was part of the clique. The narrow parameters of group inclusion means management-led cliques usually exclude new starters or those who find their face does not fit. Management-led cliques also surfaced in interviews with Rachel and Jessica who both worked in clothing retail. They identified management attitudes and practices as the worst element of the job because they had 'one rule for one, one rule for another', particularly in relation to pay rises linked to in-house staff training. Those in the clique could achieve pay rises without completion of the training programme while others were made to wait. Those outside of the clique were made to feel unwelcome and in the way, often ignored by colleagues and managers when they asked for help. The combination of a toxic culture among self-interested and competitive co-workers and unresponsive managers, particularly in terms of shift patterns and rotas, led Jessica to leave. Cliques led by managers imbue certain co-workers with a feeling of safety and freedom, special liberty, to willingly harm other members of staff through exclusionary practice or outright verbal violence. Daniel noted that large companies tend to have a 'massive element of unfairness' and favouritism whereby cliques emerge and those unwilling to 'dance to their tune' suffer. Jade acknowledged her co-workers were emboldened by their close relationship with the manager. Jessica found similar issues in her work, judged by colleagues for not 'looking your best', marginalised as the odd one out and ignored by co-workers. The competitive atmosphere within organisations leads to exclusionary behaviours. For those inside the group, they would undoubtedly report close working and social relationships as well as a positive atmosphere. For those not included, exclusion, bullying and intimidation by co-workers become part of working life. In both Jessica and Jade's case, this was not sustainable and both moved on to other jobs.

The use of part-time and temporary contracts becomes a greater issue when linked to management favouritism and cliques. Managers will bring personal relations and specific agendas to the process of overtime allocation and favourable working times. As Price (2016) notes, managers and supervisors within retail and service work reserve the ability to change rotas; those employees unpopular with managers found shifts reduced. Managers who control access to working hours control the employee, something particularly important for precarious, low-paid workers. However, beyond the narratives of control, the philosophical notion of the 'negation of the negation' plays an equally powerful role. The control thesis suggests employers manage unwilling workers through control of functions such as overtime, role and pay. The Hegelian 'negation of the negation' acknowledges this but also identifies the role of the subject. The negation of capitalism's exploitation of workers through the labour market conditions presented to the subject (McGowan, 2016) would be the resistance valorised by Foucauldian labour process scholars determined to identify struggles within the workplace (Thompson and Smith, 2009).

However, the structural reality of capitalist society – rent, mortgages, bills, children to feed, medications – negates the desire to resist the controlling nature of work. Employees will not resist working conditions in a precarious, competitive culture where jobs are scarce and unstable, bills and outgoings do not diminish, while the consolations of capitalism in the guise of consumer culture, entertainment and reality TV, act as solace against the worst iniquities of work. That we actively solicit the consolations of and immersion within the circuits of consumer capitalism, means the subject is as complicit in narratives of control as the employer. Employees are, in varying degrees, emotionally invested in the Symbolic Order of neoliberal market capitalism; some employees join management cliques because their competitive individualism recognises the benefit of group acceptance. This permanently postpones the negation and acts as capitalism's successful 'negation of the negation'. They know the workplace is exploitative so they seek gains where they can find it; if that means this comes at the expense of co-workers then so be it. Co-workers, as seen in the discussion of Abbie's bonuses in Chapter Three, are competition; self-protection and subjective distancing makes sense and reflects the psychosocial and ethical consequences of hegemonic neoliberalism.

The absence of stability cultivates a culture of competitive self-interest as employees seek out ways to maximise market shares at the expense of co-workers. This contradicts the often stated assertion that co-workers reflect the best thing about contacts' service economy jobs.

However, this requires that we look again at the way ideology works, at the level of action, not thought (Žižek, 1989). The unconscious motivation to act within precarious labour markets inevitably moves towards self-preservation; we may say one thing but act in completely the opposite way. In a culture or ideology which valorises competition, individualism, self-interest and achievement, the unconscious solicitation of these values motivates and drives actions which, on a conscious level the individual may reject or deplore yet at the level of action *they still do anyway.*

Cliques reflect the positive motivation to harm in two ways; first, exclusion of the Other from workplace cultures, which serves to marginalise the individual, and, second, the absence of ethical responsibility for the other. As noted earlier, if morality shifts from collective learning and doing towards individual feeling (MacIntyre, 2011) then those co-workers who bully colleagues not only demonstrate this ethical shift but also actively hamper their co-workers ability to flourish as well as deny them the recognition they seek as part of the team. A further harm of instability also exists as those excluded from the group fail to acquire the material resources needed to find a degree of fixity in work routines. The failure to secure overtime and management support for rota changes demonstrates clear harms within these workplaces. Bullying and intimidation were not the only forms of harm inflicted on employees by their co-workers, some went as far as to actively undermine co-workers' ability to hit targets and make bonuses.

Stealing sales

The reconfiguration of labour markets in accordance with demands of flexibility creates a two-tiered workforce within certain areas of the service economy. The ability to meet seasonal demand through temporary hires allows employers to bolster core staff with transient labour. The influx of supplementary personnel creates further competition for sales and target-driven employees, albeit the customer base usually expands during this period too. However, the fixed-term nature of temporary staff justifies those possessors of special liberty to inflict harm in their instrumental pursuit of market shares and targets.

Commission or target-based sales and retail work provides opportunities for employees to make financial gains without necessarily doing the work. As noted earlier, Leanne and James acknowledged that sales personnel could benefit from 'free sales' if cashiers attached processed sales on a colleagues sales number, even when that colleague did not participate in the sale. The negotiation behind the allocation of sales to particular personnel had a more invidious side which tapped into the flexible use of temporary workers to meet peak demand (Standing, 2011) and reflected the negative and asocial culture engendered in workplaces driven by targets and performance. This was known as 'stealing sales' and happened in several ways.

For some permanent staff, the impermanence of temporary colleagues contrasts with their vital role within the company. Naturally, they become more entitled to reap rewards from good sales. An inexperienced temporary worker may cultivate an expensive sale with a customer, sell additional items, extended warranties and provide a high level of customer service. More experienced members of staff, those imbued with a degree of entitlement derived from their acknowledged position as 'successful' sales personnel, were observed 'stealing' sales from temporary colleagues.

This was done in numerous ways but most often occurred when the experienced sales person would approach a new colleague during the sale and offer to 'help'. Strategies aimed at stealing sales were numerous. This included the experienced colleague developing rapport with the customer by appearing friendly and offering advice to an inexperienced member of staff. At some point during the interaction, the experienced sales person would leverage the situation to their advantage, taking over the sale and sidelining the colleague who had cultivated the transaction. The temporary colleague received no acknowledgement or recognition for laying the groundwork or developing the sale. The sale would be allocated to the experienced member of staff and count towards their personal sales target. Sometimes, the sale would be 'stolen' at the cash desk. Experienced members of staff would solicit the support of cashiers; if the two sales staff arrived at the cash desk with the customer, the cashier may inadvertently assume it was the experienced colleague's sale or the sales person would collude with the cashier to switch the transaction.

The role of the customer is important. The customer could, on the arrival of a new sales person attempting to inveigle their way into the encounter, insist that the original member of staff was managing the transaction adequately and the experienced colleague was not necessary. Of course, the employment of emotional labour in a customer-facing interaction, coupled with the status pressure existing between permanent and temporary staff, could prevent the temporary colleague asserting authority and rejecting the experienced colleague's involvement. The colleague in possession of special liberty sees no ethical problem in exploiting these circumstances and profiting personally. Neither does he or she see an ethical problem in negatively disadvantaging a temporary colleague who requires good sales figures and the attainment of targets to stand any chance of earning a permanent contract.

This is the ultimate harm from stealing sales. Within the service sector, there are inducements to temporary colleagues, particularly Christmas 'temps', in terms of potential permanent positions. Earlier we noted Amazon expected to retain less than 10% of temporary staff; this is usual, largely as a measure to combat turnover. This generates competition between the temporary hires, many of whom want a permanent position. In order to secure a permanent post, temporary staff must agree to work whenever management require, be seen to fit in with the organisational culture, acquiesce to senior and more experienced colleagues, and perform well. This performance is measured, of course, through statistics and targets. When permanent colleagues steal sales, this negatively affects performance and harms the temp's chance to secure a permanent contract.

It is pertinent to consider the role of managers while those possessors of special liberty wantonly harm their co-workers. High-performing sales personnel are often valued by store managers and, unless any personality clashes or status insecurity generate antagonistic relations, as in Daniel's case mentioned earlier, managers and supervisors turn a blind eye to the behaviour of their 'favourites'. In a culture driven by results, managers tacitly accept the harmful behaviour of those colleagues who they believe are best positioned to achieve results. The target-driven culture within retail and other service sector employment generates and reflects wider cultural imperatives towards competitive individualism, status and achievement. As long as high-performers continue to perform, their mistreatment of temporary colleagues does not matter; in all likelihood, they will not be with the company for long anyway.

This section has shown how relationships between members of staff matter in the negotiation over sales recognition and the pursuit of targets. It proves economically beneficial for sales personnel to cultivate positive relationships with cashiers who may then be inclined to allocate 'free' sales to their favourite sales person and boost his or her figures. The relative degree of freedom around this process also provides the platform for those who possess 'special liberty' and are positively motivated towards the maintenance and maximisation of their wages and position through any means necessary. This also includes outright harm in terms of stealing sales. This practice is seen as entirely justified due to a sense of entitlement and seniority but underlines the vapid, asocial culture within workplaces dominated by competitive individualism, insecure contracts, flexible pay and individual targets, and management concerned primarily with profitability. Within these conditions, it is perhaps no surprise that some co-workers inflict harm on their colleagues without compunction. The positive motivation to harm is reflective of the absence of any sense of moral responsibility or ethical duty to one's colleagues and co-workers (Smith and Raymen, 2016). Co-workers may be fun and friendly but they are also competition and competition overrides any sense of virtue or ethics. In some retail and service sector companies with large numbers of employees, it is likely that employees will find some colleagues they like but also likely that there will be a large number of people they simply don't give a shit about and will harm in order to maximise their own self interest.

The absence of a positive culture provides the platform for these behaviours. Some suggest management strategies built on 'fun' and vibrancy encourage employees to bring their personalities into the workplace (Fleming and Sturdy, 2011). However, the incorporation of personality into the workplace does not facilitate a 'positive culture' but is instead reflective of a process whereby personality, character and emotion are drawn into circuits of consumer capitalism and commodified as components of affective labour (Berardi, 2009) and communicative capitalism (Dean, 2009; Hill, 2015). The logic which underpins the clamour for a workplace culture infused with personality and fun remains the exchange relation and profit motive which drives target attainment and management pressure. Attempts to overlay the cold logic of exchange and competitive markets with a veneer of personality fail to counteract the libidinal energy of capitalism's generative core. Instead, it demands more of the employee who is expected to perform and criticised for failure to demonstrate the 'right attitude' (Callaghan and Thompson, 2002). The problem is not with the culture of the workplace, the problem is with the individual employee (Cederstrom and Spicer, 2015). Within these spaces, instrumental and harmful behaviours exist between employees, supervisors and managers who exploit the negativity for their own benefit.

Harmful customers

As established in earlier chapters, many service economy encounters take place against the backdrop of inauthentic social interaction. The employee is driven by targets or management pressure to provide excellent service and is therefore expected to employ emotional or affective labour. The 'knowing consumer' is aware of this; the exchange of socially expected dialogue governs the interaction. "Can I help you?" "No thanks, I'm just looking." This routine is entirely appropriate for service sector encounters but is also almost always false. A consumer who desires a particular commodity or object engages a sales person driven by management imperatives or targets to ensure the exchange relation occurs successfully. It is a substanceless interaction, as the customer and employee are focused on the self, on what they can derive from the exchange (Baudrillard, 1993). In a culture underpinned by exchange but experienced through the symbolic of interpersonal interaction, the symbolic is always on shaky ground; if one party fails to achieve appropriate resolution, the veneer of socially acceptable relations can break down spectacularly, and reveal the reflection of the capitalist Real which drives the encounter.

The positive motivation to inflict harm is, of course, not limited to co-workers and managers. Often customers display willingness to inflict verbal, symbolic and physical harms on service economy workers. Service economy workers experience customer abuse relatively frequently and deal with it as 'part of the job'. Korczynski and Evans (2013) suggest that 'customer sovereignty' generates a level of 'enchantment' within the shopping experience which often clashes with control elements within a service interaction. These clashes lead to 'disenchantment' as the illusion of customer authority is shattered; service workers are particularly threatened by abuse because they lack power and display a weak 'status shield' whereby customers look down on them. Williams (2006) places customer abuse within a hierarchy of class, race and gender. In the context of US toy stores, Williams suggests that white middle-class women engage in abuse of retail workers through a sense of entitlement often not visible among black men and women. Both studies attempt to place customer abuse within a wider sociological context but this section places customer abuse within the ultra-realist harm schema.

From intoxicated customers who raged against her unwillingness to serve them to angry customers who decried her for 'ruining Christmas', Jade could immediately recall incidents where she had been the victim of customer abuse. One incident stood out in particular,

> 'There was a woman, about a month ago, she turned up the Wednesday earlier than she needed to be to pick up a parcel and the parcel wasn't even in the store, and she "shushed" me. In my face, she went, "shush". Four times. Just "shush". You're not important, I need a manager and

I want someone who I normally deal with, not someone stupid like you. And I went, "Right." So that is quite, I do take it really personal. Especially when I was right. I get, as well, Christmas is stressful. I get that people have ordered things for a particular reason so if that parcel isn't there when they come and turn up for it, I'd be angry as well. But it's more the personal digs that, like, come on? Really? You're talking to another human being that actually has feelings and I think that that's the problem with customers. The majority of people are lovely and they are so understanding, they're like, right, fine, I totally get it, but others just see you as this robot, you are there to just sort their needs out.'

To 'shush' another human being is not only dismissive and rude, it is also a harmful denial of recognition. Whitehead (2018) discusses the historic socioeconomic origins of 'othering', a process whereby groups and individuals are filtered, graded and sieved; determined to be alien to 'the likes of us', regarded as dangerous and problematic, worthy only of disdain and marginalisation. Under neoliberal capitalism's competitive individualism, the pyramid of social inequality, underpinned by class, race and gender differences, marks out the Other as socially inferior and therefore reduces any moral or ethical responsibility. The negative culture of neoliberal workplaces is marked by social and subjective distance. Within service economy encounters in this study, the structural distance between employee and customer is often imperceptible. However, it is *felt* within some interactions. To demonstrate authority and sovereignty over a minimum wage employee within a service interaction gives the precarious customer a sense of superiority and temporarily assuages any sense of precarity or anxiety in their lives. It also demonstrates the central components of neoliberal subjectivity – competition, status, self-interest – rising to the surface of personality and social interaction.

Customer abuse can also manifest itself racially. Sam explained that his years in retail have been punctuated by racially motivated abuse from customers who have openly declared, 'I don't want to be served by a Paki.' Sam explained that this had happened recently, both to him and a young co-worker.

'There's a girl at work who had it the other day ... for me, a member of management should've supported that person, she's a young lass, she's 18 year old and she was in tears. I went over to her and said, "Look, you've got to become stronger," but why should she have had to put up with that? He [manager] didn't do it vindictively, he just lives in his own world, is all about figures and he just got another member of staff [to serve] but he [customer] totally undermined her and brought race into it, saying "I'm not getting dealt with by her," and it was blatant ... I said to the manager that it was wrong, and he said "Oh yeah I know but ..." He gets his stress head on, but I said, "You've got to realise that not everyone's as thick-skinned as someone like me who can deal with it, these are young kids and they shouldn't have to deal with it, all she wanted was a bit of support from you.'"

This excerpt raises a number of issues. Customer service interaction inevitably reflects socio-economic and cultural dimensions. Sam's response to racial abuse by customers was to look for support from colleagues and managers but not issue overt demands for solidarity. He hoped colleagues would refuse to serve the customer but had experienced situations where his co-workers had undermined him and served the customer. He also subjectively chose to make his peace with it. Meanwhile, he expects younger colleagues to 'toughen up' because they will face this in the future; a 'thick skin' is necessary for work in retail and encounters with the public, some of whom they will not get along with. In areas of economic disadvantage such as Teesside, the socioeconomic status of customers and staff is often marginal. Within a culture of individualism, achievement and competition, customers who themselves exist in precarious circumstances will seek forms of negativity to bolster their own fragile position while displaying increasingly common cultural characteristics. In Sam's case, this was racial. In other cases, it may be gender, hair colour, body shape. Yet in a culture defined by negativity, individualism and a growing subjective distancing from the bonds of sociality (Fisher, 2009; Winlow and Hall, 2013), abuse such as this will manifest in the obvious social cleavages of class, gender and race.

His manager's response to the situation reflects the unqualified centrality of the exchange-relation and profit motive. The sole objective of moneymaking renders encounters between manager and worker impersonal and instrumental. Sam accepts his managers are target-driven and have benchmarks to meet on a daily basis yet his manager's decision to find another salesperson rather than ask the customer to leave reflects what Whitehead (2015) calls the primacy of markets over morals and ethics. To replace an Asian salesperson with a white salesperson legitimised the customer's racism as well as his sovereignty as a customer; the customer is always right, and his money is more important than employee well-being. There is a clear absence of ethical responsibility for the Other on the part of the customer who is happy to racially abuse an employee. There is also an absence of ethical responsibility for the Other on the part of the manager confined within the parameters of the negativity imposed by targets, profitability and efficiency at the heart of the neoliberal workplace. His decision to replace the employee with another is more harmful than the initial verbal violence. How can an employee find value in a workplace in which a double blow of negation takes place?

The rise of the bailiff: special liberty at work

These encounters reflect the 'special liberty' exhibited by certain actors (Hall, 2012a). Hall's concept of 'special liberty', what we've already termed the positive motivation to harm, delineates an individual who actively solicits the sociosymbolic structures of neoliberal ideology; the subject epitomises the competitive individualism, envy and self-interest which fuels consumer capitalism and possesses a special liberty which convinces them of their right to maximise market shares, and protect their position from rivals, through any means necessary. The subject is compelled to act, emboldened by the belief that they are entitled by a Symbolic Order which encourages individualism, social mobility, instrumental self-interest and, above all, status, accumulation and success.

The classic image of the bailiff is of someone who takes away from others. The bailiff enforces contracts and collects debt through the removal of property, commodities and money from those unable to meet certain obligations. The bailiff is emboldened to act through structural conditions which place them in a position of superiority or authority over less fortunate subjects and, no matter how unpalatable it may be to others, are entitled to remove whatever is necessary to satisfy the obligation. The bailiffs within the service economy are also emboldened to take away from others and act with a degree of freedom and superiority. Sales staff will scam colleagues to steal sales because the workplace culture of targets fosters a spirit of competition with the added incentive of monetary reward through bonuses. Individuals embedded within a 'winner-take-all' consumer culture see sales as a way to ensure pecuniary advantage which translates to consumer commodities and experiences. Managers who have ascended to an intermediate rung on the organisational hierarchy recognise their relative precarity and seek to take away from others in order to maintain their position. To inflict harm on colleagues through verbal put-downs, bullying and emotional violence, as well as through management mechanisms such as overtime, rotas and the ability to award permanent contracts, keeps others in their place and maintains their own relatively privileged position. Customers who embody the sovereignty enshrined in the dictum 'the customer is always right' will actively harm employees in order to get what they want. They will take away dignity and recognition from others in order to ensure they gain and assert a degree of superiority.

Special liberty reflects the absence of any ethical or moral responsibility for the Other. This absence is fostered by a negative culture driven by the generative core of capitalism. Those few individuals in possession of special liberty take advantage of the absence of ethics or morality within management practice that is designed to maximise profit, efficiency and productivity through the use of targets, just-in-time staffing models, temporary contracts, and performance management. These individuals show scant regard for co-workers and employees yet shore up their own precarious position or maximise their own market shares and opportunities. It also reflects the emergence of harmful subjectivities attuned to the core values of neoliberalism; individual success, self-interest, freedom, social mobility and status become the values which motivate the subject to act. The stimulus at the heart of capitalism, the absence of satisfaction (McGowan, 2016), encourages harmful subjectivities to seek this satisfaction through the acquisition of material goods and benefits such as wages, bonuses, promotions, commodities. Those who possess special liberty believe their freedom to act in pursuit of such objectives can come through any means necessary even if it means they take away from others in order to succeed personally. The positive motivation to harm by subjects in possession of special liberty is a reflection of the culture of negativity associated with neoliberal capitalism. The connection between subjective motivation and structural or ideological conditions is clear.

Conclusion

Special liberty and the positive motivation to harm, the absence of a moral duty or ethical responsibility towards the Other, accounts for the motive behind workplace bullying, stealing sales, co-worker disputes and customer entitlement to mistreat staff. It also epitomises the release of amoral forces of neoliberal capitalism, reflected in and reproduced at meso and micro levels of organisations and subjectivity.

It is clear that those actors emboldened by their possession of special liberty have a significantly harmful impact on others. Daniel's tale demonstrates this clearly. When studies note a decline in levels of job satisfaction or low levels of positive employee well-being, it can be easy to overlook the significance of these statements. The organisational practice and culture within the service economy creates a platform of targets, pressure, profitability and efficiency wherein some actors capitalise on the competitive individualism pervasive within modern culture and contemporary workplaces to significantly harm co-workers. Managers, employees and customers each play the bailiff; taking away from others in order to advance one's own position. The negativity associated with the primacy of market forces and profit *at the expense of everything else* creates harmful subjectivities.

The importance of this chapter is in the connection of macro-level considerations of structure or ideology, the injunction towards individual freedom, mobility, competition and status, with micro-level actions such as management mistreatment, customer abuse and co-worker conflict. Much of the harm literature convincingly demonstrates the impact of capitalism or neoliberal ideology on social structure and daily lives (Hillyard and Tombs, 2004; Pemberton, 2016), but it often fails to account for subjective motivation to inflict harm. The synthesis between social harm perspectives and ultra-realism allows this chapter to demonstrate that the negative culture of neoliberal capitalism and its ideological contours shape both the objective conditions of employment but also the subjective attachment to a Symbolic Order which encourages and motivates the individual to act in harmful ways. The absence of any sense of ethics or morality within the generative core of capitalism is also absent from the organisational imperatives within the service economy, and often absent from the interactions between managers, employees and customers. The absence of ethical or moral responsibility for the Other creates the conditions within which those in possession of special liberty sense an entitlement to deprive others of material, symbolic or emotional resources. Within this context, precarious conditions generated by the absence of stability and employee well-being, affected by the absence of ethical obligation suggest a third absence: an absence of protection.

SIX

Absence of protection

Introduction

The absence of stability creates inherently precarious and insecure conditions for many employed within the service economy. Workers report problems of instability in contractual arrangements, the use of overtime, just-in-time staffing models and progression into a steady career. The absence of an ethical obligation to the other within a negative culture of competitive individualism creates space for harmful subjectivities to emerge and deprive co-workers of material and emotional resources. This reinforces and bolsters the instability associated with insecure employment conditions and is further aggravated by an absence of protection. We return to systemic violence and an additional causative absence with significant harmful consequences for low-paid service economy employees. Inadequate protections negatively affect emotional and physical well-being.

Employees shorn of employment protection find the minimum statutory rights afforded by legal strictures can fail to materialise; service economy workers provide undervalued and free labour to employers. Legal protection is often absent too; workers unaware of their rights are exploited and adversely affected by employers who heap responsibility onto the employee and leave the worker to deal with the aftermath of negative outcomes. The absence of physical protections in the intense struggle to meet targets and deadlines also has a harmful impact on the individual through inadequate health and safety restrictions (Tombs and Whyte, 2007). Absent protections in relation to redundancy also ensure negative outcomes for the employee. When the creative destruction of the market accounts for the demise of an organisation, its employees face harmful consequences. This chapter emphasises the continuum of legal and illegal practices that constitute much of the social harm agenda; some absent protections are legal, other forms of harm employ illegal means to exploit absent protections yet both forms of harm stem from the same imperative to remain competitive and generate profit (Scott, 2017). The fundamental absence of protection for employees raises serious implications around the mental health and well-being of workers trapped in low-paid, insecure and flexible forms of work.

Employees desire a future satisfaction that often appears unmanageable while the present remains the constant struggle to pay immediate bills and feed families.

Working for free

Harvey (2010) describes 'accumulation by dispossession' as a routine process within capitalist economies whereby the capitalist class earn leverage, advantage, assets and capital. An advance on Marx's (1990 [1867]) concept of 'primitive accumulation', Harvey suggests that 'accumulation by dispossession' is not a one-off process at the outset of the capitalist project but rather an ongoing practice at the heart of capitalism. On one level, the privatisation of Royal Mail by the British government in 2013 placed a public service in private hands for the purposes of profit making. On a more routine level, we can see acts of dispossession in relation to the rights and guarantees supposedly held by service economy employees. The imbalance between employers and employees, noted earlier, is more pervasive than simply the use of temporary contracts or the absence of sick pay. Jason was 21 and worked for an independent clothing retailer. As a full-time student who still lived with parents, Jason regarded his employment as little more than an opportunity to pay for clothes, holidays and nights out. He had worked for his employer for four months but could already point to several examples where he was dispossessed of the few workplace rights he did have. At the time of the interview, the minimum wage for workers aged 21 and over was £6.70 an hour. Jason earned £6.50 an hour and worked three shifts a week. He was unaware of his exploitation but his attitude was clear,

> Interviewer: 'Minimum wage is £6.70.'

> Jason: 'Is it £6.70 now?'

> Interviewer: 'Yeah, so £6.50 ... they're paying you under the minimum wage.'

> Jason: 'It's only twenty pence, man.'

The flexibility at the heart of the service economy can be beneficial for students, Standing's (2011) 'grinners', yet the transient nature of student labour ensures employers can exploit young workers who are either ill-informed or simply uninterested in any rights that may apply to a temporary job. Jason and his employer epitomise this. Jason suggested that he would be looking for a new job within the next few months anyway; why worry about 20 pence? He liked his job, largely because it compared favourably with previous work experiences and it required very little of him. ("It's a bit boring and it's repetitive but it's not actually hard graft.") His shifts are usually quiet ("On a weekend it's busy but d'you know, on a weekday some days we've had one sale all day, [laughs]") and he has fun with his co-workers. For Jason, this is enough to compensate for his exploitation. He had signed no contract, did not know whether he paid tax or deductions and seemed to think his manager paid him through direct bank transfer each week rather than BACS. From what Jason could or would impart during the interview, his employment was off the books. This was further established when asked about his early experiences in this job,

> Jason: 'No interview, no nowt [nothing]. He gave me a trial period, three days, but I didn't get paid for the three days and, like, the trial period was like, they expected me to learn everything in three days and obviously it wasn't going to happen. I don't know what job you learn everything in three days …'

> Interviewer: 'Once you got through the trial and he took you on permanently did you get paid for those three days?'

> Jason: 'No, no. I got my lunch, I got a fiver a day. [laughs]'

> Interviewer: 'So he got three days free work out of you?'

> Jason: 'Yeah.'

His employer extracted three days of free labour from Jason before he agreed to pay him an hourly salary lower than the national minimum wage. Tellingly, this is not the only experience Jason has of this, having been on trial in a recycling factory which paid him £50 per day for working 11-hour shifts. The use of 'trial' periods to determine suitability serves unscrupulous employers and dangles permanent work in front of potential employees. That Jason laughed when he recounted his unpaid trial is testimony to both the normalisation of precarious and nefarious employment practices within the service economy and his lack of identification with any form of low-paid service employment. It was all temporary. His aim was to get his degree and find a job where, in his words, he would 'get to wear a suit' and could leave behind the trail of hard and meaningless jobs and exploitative practices that have characterised his working life to date.

Lee was 18 and sitting his A-levels. His part-time job in a takeaway was cash in hand and, as with Jason, below the minimum wage. He received £30 a night for working seven-hour shifts. Lee complained about his bosses being 'arseholes' and, after 18 months of employment, would still tell "Me, I'm doing shit wrong." He felt that his salary was "Fucking shocking ... don't turn up and you don't get paid but I can say a week in advance that I'm going to need next week off but I don't get paid so it's off my back really ..." but despite these drawbacks it "keeps me in fags and drink ... barely". As far as Lee was concerned, his job was necessary but he had plans to finish college and then either attend university or look for apprenticeships. His current employment barely registered in his future. The transient nature of youth employment in an age of extended educational pathways provides employers with a supply of cheap labour who have no long-term commitment and more likely to put up with inconvenience and exploitative conditions.

The erosion of overall employment protection negatively affects *all* workers within the service economy. It also generates opportunities for those employers at the bottom of the low-level service economy to maximise profitability if they exploit and underpay young workers who seek temporary work. Ahmad (2008) identifies this as particularly acute within migrant labour but this practice is not limited to migrants. Working for free and paying under the minimum wage is exploitative but beneficial; they avoid the need to declare these employees and thus evade tax and national insurance contributions. The loss of protection at the lowest end of the labour market is evidently harmful to employees who have little recourse to ensure nationally mandated levels of remuneration. They sacrifice their labour for free or at vastly reduced rates in order for the customer to enjoy the satisfaction of their commodity or experience (McGowan, 2016) while the employer exploits the lack of protection available for low-end workers in order to maximise tight profit margins. From a harm perspective, the motivations and processes which drive these entirely illegal practices reflect the systemic imperatives of consumer capitalism; profitability, since Marx, has derived from surplus value, the distance between the cost of labour and the work produced. To maximise margins through the exploitation of labour reflects not only nefarious employment practices but also a clear adherence to the rules of the game; seek profit above all else and increase margins where possible, even at the expense of employees. Some employers can maximise profit through cuts to wages, benefits and employment conditions in entirely legal ways; others who perhaps find margins much tighter, resort to illegal means.

Physical and legal protection

Daniel's work history is an exemplar of low-paid service work. Alongside an educational trajectory which culminated in a degree towards the end of his twenties, Daniel variously worked for call centres, retail, and supermarket distribution. His account of call centre work matches much of the academic literature related to the post-industrial assembly line (see Lloyd, 2013, 2016). His experience of retail illustrated the previous chapter. His time in supermarket distribution matches recent media accounts: workers timed for picking items, performance managed against their outputs, as well as the harms which occurred when employees cut corners to achieve targets and satisfy management. His desire to work flexibly to fit around his college course resulted in a move from a specialist team to a generic stock picker.

> 'If you're on flexible hours you have to go on the shop floor. And that didn't mean going on forklifts, it meant going on the pick. Slave labour. It was ... if you know anybody that's been at that place and you ask them what it's like to be a picker, it's awful. Round and round in circles all day, they time you, you have to keep to a good time. It's dangerous. I ended up having two accidents while I was there. I was unhappy with that but I had to do it, at the end of the day. You'd go around on a truck and this was a massive massive warehouse. Obviously people, just like on the roads, take risks, they act a bit daft and, you know, because you have to stick to a time. If you don't get time you get managed for it and all sorts of things happen to you. You have to make sure what you pick is right, okay? So I used to ... my picks were 100% correct but my timing was poor ... I hated it so much and I was crap at it, apart from anything else.'

Daniel had two accidents at work which ultimately signalled the end of his employment for 'failure to discharge his duties'. First, he was hit by a truck in the warehouse and second, someone crashed into the back of his truck and injured his neck. After a significant period of sickness, he was assessed and asked when he would return to work. Despite continued reliance on painkillers, Daniel suggested a modified assignment to get him back to work; this was rejected because 'you're a picker, you have to come back and pick'. When his employer suggested he could work reduced hours for two weeks only, Daniel asked what would happen if he failed to hit his targets. His employer told him he would face a performance review, as every other employee would. Given his still considerable pain level, Daniel refused and was sacked. When asked about his employer's lack of flexibility, Daniel's theory was,

> 'I think they were just like "come back now or don't come back at all because we can easily replace you with someone else who's going to go and do it for less money from an agency."'

Daniel decided there was 'no point in pursuing it' because he could not physically perform the role his employer demanded from him. Even with union support, he lacked protection in relation to his contractual status and lost his job. Meanwhile, the work intensification characteristic of low-level service economy distribution centres failed to protect Daniel's physical safety. The time restrictions and performance management associated with picking items for distribution inevitably leads employees to cut corners in order to meet targets. An employee who operates heavy machinery such as a forklift truck presents risks to the health and well-being of co-workers when they choose to cut corners. Physical trauma, considerable time off work, the management of pain via prescription medication, and, ultimately, job dismissal reflect the harmful consequences associated with the absence of protection, both in terms of Daniel's person and the conditions of his employment.

Katie, 30, had worked as a courier before she decided to heed the call to self-employment and independent work arrangements offered by an advert to become a driving instructor. Frustrated at the lack of progression in her courier role, Katie recognised that her ambition to own her own home and acquire a steady standard of living would require more income. An advertisement which offered up to £30,000 a year as an independent contractor associated with a national chain led to a particularly unhappy and complicated personal and legal struggle. Katie paid £3,000 to complete the training and passed all of her tests. Within a few months as an instructor, the company she was franchised to went into administration and were bought by another national driving school. Nobody had known how precarious the company's position was. This closed the storefront office on Teesside where Katie used to gain clients,

'I used to get quite a lot of clients because I'd just go and sit and talk to the girls in the office and if someone walked in off the street I'd be like "Oh hi, I'll take you out." They basically had 27 instructors at one point out of that office which you're never going to be able to earn the £30,000 because you'd have to be working full time and there's just not the clients available. So I was beginning to get less and less work, obviously the pupils I had at the beginning were passing their tests and ... not getting replaced. It went on and it was just less and less people and I was like it's not actually viable for me to continue. I just can't do it. I obviously tried my own advertising. I just thought no I need to get out because I'm nearly bankrupt. I'm earning no money. I'd actually moved out of home at that point. For six months I was renting a place with two friends and my Mam was paying my rent for me. She was like "Yeah, you're going to have to move home because I can't afford to pay your rent." I was near enough bankrupt. I was living off credit cards and, yeah, gave it up.'

The capitalist promise of the future is clearly visible in the advertisements promising £30,000 per year and the chance to effectively work for oneself. Enjoy the freedom associated with setting your own hours and earn good money doing it. Katie's dissatisfaction at the lack of progression in her previous employment fuelled the desire to try something new in order to reach her goals and ambitions. Given the number of driving instructors working out of the same office, Katie was not the only person to buy into this. As the ideological freedom associated with self-employment and on-demand work spreads throughout the labour market (Friedman, 2014), the competition for work and contracts intensifies (Scholz, 2017). A finite pool of potential clients and a large number of instructors inevitably fails to add up to the standard of living offered in the promotional material. Of course, failure to meet those levels of pay is a reflection on Katie, not the company which see its role as providers of opportunity.

Due to the competitive nature of the market, Katie came to see her fellow instructors as competition to be beaten and outsmarted. She tried her own advertising to gain a competitive advantage. When this failed, Katie relied on parental support and credit cards to get by. At no point in her 12 months as a driving instructor did Katie earn the income promised in the advertisements. Initially, Katie was paid hourly and the company deducted its cut from the client's payment.

After fuel deductions, which Katie paid, she was earning around £6 an hour, slightly under minimum wage. At this stage, she had enough clients to work full time and was convinced to sign up to a premium franchise which involved a weekly fee to the company while Katie kept the remainder of the income.

> 'It was £300 and that covers your car, they run your business for you, they'll help you with your accounts at the end of the year, which they didn't. Promise you all sorts and deliver nothing. So this was £300 a week, it would come out, you would get certain pupils that would pay block bookings, so ten lessons for however much money so every week they sign off and that credit comes off your £300. Obviously any cash in hand you were supposed to pay in every week but I got to the point where it was like, well, I'm not paying it in because I need to live and I need to buy fuel. So this £300 a week built up and up and up. By the end of it, the last four weeks I was there, I think I did six hours a week lessons and only one of them was cash in hand. So I was living off £21 a week, technically. I knew when I left that I owed them a good amount of money. I got a letter through my door from a debt collector company saying you owe us £2,400. I mean it did scare me. I went to Citizens Advice. I still had all my contracts and stuff and they went through it and were like, "No, I don't think you can get out of this. I think you're going to have to pay." I'm not paying it out of principle in that they didn't supply the pupils to be able to cover the amount, this £300 a week I was supposed to pay. They hadn't stuck to their side of the contract.'

Katie refused to see a debt management company and eventually procured free legal support which encouraged her to challenge the outstanding debt. The debt collection agency continued to contact her by letter and phone but, after the intervention of Katie's legal advocate, the company backed away. The driving school successfully convinced Katie to double down on her wager that driving instruction would be the gateway to the life she desired. In selling the prestige franchise to her, the company earned a guaranteed £300 per week and left Katie to work out how best to ensure she could pay it and earn a living at the same time. This proved impossible. However, the contractual agreement with the driving school meant that Katie not only incurred debts, was forced to move back into the family home, had little income to live on, and eventually had to leave and spend four months unemployed, but also had to pay back what the driving school claimed she owed. Only her persistence in seeking legal support negated that contractual obligation to pay back nearly £2,500. Given that Katie also paid £3,000 for her training, her experience as an independent contractor proved financially and emotionally costly.

Katie's dream of a steady income to finance the purchase of her own home turned into a nightmare. The absence of any sort of protection in relation to guaranteed work and a minimum number of clients meant that Katie had a fixed weekly outgoing to her contractor without any guarantee she could pay it and have money left over to live on. The contract effectively tied her financially to the company but failed to protect her. Harvey et al (2017) characterise this sort of contract as 'neo-villeiny'; in feudal times, a villein characterised the relationship between serf and lord whereby the serf was bonded to the lord, paid rent to the lord and had no guarantee of any income. Harvey et al (2017) suggest that neo-villeiny is an extension of hyper-flexible working arrangements which creates a new level of precarity and exploitation. In their example of personal trainers, they argue that neo-villeins, as self-employed operators, pay rent to the gym in return for an opportunity to engage clients. Katie does this with her driving school. She is bonded to the company who offer her some token support in terms of vehicle upkeep and business guidance but essentially offer her an opportunity, for a price. This price binds Katie to the company, generates revenue for the company and leaves Katie with no guarantee of income. It is cheaper for the driving school to employ flexible contracts rather than maintain a full-time workforce. This is similar to the use of brand concessions within retail, as noted in Chapter Three. The driving school profits and the contractor absorbs the risk of reduced demand. If the contractor fails to pay the weekly fee and terminates the agreement, legal proceedings follow.

There is a clear absence of protection for an employee left in a position of insecurity and precarity, bonded to a company yet expected to find their own clients and income. Flexibility benefits the employer, the employee faces precarious and unstable work patterns which belie the myth promulgated by companies such as Uber that suggest contractors are free, independent and able to earn what they want, when they want. The 2017 court proceedings against Uber reflect this absence of protection; contractors seek the status of employee in order to find a measure of protection in uncertain and precarious working lives.

Redundancy

Within neoliberal economics, growth is more important than employment (Harvey, 2005). The repeated rounds of quantitative easing introduced by the central banks of the UK and US have attempted to improve liquidity within a financialised economy which has proved incapable of sustained growth. Although profit is visible, economic growth remains sluggish. Harvey (2010) suggests that capitalist economies require a minimum of 3% annual growth in order to comfortably recycle surpluses and keep the system moving. This has largely failed to materialise since the financial crisis. The knock-on effect for the service economy is palpable and clearly demonstrable on the high street. The crash raised unemployment levels significantly (O'Hara, 2014). The austerity response has ensured cuts to services and jobs which also affects spending power (Dorling, 2015a). The replacement of well-paid, secure and stable employment with considerable underemployment in low-paid and flexible labour markets may mask the unemployment figures (Streeck, 2016) but it also damages the spending potential of consumers. The inability to grow the economy hits wages badly and consumers have continued to spend via the extension of credit; private indebtedness continues to grow while wages fail to rise. The service economy has been characterised by spikes in closures and redundancies, often in larger chains and companies, while micro-businesses attempt to fill the void.

Bauman (2004) suggests that the word redundancy denotes disposability; workers discarded because they are disposable, unneeded and supernumerary. In the world of global financial capital, more and more suffer redundancy because the mechanisms for profit can function efficiently without a global workforce. Disposable bodies pile up as firms outsource, downsize or fail to survive. In the service sector, the long-term economic stagnation which followed the financial crisis has borne witness to the failure of numerous high-street retailers, restaurants and other service economy enterprises. While Bauman is right to suggest that, in terms of labour, human waste piles up, their redundancy is not complete; they remain a reserve army of consumers, thoroughly interpellated within the Symbolic Order of consumer capitalism and wait for the chance to consume like those fortunate enough to remain in paid employment (Winlow and Hall, 2013).

Redundancy was a theme in this study, as the service economy of the North East, similar to many other parts of the Western world, has suffered badly since the financial crisis. Many contacts had suffered redundancy. One of the additional pressures associated with the absence of stability, particularly in terms of contracts and employment conditions which favour capital over labour, is further exacerbated by redundancy. The plethora of part-time and flexible contracts employed within the service economy has consequences for redundancy pay. Martin had spent nine years working for a retailer that entered administration. His account serves as a good example of my contacts' encounters with redundancy. Rumours had circulated about financial difficulty and the threat of closure but ultimately employees were given one week's notice that their employer was going out of business

> 'I never felt any sort of personal upset about it, it was just very weird, I'd never been in that position before where I genuinely thought my job was under threat but it was upsetting seeing people who had worked there twenty, thirty years who were all of a sudden were going to be out of a job, it was all that they'd ever done. All of a sudden, because we knew we were going out there was no sniping, no, obviously target grabbing, because it was all pretty much pointless by then and everybody just sort of relaxed so it was, yeah weird, it was upsetting because we were losing the jobs but I think everybody thought, we can't do anything about it ... I was made redundant at the end of November and I decided to take December off because I'd never had a Christmas to myself for about nine years so I got my redundancy pay, took December off and then started in earnest for a job in January. I didn't get the next job until about ... if I finished at the end of March and I was there for about eight weeks ... it'll have been the beginning of February so in total I was jobless for about three months, I was looking for about two months.'

Over the course of his employment he had worked flexible hours, regularly over thirty and as high as fifty over the peak Christmas season. However, he was employed on a sixteen-hour contract. When the company closed, his redundancy pay for nine years' service failed to reflect his contribution to the company,

Interviewer: 'Do you feel like it reflected –'

Martin: '– [interrupting] No. Not at all. Because I was only ever minimum sixteen-hour contract and it was never upped so I only got paid my minimum contract. And, considering, over Christmas you're doing fifty-, sixty-hour weeks and most of the time I was doing double my contract, thirty-two hours and above, no I don't think my pay reflected what I got ... I mean, I think in total for nine years' service I got about two and a half, three grand, something like that. And, even though it's still quite a lot of money but when you look back at the amount of hours or whatever you did and you were judged on the minimum contract. What would've been a lot fairer would've been an average of what you worked then yeah, I don't think it reflected it at all.'

The fact that Martin saw three thousand pounds as a lot of money reflects the normalisation of minimum wage work. Thirty-two hours per week at minimum wage yields a relatively low monthly wage; a three thousand pound redundancy payment seems like a lot in comparison. The absence of employment protection leaves low-paid workers subject to the vagaries of the market. Those companies unable to stay afloat in the turbulent waters of post-crash consumer and labour markets inevitably sink and employees are left to scramble for a life raft. Once redundancy strikes, service economy personnel often find new employment in similar roles and occupations. Some suffered periods of unemployment and no choice but to apply for Job Seeker's Allowance. When work does present itself again, it bears a remarkable similarity to previous occupations. Phil had worked in retail before his redundancy. Similar to Martin, his redundancy pay was based on his contracted hours, in this case four hours per week, rather than the regular shifts he worked. Phil subsequently found work in clothing retail, only to be made redundant again within a year. When we spoke, he was about to start an apprenticeship after making the decision to move away from the service economy and access a skilled trade.

Employees who suffer redundancy are temporarily discarded from the labour market, waste products in the market's process of creative destruction. As labour markets contract in times of low growth, the ability to find a new position shrinks. The absence of protection against redundancy, aside from a legal right to redundancy pay, creates chaos in the lives of low-paid service economy workers. As noted above, many find subsequent work within similar areas of the labour market. They capitalise on skills and networks to find employment in different call centres, other shops, new bars or distribution centres. Within a precarious local and national economy, the spectre of redundancy and market failure is visible. This spectre pushes managers to impose targets and strategies for profitability. The absence of stability within the service economy has a causal impact on redundancies, the absence of protection in the event of redundancy harms those individuals tossed into unemployment.

Mental ill health

Work and diminished mental well-being (see Wilkinson and Pickett, 2009) have been intertwined ever since Marx and Engels (2011 [1932]) positioned the alienated subject as divorced from the product of labour. More recently, Fleming (2015) notes the spike in suicides among professional workers overburdened by stress and anxiety in what he identifies as an 'I, Job' society: the subject and their work are entwined, the pressures of work inescapable. At the other end of the labour market, those egregiously deemed 'fit to work' through capability assessments are increasingly linked to elevated suicide rates; deaths linked to the injunction to find work become more common with successive rounds of benefits cuts and welfare reforms (Butler, 2015; Cooper, 2015). Different labour markets undoubtedly generate different stressors and triggers for anxiety and ill health. The capitalist work ethic (Weber, 2012 [1905]) couches labour in moralistic tones. Under neoliberalism, productivity and work is seemingly fetishised. However, inequality continues to rise and many seek to keep their heads above water through increasingly low-paid, flexible and insecure forms of labour. At one level, we are compelled to work while, on another level, exploitation and work-related harm can perhaps be linked to a rise in mental ill health.

According to NHS Digital (2017), approximately 2.6 million people in the UK were in contact with secondary mental health, learning disabilities and autism services across 2016-17. This represents almost 5% of the total population. By the end of 2015, just over 1 million people were referred to IAPT (Improving Access to Psychological Therapies) services for help with anxiety and depression, 60% of whom were women and 46% were under 35 years of age (NHS Digital, 2015). Figures for 2014-15 show an almost 10% increase in the number of people detained under the 2007 Mental Health Act. From a fiscal perspective, prescriptions for anti-depressants cost the NHS in excess of £285 million (NHS Digital, 2016). Indicative of a crisis in adolescent mental health, six in ten children and young people in the UK failed to receive treatment for anxiety and depression (Campbell, 2016). In the US, a long-term problem with prescription drug addiction (Maxwell, 2011; Nargiso et al, 2015; Quinones, 2015) points to a desire to medicate away the effects of difficult social conditions and fractured lives. Prescription pain medication was ranked alongside heroin as the biggest drug threat in the US in 2015, according to the Drug Enforcement Agency (Caldwell, 2015). The biggest cause of death among middle-aged men in the UK is suicide (Hemmings, 2016) and female suicide rates have recently reached the highest level this century (Agerholm, 2016). Suicide rates in Europe have increased dramatically since the financial crisis (Antonakakis and Collins, 2014), a similar situation to the US (Philips and Nugent, 2014). Suicide reflects the most severe response to increased mental distress in complex personal and social circumstances (Durkheim, 2006 [1897]). However, we can broaden the relationship between precarious socioeconomic circumstances with mental ill health more generally to consider the impact that an absence of protection can have on subjective well-being.

Sarah worked for a local authority when austerity bit and reduced her hours to the point of financial impracticality. She found work at an independent cake shop which specialised in cakes for weddings and birthdays, employed as a customer adviser. Her partner worked for an IT company in York but had recently decided to set up his own business closer to home. The reduction in Sarah's income plus the uncertainty around her partner's work took a heavy financial toll and had emotional impact on Sarah as she tried to raise her infant son. Sarah wanted some stability in her work. Even though she acknowledged the long-term prospects with her current employer were very limited, this stability would be important while Richard set up his own business. Sarah and her family were in the middle of a very tough period,

> 'Our son doesn't know any different right now, it's not like we've given him everything in the world and then we're taking it away. We do stuff that's free and cheap, we've only just qualified for tax credits because of the way Richard pays himself through the business so we've got free childcare now which is where he is this morning but that frees up £200 that we don't have to find this month ... we only have £150 for food a month and that includes, it's the third week in potty training so that includes nappies.'

It is clear from Sarah's description of their circumstances that job uncertainty created financial pressure but compelled them to undertake further temporary hardship which they hoped would pay off in the future. McGowan's (2016) insight that capitalism creates psychic investment in the future is clear here; their long-term goal is the object of desire and future satisfaction while current circumstances are a barrier to be overcome. However, those material barriers create conditions which affect the emotional and mental well-being of the individual. In Sarah's case, the absence of stability and protection in their working lives and financial situation required medication,

> 'I'd say probably around November last year which is when things were getting a bit rocky for Richard at work. I started having a bit of a decline myself and now I'm on anti-depressants because the stress of everything that's been going on and the way that we've had to tighten tighten tighten our belts. We've found that we feel caged because of the financial situation that we're in, we've got a little boy and we've got to keep a roof over his head and food in his tummy, clothes on his back. So we've sacrificed a lot of stuff, there are nights when we've said do you know what, we'll just have toast for tea tonight and at least he's [their son] got a warm meal in his belly. It just got to the point where I was so overwhelmed with feeling caged that I was ... the doctor's told me I'm not depressed, I have low mood because it's an environmental thing, it's not a chemical reaction in my head, it's an environmental reaction so he's put me on a very very low dose of something to help give me a bit of pep to get the focus to address what I need to address. And it's helped, I feel like the cage is there but I've got a bit of space, do you know what I mean?'

Sarah clearly identifies her external environment and the pressures associated with her precarious life as the cause of her mental ill health. The iron cage she acknowledges prevents her ability to access the freedom at the heart of neoliberal ideology; her future satisfaction is predicated on the ability to achieve the freedoms advertised by capitalism. Structural barriers constrain individual desire and require a medical solution. The limits of neoliberalism in relation to its ability to offer subjects not only the promise of future satisfaction but the remote possibility of offering anything other than precarity and insecurity become clear; as a Symbolic Order, neoliberalism loses its efficacy but for the subject, the lack of symbolic coherence, the gap between ideology and reality places Sarah in close proximity to the Real, a proposition which has harmful consequences. McGowan (2016) emphasises capitalism's gesture towards the promise of future satisfaction. As they seek an avenue to that future satisfaction, Sarah acknowledges a focus on the here and now rather than past accomplishments as well as bouts of insomnia countered by periods of inactivity when sleep finally arrives. She acknowledges a desire to work hard and recognises that the world does not 'owe us a living' but she also clearly internalises their indeterminacy, and its subjective manifestation in mental ill health is the result.

The scramble to stay afloat amidst significant economic precarity overwhelms millions who live in areas of permanent recession. This pressure is felt subjectively and blame is assigned personally; note that labour market conditions are not to blame for their situation, it is their own expectations that cause the problem. What should be considered as structural and social factors are explained in relation to personal ambition and opportunity. Within this context, Sarah's emotional well-being suffers; she is responsible for the situation she finds herself in, she was too optimistic or ambitious regarding what was possible, she is to blame. While Sarah's mental well-being was challenged by what she termed the 'cage' of financial restraint which boxes her in, Daniel's mental well-being was adversely affected by the behaviour and practice of his managers.

In the previous chapter, Daniel's mistreatment at the hands of managers and supervisors led to a number of psychological responses. He was diagnosed with stress-induced depression as a result of what he regarded as outright bullying by managers within a culture whereby his co-workers and colleagues were either unaware or misidentified it as standard management pressure to perform. His return to work signalled the onset of a period he describes as 'paranoia', the evil machinations of his oppressors became visible in the most benign acts, which he self-managed and medicated through nicotine and over-eating. Jade and Sam were among a number of interviewees who describe working conditions which at times reduced them to tears. Even those who readily admit that jobs were not long-term still found the pressure and strain of work to be enough to elicit an emotional response. That some had to resort to medical support to manage emotional responses to working environment reflects on the management practice and organisational culture of the service economy. The objective conditions of employment, temporary and zero-hour contracts, instability, low pay, as well as the objective conditions of work, management strategy, targets, performance management, emotional labour, collectively combine to produce a set of extant circumstances which, in some individuals, provoke an adverse psychic and physical response.

How do we begin to explain this rise in mental health issues and suicide? Durkheim argued that an abundance of evidence for a particular social fact reflected the 'normal' function of society rather than a 'pathological' anomaly; the figures presented earlier indicate that anxiety, depression, mental health problems and suicide are increasingly normal within late modern neoliberal market capitalism (Sedgwick, 1982; Fisher, 2009). Fisher's (2009) thesis on capitalist realism and the depressive hedonia exerted by young people rendered impotent by horizons reduced to the contours of capitalism without coherent alternatives which exist 'beyond the pleasure principle' (Freud, 2003 [1920]) has characterised youth today as an illness. Sedgwick's (1982) prescient analysis of mental illness suggested that capitalism would continue to create an undercurrent of discontent which would fuel melancholia, neurosis and mania.

The symbolic efficiency of neoliberalism is in decline. On a subjective level, the intransitive realm of depth structures is felt on a daily basis; the insecurity, precarity and absence of protection characteristic of low-level labour markets enters the level of practical knowledge. Meanwhile, neoliberal ideology continues to extol the virtues of choice, freedom, opportunity and mobility. For more and more people, structural impediments prevent acquisition of any modicum of socially or culturally validated 'success'. On a political level, this failure of symbolic efficiency may result in a challenge to the status quo (see Chapter Seven) but on a subjective level, it raises questions about mental health. Leader (2012) suggests that 'madness' reflects the subject's inability to engage with the Symbolic Order of meaning. The subject who solicits the current Symbolic Order increasingly finds a disconnection between the symbolic fiction which governs our existence and the repeated encounters with the shadow of the Real. The failure of the Symbolic Order, the collective lie that prevents encounters with the Real, is reflected in the increased levels of anxiety, depression, stress, emotional turmoil and mental illness outlined earlier. The adverse mental well-being demonstrated by some of the interviewees in this book is both a result of objective conditions of precarity and insecurity and a subjective response to the failure of neoliberal ideology to provide a set of norms, values and narratives that function in contemporary post-crash capitalism. A process of 'subjective distancing' (Fisher, 2009) or 'cynical disaffection' (Stiegler, 2013) takes place as the subject withdraws in the face of social dislocation, precarity and limited social obligations; the retreat into subjectivity ensures that crises are shouldered personally and not laid at the door of social structures or institutional failure.

The absence of protection within low-paid insecure labour markets is not felt politically or socially; it is felt personally. Conditions and experiences are somehow the responsibility of the individual, either to set realistic goals and ambitions, as in Sarah's case, or to find an appropriate way to deal with workplace abuse and bullying, as in Daniel's case. If the work environment is toxic and causes emotional distress, the subject should employ coping mechanisms or leave; changing the environment is not an option (Cederstrom and Spicer, 2015). Within a harm framework, this disconnect between neoliberal ideology and daily reality engenders psychic harm on subjects who face precarious objective conditions and libidinal investment in a socioeconomic and psychic order that fails to provide adequate opportunity to realise goals and desires. Flourishing is a remote possibility.

Conclusion

Low-paid and insecure workers face an absence of protection which has harmful consequences. As this chapter has shown, protection can come in a number of forms and its removal can be problematic. The 'accumulation by dispossession' (Harvey, 2010) at the heart of the capitalist project deprives low-paid workers of holiday entitlement, pay and other benefits. The entirely legal change to employment legislation designed to facilitate the expansion of capitalism's generative core, at the expense of the worker, has harmful effects on those employees who lose out (see Lloyd, 2013). Meanwhile, wholly legal socioeconomic processes of efficiency, productivity and profitability also drive entirely illegal practices which also harm workers who are denied rightful levels of pay and security. Cash-in hand employment, work trials, failure to pay minimum wage and other practices exist in the shadows but emerge from the same generative processes at a political-economic level.

Radically recalibrated employment relations such as on-demand work, independent contractors and enfranchised workers also reflect a considerable absence of protection. Uber drivers reflect the disruption of the employer-employee relationship and bear all of the risk and responsibility from precarious and flexible relationships (Scholz, 2017). Katie's brief sojourn into driving school was a litany of disastrous decisions and unprotected work arrangements which left her emotionally and financially damaged. Meanwhile, redundancy looms over a labour market still driven by consumer spending within a slow or zero-growth economy where wages still fail to rise in line with inflation. Service economy businesses require the targets and performance management outlined earlier because the competitive marketplace and sluggish economy threaten their existence. Many of my contacts had experienced redundancy, often at short notice and with financial settlements incommensurate with their contribution to their employer.

Finally, the precarious and insecure nature of the service economy creates a set of conditions which can have an impact on the mental well-being of employees. The straitened labour market conditions and precarious circumstances had a psychical impact on Sarah's well-being and medication proved the necessary step to find some space within the 'cage' she inhabited. Daniel's stress-induced depression was entirely the result of his bullying at the hands of managers who systematically destroyed his self-esteem, confidence and mental stability. Other contacts reported stress, anxiety, emotional disquiet and tension as a result of management pressure, customer abuse and the objective conditions of service economy work. The limits of a deaptive ideology (Johnston, 2008) which lingers long after its symbolic efficiency has waned becomes clear and undeniably points towards harmful conditions. Neoliberalism fails to provide even the remote possibility to achieve its ideological goals as more and more people live in the shadow of the Real. They subjectively retreat and face problems alone. The absence of protection leaves some service-economy workers mentally distressed, undoubtedly the victims of harm. If neoliberalism increasingly fails to provide coherence in contemporary society, is it possible to identify opportunities for change? The final chapter will look at the barriers and opportunities presented by this question.

SEVEN

The violence of ideology

Introduction

The evidence presented so far locates the low-paid service economy employee within the context of global political economy, restructured labour markets and neoliberal ideology. The reality of life in the labour market's lower echelons has been illustrated through exploration of management practices, organisational culture, working conditions, employment conditions and relations between employers, employees and customers. Within this context a number of absences, imbued with causative potential, become apparent. The absence of stability, an ethical responsibility for the Other, and protection all indicate a set of problematic conditions and experiences that demonstrate the impact of neoliberal ideology and market capitalism. Inequality, precarity and indeterminacy reign. Meanwhile, the transcendental materialist subject actively solicits the dominant Symbolic Order of neoliberalism and reflects the supreme values of competition, individualism, status and self-interest. Workplace cultures reflect these values and subjects simultaneously shape and are moulded by these precepts.

From our harm perspective, the conditions outlined so far and the causative absences elucidated throughout these pages illustrate a number of pertinent issues. First, harm occurs across a number of levels. The systemic violence of neoliberal capitalism and reorganised labour markets creates a set of drivers and imperatives that fuel both legal and illegal practices, both of which inflict harm on individuals and communities. The unintentional *negative motivation to harm* ensures that the deep level restructure undertaken as part of the neoliberal project to free capital from regulatory restraints results in harmful consequences related to stability and protection. This indeterminacy actively undermines the quest for recognition and flourishing. Second, the *positive motivation to harm*, the 'special liberty' that emerges from a culture of self-interest, competition and individualism results in a series of harms perpetrated against individuals by employers, co-workers and customers. The absent ethical responsibility for the Other denies intersubjective recognition as the subject fights to maximise market shares.

However, a further absence exists, one which also fits within the harm perspective delineated in Chapter One. The triumvirate of violence outlined by Žižek (2008) included not only systemic and subjective violence, already analysed in previous chapters, but also symbolic violence. The symbolic violence of ideology forecloses alternatives to the status quo, dimming horizons to the confines of 'capitalist realism' (Fisher, 2009). If we know inequality exists under neoliberalism (Dorling, 2015b), if we know capitalism's default position is to grow inequality (Piketty, 2014), if we can identify the deleterious effects of inequality (Wilkinson and Pickett, 2009), if we acknowledge that social inequality generates indirect and direct social harms (Pemberton, 2016), why is this situation allowed to persist? The absence of a coherent alternative to neoliberalism fosters significant harm as individuals trapped in low-paid, insecure jobs shrouded in competition, self-interest and precarity, are denied access to a different language, an alternative conception of social organisation that perhaps better enables human flourishing or actively facilitates subjective recognition. As this book moves towards its conclusion, this chapter will first outline the nature of this absence as well as its harmful consequences, but also begin to identify ways in which the harms of work may be fixed.

Ideology

At an epistemological level, the origin of ideas ranges from the idealism of Hegel and Kant to the materialism of Marx and Engels. In *The German Ideology,* Marx and Engels (1998 [1845]) contemplate the inability to see things as they really are. Ideas emanate from the human subject yet escape the individual's control and begin to exert their own force or control over the individual, as processes and commodities do in the sense of alienation and reification. Ideas and thoughts that emerge from subjects and social practice are autonomous entities and form the basis for our conception of false consciousness. By *Capital,* ideology had become a duplicitous and deceitful reality; falsity is no longer the fictions of the mind but the structural effect of capitalism. The political ideology associated with Marx's later writings suggests the illusory values of ideology are grounded in the real contradictions of material reality. Capitalism is explained and overcome by a materialist theory of ideology and revolutionary politics. The ideas of the ruling class stem from material relations and superstructure. The political ideology is a limited historical phenomenon, overcome when capitalism is replaced with communism, an idea challenged by Gramsci's (2000) notion of 'hegemony'.

More recently, the 'reversal of ideology' attaches the subject psychically to the material realities of neoliberal capitalism and presents us with a critical opportunity to consider the symbolic violence of ideology in relation to the harms demonstrated above. Slavoj Žižek's (1989) interpretation of ideology flips Marx's 'false consciousness' on its head. Žižek suggests that the legacy of postmodernism within contemporary culture lies in the incredulity towards meta-narratives, a widespread disbelief in the universalism of grand theories and value systems which attempt to explain human essence and social reality (Lyotard, 1974). The world is too complex for overarching explanations. We cannot be duped by ideological state apparatuses (Althusser, 2014) and belief systems such as communism or religion. In this sense, we may have reached a 'post-ideological' age. However, this is to misrecognise the way ideology works (Žižek, 1989) and brings us back into the realm of ultra-realism and transcendental materialism.

For Žižek, ideology is an unconscious fantasy which structures social reality. That fantasy is the *libidinal drive* encouraged and structured by the Symbolic Order of consumer capitalism; our desire for commodities and objects provides the energy that fuels neoliberal market capitalism (Žižek, 1989; Hall, 2012a). The function of ideology is 'not to offer us a point of escape from our reality but to offer us the social reality itself as an escape from some traumatic, real kernel' (Žižek, 1989: 45). As the subject seeks to avoid confrontation with the Real, we unconsciously solicit the ideological coherence provided by the Symbolic Order. The illusion, the fantasy, takes place at the point of *action* as opposed to *knowledge:* the illusion structures our social reality and social relations; at the level of thought, we believe we know how things really are but at the level of action, we continue to act as though we do not know. To act as if one does not know represents a *fetishistic disavowal.* The subject continues to believe that it is not exposed to the exploitative practices of capitalism, that we know how to navigate the ethical dilemmas of the market, yet we continue to act as if we do not know these things. There is a need for exploitation at the heart of capitalism which, to some extent, we are all aware of; however, we disavow this knowledge to continue our instrumental journey (McGowan, 2016). While on one level I know workers are exploited to mine the natural resources essential for my next smartphone, I disavow this knowledge and act as if I don't know it; this allows me to temporarily enjoy my consumer purchase.

How this disavowal functions will have an impact on the political or collective will to challenge the harms and inequalities of contemporary capitalism. We could argue that disavowal takes place at a collective

139

level (Žižek, 2008). However, we can go further; Kotzé (2016, 2019 forthcoming) argues that there is variable adherence to a 'dream myth' of incremental liberal progress. Akin to the fetishistic disavowal, the dream myth allows the subject to exist in the world yet retain access to a comfortable delusion of reality. Assimilation within this ideological fantasy or dream myth is variable, dependent on, among other things, proximity to capitalism's obscene Real. Devoid of confronting the daily reality of crime, harm and inequality, some groups and individuals can continue to act as if they do not know or, in Kotzé's (2016, 2019 forthcoming) parlance, continue dreaming comfortably. Some are partially assimilated whereby their proximity to the Real is negated and diluted by the sociosymbolic comfort of the ideological fantasy, which enables them to disavow what they do not want to know. For others more proximate to these deleterious effects, assimilation proves impossible. The following section will consider how disavowal and assimilation within the sociosymbolic affects the task of finding genuine solutions to a wide range of actual or potential harms.

From political economy to 'tinkering at the edges'

In terms of solutions to the problems illustrated throughout these pages, the key question must relate to the level of intervention required to fix these interrelated social problems. How far should we go? Across Western neoliberal societies, the 'post-ideological' thesis (Ranciere, 2007) appears ascendant. Political economy and dialectical tension between opposite ideological visions has given way to the negative ideology of 'capitalist realism' (Fisher, 2009); capitalism has become naturalised, market economics as fait accompli and political decision making reduced to the efficient administration of the status quo (Mitchell and Fazi, 2017). Even the populist turn which reached its apogee with the election of US president Donald Trump and the repudiation of the EU in the UK referendum fails to signal a turn away from market-based capitalism (Winlow et al, 2017). Although the resurgent left under Bernie Sanders, Jeremy Corbyn and others signals a willingness to embrace ideas beyond the mainstream, in the main, capitalism's systemic violence continues and political intervention fails to address the underlying issues.

Within the mainstream media, politics and academia there is a widespread disavowal of the knowledge that society faces significant challenges that require bold solutions. There is also incredulity and disbelief within a growing section of the population that increasingly rejects the liberal narrative of freedom, competition, multiculturalism and tolerance. According to Thomas Frank (2016, p 39), 'those who succeed in a professional discipline are those who best absorb and apply its master narrative'. A number of significant issues on which evidence presents a strong case for change are often ignored or disowned by those who control the levers of power. The harms of low-paid service work represent just one. The political class continues to act *as if they don't know these things.* In an account of his ill-fated spell as Greek finance minister responsible for bailout negotiations with the troika, Yanis Varoufakis (2017) expertly outlines the collective disavowal of career technocrats and politicians. In private, officials agreed with his analysis of Greece's situation and enthused over his strategy of debt reconstruction, yet the same officials publicly disavowed this knowledge to blindly repeat the EU's mantra that Greece must honour its debts.

We can identify the collective disavowal of political elites, their assimilation within the master narrative of neoliberalism facilitated by their physical and mental distance from the ravages of the obscene Real of global capitalism, and the harm, crime and inequality perpetuated on a daily basis. Investigation of the worst effects of post-crash neoliberal policy and identification of the problems and harms which adversely affect huge swathes of the population is not hard to find (see Briggs and Monge Gamero, 2017), and the evidence of a plethora of intransigent social problems exists in the public realm. Those politicians who recognise this evidence but reject it clearly show a partial assimilation (Kotzé, 2016, 2019 forthcoming); their solicitation of the sociosymbolic reality of neoliberal ideology negates and dilutes any proximity or experience of the Real.

Change for liberals often amounts to modification of the extant legal frameworks in a way which would guarantee a degree of freedom or equality to those who suffer under the yoke of capitalist exploitation. The liberal project has, since the Enlightenment, focused on individual freedom (Tarnas, 2010). The belief in science, knowledge, politics and law as mechanisms to liberate the subject from the confines of myth, magic, tradition, class, background and culture is crucial to the liberal agenda. The liberal right seek freedom and liberation in economic terms, the liberal left demand liberation and freedom in cultural terms, particularly in relation to identity (Dworkin, 1997; Hall, 2012c). Piecemeal reform, over time, began to fix some of the problems associated with capitalist excess; the regulatory sleeve wrapped around the generative core of capitalism following the Second World War reflects this process. Upon the twin shocks of the failure in Keynesian polity and the collapse of the Soviet Union, the left has increasingly shifted to the centre in relation to the economy in order to gain concessions in the field of culture and identity; the New Democrats and the UK's New Labour accepted market freedoms and promoted cultural and individual freedoms associated with social mobility, gender, race and sexuality. This incremental search for freedom through legal reform works within an extant political-economic order and fails to seek or countenance a genuine alternative to the status quo. A human face on capitalism was better than uncontrolled free market capitalism. However, as Pemberton (2016) notes, to graft a human face onto capitalism still leads to a plethora of harmful acts.

Reform advocates who seek to fix the immediate violence and harm before their eyes offer piecemeal and pragmatic responses which fail to address the underlying systemic violence of capitalism and the symbolic violence of 'capitalist realism'. The failure to see beyond the confines of liberal democratic market capitalism ensures that pronouncements and measures will ultimately fail to achieve their intended goal because they tackle symptoms, not causes. Poverty will not be alleviated by welfare programmes because economic inequality is intrinsic to the capitalist mode of production; in a culture of competitive individualism, social mobility, status, display and anxiety, neoliberal subjects interpellated within this non-ethical framework increasingly resent welfare payments to those unable or unwilling to work. The liberal class does not advocate an alternative to capitalism because it is largely incrementalist in nature but also because the status quo has provided them a reasonable degree of personal and professional success and stability. To disavow the concrete realities of harm, crime and inequality at the heart of neoliberalism is to demonstrate assimilation into its dominant Symbolic Order. This, in turn, ensures that the ideological fantasy of freedom *from*, individualism and competition trumps the glaring negative outcomes foisted on large swathes of the populace. Either their proximity to this Real nourishes their disavowal or the power of ideology negates confrontation of reality. In any event, this places limits on political intervention; the fundamental fantasy of progress and freedom shapes political responses yet fails to go far enough in dealing with root causes.

The visible harms of street violence, poverty, obesity, terrorism, failing schools, unemployment, underfunded healthcare or lack of health insurance, are often met with a rush of action or activity as the progressive elements within society heed the call to do *something*. Progressives identify as being agents of change who seek to support and protect the best interests of poor and marginalised people, yet often advocate little or no change to the status quo. Considerable time and effort is expended on the symptoms of capitalist exploitation and harm yet little time or attention is devoted to root causes as the solicitation of the dominant Symbolic Order limits the willingness to challenge the deep structures of neoliberalism. The analytical lens often fails to focus on the wider macro-level issue of the constitution of society and economy and its attendant social relations. The intervention and determination to alleviate poverty through small-scale policy pronouncements often serve to attach a sticking plaster to the gaping wounds which drain the lifeblood from the remnants of the welfare state.

This works in capitalism's favour. Those who are poor and marginalised, the precarious multi-ethnic working class exploited by capitalist excess may recognise the conditions of their existence but largely fail to act, particularly in an increasingly post-social world. This is the genius of capitalism, negating its own negation by tying individuals to the system in a way that mutes their anger and resentment. First, one cannot fight for improved conditions in a precarious labour market when one has bills to pay and mouths to feed. These subjects may no longer solicit the dominant ideology but their precarious position negates any challenge to the status quo. Second, subjects who have actively solicited the Symbolic Order of capitalism are not motivated to change the world, they are motivated to succeed and make the best of their situation. To get through life unscathed often requires a single-minded focus to secure a way to maximise one's own potential and situation, not seek collective solidarity or a thorough analytical interrogation of the logic of capital. A Symbolic Order that encourages individual achievement, competition and social mobility ties individuals to an ethical system devoid of moral responsibility for the Other (Smith and Raymen, 2016). Bursts of solidarity can emerge in moments of crisis, such as the aftermath of a terrorist attack, but are largely unsustainable in a wider culture and Symbolic Order built on competition and individualism. The subject is emotionally invested in consumer capitalism and its attendant Symbolic Order. This investment negates the desire to protest too much.

Climate change represents the clearest example of a collective disavowal; the ideological attachment to a Symbolic Order negates the weight of evidence that suggests climate change represents a clear and present danger to our current way of life (Parenti, 2011; Klein, 2014; Nurse, 2016). With regard to low-paid, exploitative and harmful work, the political class continues to disavow knowledge that the minimum wage is insufficient, as is the living wage. Low unemployment figures are heralded triumphantly but fail to address the vast growth in under-employment (Streeck, 2016). The shift from security to flexibility noted throughout this book is dismissed as a positive for workers who now have freedom to set their own terms. In their advocacy of market stability and growth, politicians often overlook the resultant impact on the employee. What is good for business is good for Britain and the economy. Climate change will present both challenges and opportunities in relation to work and labour markets; challenges from the disruption and upheaval caused by migration and competition for work, opportunities in relation to emergent labour markets designed to prepare for climate change or tackle its effects. The growth of technology will have an impact on labour markets and job opportunities (Ford, 2016; Srnicek and Williams, 2016) with predictions that automation will threaten significant proportions of jobs in the UK, US and elsewhere. Estimates suggest that automation threatens up to 35% of UK workers and 47% of US workers over the next 20 years (Stewart, 2015). Ford (2016) notes that the majority of new jobs appear in the service economy, often with work routines that are easily replicable by machines. The political elites disavow this knowledge and continue to celebrate the low unemployment figures.

If questions of *capitalist* economics are largely absent from political interventions into poverty, harm, crime and precarious working conditions, fundamental questions of political economy are also largely sidelined within mainstream social science. Aditya Chakrabortty (2012) accused sociology of a dereliction of duty in the wake of the financial crisis, as it failed to address the causes and consequences of the worst financial crisis since the 1930s. Social science has largely abandoned the economic sphere in favour of a focus on culture and identity. The sociology of work is a case in point. Sociology's founding texts address the relationship between economy and society and incorporate the role of work within an emergent capitalist economy (Marx, 1990 [1867]; Polanyi, 2002 [1944]; Durkheim, 2012 [1893]; Weber, 2012 [1905]). Employment conditions within the context of political economy illuminated the early discipline. The sociology of work was also a core component of post-war sociology which considered the lives of workers within the bureaucratic organisation (Whyte, 1956; Mills, 2002) and the factory (Beynon, 1973; Braverman, 1974).

However, since the ascendancy of neoliberalism and the coronation of capitalist realism, questions of economy are largely absent in sociological studies. The sociology of work has become a peripheral subject within the discipline, often moved towards business schools and HR or management studies (Strangleman and Warren, 2008). This results in a series of niche arguments about organisational policy and management strategy, or minutiae of the labour process and often fails to address broader issues such as the threat of automation (Ford, 2016). A focus on management practice and organisational development is coupled with a narrow analytical lens on a single site of empirical study. Attempts to connect practices and processes within a single organisation and the wider context of financial capitalism, neoliberal labour markets or the reconfiguration of society's depth structures is exorcised in the name of empirical validity. The Foucauldian turn within workplace sociology (see Lloyd, 2017) which emphasises control and resistance within the organisation reflects a focus on micro-sites of investigation, the cultural sphere and the individual subject. The connection between the subject and the labour process is more important than the connection between the labour process and the imperatives of capital.

Focus on the individual subject foregrounds identity within the sociology of work and opens up space for identity politics of race, ethnicity and gender at work, often at the expense of class and political economy. Social science has become increasingly factionalised; competition for funding takes place among different interest groups and often fails to address the greater harm and inequality associated with the class project enacted by neoliberalism in order to maintain the capitalist status quo. The narrow focus on factional identities means social science often ignores the more fundamental issues which must be faced immediately and will affect everyone, regardless of gender, ethnicity, sexual orientation or class. What will work look like in a future which undergoes radical change as a result of climate change? What impact will automation have on the workplace? Meanwhile, with few notable exceptions (Tombs, 2004; Scott, 2017), few scholars contemplate the workplace from a harm perspective, despite the myriad harms visible in the neoliberal workplace.

This identitarian orientation extends beyond the academy as liberalism has increasingly focused on issues of culture and identity, as well as poverty reduction schemes. This has had disastrous consequences for the left's relationship with the working class, the traditional base of leftist politics in Europe and the US (Frank, 2016; Winlow et al, 2017). The equality of opportunity argument at the heart of liberalism suggests that each minority group should be elevated to higher positions within the social hierarchy, given their previous subjugation. Nancy Fraser's (2017) term 'progressive neoliberalism' sums up the increasingly hostile competition for resources among marginal and minority identity groups. For many on the traditional left, this apostasy has often come at the expense of a wider working class project (McKenzie, 2015; Winlow et al, 2017). However, more importantly for this discussion, the equality of opportunity argument at the centre of liberal philosophy reinforces the arguments about meritocracy and social mobility (Frank, 2016). It reinforces the competitive individualism at the heart of a negative neoliberal ideology which channels libidinal energy and drive into competitive market forces and justifies the growing inequality at the heart of capitalism. The advocates for reform are often of noble intention but they create boundaries for debate which permanently postpones the negation of capital.

The symbolic violence of ideology creates parameters for thought, language, symbols and ideas beyond which no alternatives are countenanced. For those who demonstrate a disavowal of the obscene Real at the heart of capitalism, they reflect their solicitation of the dominant Symbolic Order which in turn limits the level of political intervention required to alleviate the worst crimes, harms and inequalities of neoliberalism. Capitalism is the only game in town. The ideological dominance of capitalist realism deprives those on the lowest slopes of an unequal social hierarchy from the language to articulate their disenfranchisement and conceive of an alternative mode of social organisation which could improve their chances of recognition and the positive rights that are necessary to flourish, or at least alleviate the worst excesses of inequality and precarity. Alternatives are shut down, the safest route of legal challenge to existing inequality and disadvantage may temper or alleviate some suffering but ultimately prevents a wider discussion which could offer the precarious working class a vision that relates to their experiences.

On a subjective level, the lack of coherent alternatives renders the subject beholden to the dominant ideology. The transcendental materialist subject actively solicits a Symbolic Order to make sense of their place in the world and avoid a traumatic confrontation with the Real. The violence of ideology in an era 'beyond ideology' prevents the subject from an encounter with an efficient and functioning alternative Symbolic Order, a divergent set of ideas and beliefs tied to an operative ideology around which the subject could 'traverse the fantasy' (Žižek, 2000), make the painful break from neoliberalism, encounter the Real and come out the other side firmly embedded within the circuits of an alternative to capitalist realism.

As an ideological force, symbolic efficiency has waned considerably as the material reality of post-crash, low-growth, austerity-driven capitalism fails to offer emotional and practical consistency or sustenance to a significant proportion of the population. As the frayed edges of the fantasy grow wider, a considerable section of the population has sought means to establish a new set of social relations which may work in their favour. The rise of both right and left in the

UK, US and Europe demonstrate a clear willingness to demand more than 'more of the same'. The shocks and irruptions of Brexit and the election of Donald Trump signalled a widespread dissatisfaction with the current political configuration (Winlow et al, 2017). Communities which had been marginalised and ignored for decades supported issues and candidates who represented an opportunity for change. The rise of the right has historically been a boon to capitalism as authoritarian states rarely impose restrictions on the market or the function of capital (Winlow et al, 2017). On the left, the Sanders and Corbyn movements have emboldened progressives and radicals to demand changes which work in the favour of the many. However, if ideology acts as a fantasy to prevent an encounter with an unpalatable truth, the collective disavowal of large sections of the political class and mainstream media reflects a neoliberal ideology which clings to power and fails to face reality. In this instance, harms will not be fixed as interventions will fail to go far enough and only scratch the surface. The symbolic violence that prevents access to an alternative Symbolic Order will continue to harm individuals and communities who fail to access positive rights and opportunities for genuine flourishing. The final section will contemplate ways in which harm can be alleviated.

Fixing the harms of work

We return to the question posed at the start of the previous section: if we are to fix the myriad harms we face in contemporary Western society, what level of intervention into the social structure and economy do we require? The previous section demonstrated the symbolic violence of ideology that contains intervention at a level that fails to challenge the status quo and is inadequate in its attempts to alleviate significant harm and inequality. This section, in restating the question, will attempt to offer one or two tentative suggestions for discussion, ideas that require intervention at the level of neoliberal depth structures and force us to consider alternative ways of thinking about intransigent social problems.

We require nothing short of a fundamental reconsideration of our socioeconomic and ethico-cultural platform (Whitehead, 2015, 2018). In relation to the workplace, we require more than mere incremental or technical change; suggestions to rename 'welfare' as 'social security' to remove stigma are not enough. Piecemeal change to fringe benefits for low-paid employees is insufficient. Celebrations of apparent 'organic resistance' in exploitative labour markets should be judged carefully and not regarded as clear evidence of protest (Lloyd, 2017). Instead, new 'concrete universals' are required to move beyond narrow self-interest and competitive identity politics. In relation to the harms of work, we can identify zero-hour contracts, employment instability and low pay as universals which affect *everyone*. Rather than operate on the basis of external signifiers such as age, race, gender and sexual orientation, we can think more broadly about the harmful nature of zero-hour contracts and employment instability and use these as the basis for a platform to address the harms of work.

The collapse of symbolic efficiency at the heart of neoliberalism provides a vital opportunity to reconstitute public debate around a particular set of progressive ideas which are grounded in ethics and a moral responsibility for the Other, stability and protection. The transcendental materialist subject is non-essential; the Symbolic Order provides a veneer of order and consistency that constitutes the subjectivities we encounter on a daily basis. The subject is not fundamentally 'good' but, as Adorno (1973) suggests, it has the potential to be so. As neoliberalism increasingly fails to offer a degree of stability and consistency in the lives of millions of disaffected, insecure and precarious people across the West, a radically progressive and morally centred ethico-political Symbolic Order is needed. The stakes are high. As neoliberalism fails, the subject requires unconscious solicitation of a symbolic realm which provides a degree of meaning and consistency; this does not necessarily have to be progressive or positive (Hall and Winlow, 2015). The rise of far-right nationalist or fascist movements across Europe and the US reflects an aching melancholy among subjects ejected from the exclusive club of economic and social success and stability (Winlow et al, 2017). As the social breaks down, as symbolic efficiency declines, the subjective retreat to a place of consistency and meaning has found a clear political narrative on the right and generated major electoral success. The left needs a coherent set of values, ethics and politics to counter this challenge.

Fortunately, those who are dispossessed, disaffected and precarious have also begun to identify with a slowly renewed call for social-democratic or socialist policies. The energy of the Sanders campaign was snuffed out by the centre-left liberal establishment in 2016 but the Corbyn-inspired Labour revival at the 2017 election demonstrated a potential awakening of left-wing sentiment, possibly based on the lacklustre and negative campaign of the Conservative government but also, crucially, as a result of a progressive and positive manifesto for wholesale political change. The transcendental materialist subject is neither good nor evil; a Symbolic Order must be created which moves beyond the competitive individualism, self-interest, status-driven, market-inspired, negativity of capitalism. It is the role of the left to begin the hard work needed to shape this debate and find these solutions.

It is imperative that we consider the way a capitalist economy operates. Wolfgang Streeck (2016) calls on sociology to affix political economy to the heart of its project. Streeck suggests that sociology has the power and conceptual tools to acknowledge that both the state and market are not 'natural' but instead politically constructed and publicly instituted. The 'natural' laws of the economy project social power relations as ideologically technical necessities. The *capitalist* economy has been reconstituted as simply the 'economy' therefore a project to embed the economy at the centre of sociological analysis becomes essential if we are to make sense of changes to institutions, cultures, communities, identity and belief. As capitalism inverts social relations, appreciation of the mechanisms within which capitalist economics shape social relations between various marginal, class and identity groups is a positive step. Capitalism's tendency is towards more insecure, flexible and low-paid work while consumerism acts as entertainment in an increasingly post-social arrangement (Streeck, 2016). If we wish to fix the harms of work, social scientists and politicians must address the underlying reality of capitalism in the early 21st century. Streeck moves us beyond capitalist realism as he clearly predicts capitalism's demise. However, his predicted return to the 'dark ages' should be heeded as a warning.

Modern monetary theory

One way in which it is possible to reconnect issues of social inequality, poverty and low-paid work with a wider appreciation of capitalist economics comes from the emergence of modern monetary theory (MMT) as an alternative conception of economy (Mitchell and Fazi, 2017). Economic orthodoxy repeatedly asks us to consider government budgets in the same way we consider household budgets; if we spend more than we earn, we incur deficits. We also believe that public spending is linked to tax revenue; if we want well-funded public programmes, it requires unpopular tax increases that reduce household income and prevent business growth, profit, job creation and so on. MMT reminds us that the government, as sole manufacturer of currency, whose debt is denominated in that currency, can never become insolvent. If the government can issue fiat currency, no amount of debt will bankrupt the state because it can simply issue more (Mitchell and Fazi, 2017). The austerity argument falls down repeatedly in the face of numerous examples whereby the UK and US governments have shaken the magic money tree when required – the Conservative government's £1 billion deal with the Democratic Unionist Party (DUP) following the 2017 election is a prime example.

The government's ability to issue fiat currency is accompanied by a reversal of the revenue-spending relation. Rather than collect taxes and then distribute that pot as public spending, limited by the total income from revenue, if spending comes first then there is no limit on public spending (Mitchell and Fazi, 2017). State investment in infrastructure, job training, job programmes, living wage and other socially beneficial mechanisms that could reduce precarity, insecurity and low-paid jobs are all fundable. As is universal healthcare, fully funded education and national defence. More currency floating around the system raises the spectre of inflation yet this can be combated by ensuring spending is in service of the pursuit of full employment and no higher, then setting tax rates at an appropriate and progressive post-hoc level, as well as personal savings and imports helping to find economic equilibrium. Public debt automatically means there is private credit in the economy and, as noted at the beginning of this book, spending drives the economy. More money in workers' pockets increases spending.

The key principles of MMT refashion our approach to economics and open up a wide range of possibilities in relation to work and labour markets. There is no economic rationale for austerity and recognition of this fact reveals the harms of austerity as an ideological weapon. Low-paid, insecure, flexible work is under threat if governments commit spending towards full employment. Well-paid, secure national job programmes and infrastructure projects could ensure a living wage for many. If capitalism generates vast inequalities, MMT offers an alternative way of redressing this balance and ensuring a degree of stability, fixity and protection, all of which reduces harm.

Universal basic income

An alternative approach comes in the renewed calls for a universal basic income (UBI). Originally proposed by the political right in the 1960s and 70s, UBI fulfils the libertarian dream of freedom and the end of welfare but it also addresses human flourishing, precarity and a significant reduction in poverty. Debate persists about the level at which UBI should be set with conservatives advocating lower payments and the left calling for higher payments. There is also discussion about how UBI is paid for. However, it falls into the trap identified by MMT above, particularly in relation to the argument over revenue and payment. How will we pay for UBI? Increased taxes, reduction in other welfare payments? MMT suggests that this is a false argument as the state maintains the means to pay for UBI at any desired level. There is also a degree to which UBI could fail to tackle inequality as a guaranteed payment to everybody will simply raise everyone above the poverty line rather than deal with structural and entrenched inequality. Mitchell and Fazi (2017) suggest that UBI will actually *increase* low-paid work as the UBI subsidy exacerbates a trend away from full-time work. Economically, UBI risks an increase in demand but a reduction in supply as more people opt out of the labour market.

In an attempt to contemplate UBI within the context of the future of work, Srnicek and Williams (2016) look past 'tinkering at the edges'. Their ambitious 'post-work' agenda recognises and acknowledges the plethora of harms associated with precarious, flexible realms of underemployment and global surplus labour. A 'post-work' society embraces automation to render vast sections of the labour market obsolete and irrelevant. A UBI commensurate with a sufficient standard of income would compensate this loss. The reduction of the working week and a divorce from the work ethic unleashes free time and transforms collective attitudes towards human potential. Under such conditions, work would be chosen rather than forced. Employers, faced with a labour shortage, would be required to improve pay and conditions. Those endowed with extra leisure time or disinclined to work at all could invest in projects designed for human flourishing, the positive freedom *to* rather than the negative freedom *from*.

As an ambitious post-capitalist vision, Srnicek and Williams break out from the cloistered boundaries of the neoliberal status quo and demand the reader engage with ideas for a positive vision of the future, beyond the limits of capitalist realism (Fisher, 2009). At times there are echoes of the problematic 'accelerationist' movement of the 1990s. Belief in acceleration through to capitalism's end point misses Walter Benjamin's warning about the dark side to the dialectic (Noys, 2014). Capitalism's mode of production generates inequality, harm and insecurity in significant quantities yet the rails of accelerationism blindly transport us towards further disasters in the name of progress; capital accumulation will continue to eject disposable bodies as we speed up towards the future symbiosis of technology and humanity. To ignore this is problematic.

There remain concerns about UBI and its relationship to the value of work. Should we find ways to restrict the market rather than let some individuals opt out? In the wrong hands, UBI transforms into the liberal quest for personal freedom from constraint (in this case freedom from work) rather than a chance for the positive rights associated with *freedom to*. Is guaranteed stable and well-paid employment more beneficial to the subject than the ability to opt out and pursue other perhaps more meaningful pursuits? As countries begin to trial UBI, these discussions are needed.

In the critique foisted on their work, the problem of the left is visible. In the afterword to the updated 2016 edition, Srnicek and Williams outline criticisms which include a concern that their post-work utopia remains ignorant of continued inequalities of misogyny, racism and post-colonialism (pp 188–9). Srnicek and Williams clearly foreground class as the crucial unit of analysis in their work. This critique is instructive of the destructive attitude of the liberal left; women, minority ethnic groups, exploited communities in former colonies, the LGBTQ community, disabled people, those who are poor or working class, *all* are significantly disadvantaged under present conditions of neoliberal capitalism. This is the abject concrete universal which can foreground progressive politics (Hall and Winlow, 2015). The harmful and destructive nature of capital keenly felt by many, particularly those who experience the worst excesses of life in the shadow of the Real, presents a more logical analytical and political starting point, rather than the competitive and precarious demands of single groups. It would be more valuable to transform the political-economic contours of society and eliminate competitive individualism from a set of ethico-cultural relations. This could benefit *all* social groups, including the multi-ethnic working class, rather than seek to maintain the status quo of competition and solely seek to boost the market shares of one group.

Facing reality

A potentially profitable avenue for fixing the harms of work emerges from what Dupuy (2013) calls 'enlightened doomsaying' and Winlow (2017) refers to as 'catastrophism'. Rather than the collective disavowal, oblivious to the wider implications of capitalist excess and amorality, there is value in facing reality and addressing both the experiences and events around us as well as the depth structures of capitalism. This requires a little more imagination and thought from both policy advocates and social scientists. Dupuy builds on the notion of the sacred to suggest that, in facing the apocalypse, a degree of revelation takes place which allows humanity to see itself in a new light. This transcendence provides the intellectual space for the subject to acknowledge impending crisis, take an imaginative leap and work backwards from the future catastrophe to our present time and identify a way to avoid our fate. In some respects this echoes Walter Benjamin's belief that a revolution represents not historical progress or inevitability but instead an emergency brake which prevents catastrophe (Traverso, 2016). If the process of 'enlightened doomsaying' affords a vision of a future dystopia, it also bestows an opportunity to engage the emergency brake and forestall a cataclysmic outcome.

In asking politicians and social scientists to make this transcendent leap, to investigate social reality as it currently exists 'out there' in the communities, cultures and workplaces that we *think* we know about, we can use this grasp of reality in a positive manner. Rather than disavowing the worst excesses of systemic violence or misidentifying symptoms as causes, in following the logic of capitalism to its conclusion we can perhaps identify the worst excesses of a particular set of social processes – climate change policy, the migrant crisis, EU monetary strategy, austerity, labour market configuration – and consider the result and effect of continuing existing strategy, policy and thinking. In staring into the abyss, we may find the collective will and ambition to take a different course. If we systematically understand the reality around us, identify the harms which occur through systemic, symbolic and subjective violence, recognise symptoms, causes and motivations, the damaging effects of a collective disavowal on the scale identified above may be averted. A society built on foundations of growing and widening inequality and harm, with a significant proportion of the population engaged in low-paid, insecure, flexible forms of temporary and affective labour, cannot and will not be sustainable. If politicians and social scientists faced the world with a realism which accounted for the worst outcomes of logical processes and structures already set in place, it could be possible to pull back from our current course and find a different way.

In a society characterised by capitalist realism and a level of symbolic violence which shuts down avenues that lead away from the status quo, the call to 'demand the impossible' (Žižek 2013) becomes a difficult proposition. However, the suggestion that we look beyond the obvious has perhaps found receptive ears. Discussions of a universal basic income gather pace; if set at an appropriate level, this would potentially remove both the absence of stability and protection within low-paid precarious labour markets. However, Swiss voters recently rejected proposals to trial UBI while Finland did trial basic income payments to 2,000 unemployed before enthusiasm and momentum waned and the scheme was terminated (Crisp, 2018). Calls for national investment banks would circumvent the power of private capital to determine the spatial flow of lucrative investment and perhaps begin to reconnect areas of permanent recession with a realistic strategy for investment and jobs. Modern monetary theory challenges the domain assumptions of mainstream economics and its ideological hegemony. Workplace co-operatives and collective ownership have also gained support (Scholz, 2017). Although a positive step, it is not enough just to graft this onto a competitive market; the imperatives of profit, growth and competition will not allow collective ownership to flourish. Coalitions of unions and students are important too. Bringing people together around shared ethics, morality and values as well as common enemies will begin to create the sorts of movements which can channel the libidinal energy or *rage* (Sloterdijk, 2010) which often dissipates into the circuits of consumer capitalism as dissatisfied subjects cannot 'bank' their anger in a positive project or collective endeavour.

In calling for us to consider the possibility of a social system not configured according to market logic and the generation of profit, we are asking subjects emotionally invested in a Symbolic Order to look beyond those horizons and contemplate something else. This is difficult. The power of capitalism is derived from its promise of future satisfaction (McGowan, 2016); things might be bad now but we could be happy and satisfied in the future, if we just work hard enough. If we just accept that zero-hour contract, it could be a stepping stone. At the very least, it might keep the wolf from the door. The success of capitalism derives from its ability to permanently postpone the negation (Winlow and Hall, 2016); we need to look beyond short term and immediate concerns in order to ensure the arrival of capitalism's negation.

Without a coherent alternative to consumer capitalism, people invested in the existing Symbolic Order, on an emotional level, will not seek to lose their chains. In discussions with undergraduate students, the scale of this problem becomes clear. Many acknowledge the harms of capital but also identify the violence of *political catastrophism* (Hall, 2012c; Hall and Winlow, 2015); the alternative ideological constructs of 20th century politics inevitably lead to catastrophe and are therefore beyond countenance. To compound this, those students who do suggest an alternative admit that the process of getting from here to there is unknown. This step into the unknown is more terrifying than more of the same under present conditions. Demanding the impossible is hard; however, in undertaking Dupuy's (2013) enlightened doomsaying, we can begin to acknowledge that more of the same, incremental change and tinkering at the edges will lead to greater problems than those we currently face. The first task is to analyse the realist accounts of everyday life, cultures and workplaces as they exist today. From there, we can apply appropriate and multifaceted theoretical constructs which make sense of this reality. Following that, we can predict what the continuation of this will bring – and work backwards from there.

Conclusion

The violence of ideology narrows horizons and limits debate beyond what could be to a pragmatic vision of current possibilities. The true violence of ideology reflects yet another absence; the absence of an alternative. Ideology works at the level of action, not thought; we know how the world works, we know what is wrong, yet *we act as if we don't know these things*. The collective disavowal at the heart of mainstream politics – that capitalism works for the few and not the many, yet binds the subject to its force through an emotional connection at the level of desire – hamstrings attempts to seek remedies for the harms of work. The subject, terrified of a potential encounter with the Real, disavows knowledge of the way the world actually is in order to maintain a degree of psychic comfort. For those who live within the shadow of the Real, society's depth structures and intransitive realm have daily, negative impacts on their lives; the systemic violence and harm of capitalism is well-known. The decline in symbolic efficiency has hobbled the neoliberal project and the cracks have grown to sizeable holes. If a recognition of the reality of social conditions could overcome the collective disavowal, an opportunity exists to ask searching questions and restart the stalled dialectic.

The limits of language are controlled by elites who act in the 'best interests' of those worse off in society. Fixing the harms of work falls to those who have a structural advantage in a capitalist system from which they gain significantly; despite an often genuine determination to help those worse off than they, it often comes couched in both structural deficit and linguistic limits. This permanently stalls the negation required to undermine the system and represents the harm of symbolic violence. The tempered negation bars those worst off from the language, voice or set of ideas, values, blueprints and confidence to articulate an alternative and the roadmap to its implementation. Those in positions of authority disavow the worst excesses of capitalism and neoliberal ideology to plough ahead with incremental change and technical course adjustments to the journey of global capitalism. Whatever practical knowledge they have of the harms of capital is jettisoned in order to maintain the status quo.

However, there are those who have made worthwhile suggestions which could address some of the harms noted throughout these pages. New ideas in economics, particularly Modern monetary theory at least raises the possibility of debate over spending, revenue and the possibilities afforded by fiat currency. The discussion of a 'post-work' society, exemplified by surveys which indicate a global lack of engagement at work, raises important questions about the function of labour and labour markets in contemporary society (Fleming, 2015). The role of automation is an important topic of debate as it will have a significant impact on the way we work in the future (Ford, 2016; Srnicek and Williams, 2016). The amplified enthusiasm for a universal basic income reflects a widespread acknowledgement that precarious forms of low-paid work fundamentally fail those on the lowest slopes of the capitalist hierarchy and an egalitarian response to alleviate these harms may be required. The need for a new set of concrete universals, around which we can all agree, regardless of social cleavages along the lines of gender, race, ethnicity, sexuality, is vital; the eradication of zero-hour contracts and employment insecurity can potentially fill this gap. In order to address harms now, we could do worse than look to the future in a state of 'enlightened doomsaying'; given the realities uncovered by a wave of critical social scientists, the connection of daily experience with broader forces such as ideology and political economy, can we envisage what more of the same would look like? If so, is it a vision that fills us with hope or dread?

Conclusion

The reality of life in the low-paid service sector is one of insecurity, flexibility, hard work and precarity. David Graeber (2013) identified the growth of 'bullshit jobs' which emanated from reconfigured neoliberal labour markets. The well-paid jobs of the knowledge economy and professions accommodate small workforces who work progressively long hours. The rest of the working-age population is swept into increasingly precarious, underpaid and exploitative forms of temporary or on-demand labour. In an economy dominated by consumer capitalism, the service economy offers the widest range of roles and functions designed to satisfy the demand for instant consumer gratification. Organisational culture and management practice aims to meet 'just-in-time' demand with a flexible workforce buttressed by temporary staff at peak periods of high demand (Hatton, 2011). In the quest for efficiency and productivity, work routines are automated and monitored to ensure maximum effectiveness while employees face targets and performance management which incentivises activity. Rotas constrain workers who are unable to plan ahead and are reliant on managers to allocate suitable shifts. Customers increasingly habituated to their own sovereignty expect frictionless and instant service and often demonstrate willingness to assert a perceived degree of superiority on their low-paid interlocutor if instant gratification and satisfaction is not forthcoming.

These realities are the result of a series of causative absences at the heart of the service economy and labour market in the UK, US and elsewhere. An ultra-realist harm perspective grafted onto the reality of life in the service economy makes an important analytical breakthrough and provides a new lens with which to consider the bottom slopes of the labour market. It also perhaps breaks ossified thinking on low-paid work and ethico-social obligation. Through a rupture with empirical traditions which observe the presence of something, the interpretation of absence at the heart of capitalist political economy and neoliberal ideology presents new realities. The conditions within which harms emerge are a reflection of the ethical void at the heart of capitalism's generative core, the libidinal energy at the centre of the mode of production, driven by the absence at the heart of a subject emotionally invested in the world around them. Capitalism co-opts subjective desire and the hope for future satisfaction (McGowan, 2016) and fills the non-essential void with unquenchable desires and drives which releases and stimulates libidinal drives towards ephemeral objects of pseudo–satisfaction (Hall, 2012a). Neoliberalism has systematically removed the ethico–cultural strait-jacket imposed upon the generative core by the post-war settlement. The market is king, competitive individualism is cloaked in narratives of self-interest, social mobility and human capital dominate social relations, and the desire which drives the generative core is appropriated towards these ends. In order to 'restore' the capitalist class to its 'rightful' place (Harvey, 2005; Badiou, 2009), neoliberalism has systematically created a number of absences which increasingly have causative and harmful effects.

The absence of stability within labour market relations manifests through the shift from security to flexibility in employment contracts. Temporary, part-time or zero-hour contracts, employment agencies, on-demand work, low pay, and minimal benefits epitomise employment conditions within the service economy. Working conditions reflect this imbalance; stability disappears when rotas are produced 'just-in-time' with little planning or warning for employees left to arrange their own cover. Progression is dangled in front of compliant workers who face uncertain futures; the perceived stability of a promotion is often little more than a ruse to encourage 'transactional' workers (Cross et al, 2008) to invest emotionally in the company. Promotional opportunities are often limited and in reality only offer more responsibility for slightly more money. In the context of a transition to adulthood, the absence of stability at work is reflected in the difficulty in attaining objective markers to adulthood such as a house, car, career and family. Some of the interviewees in this book, such as Martin, Ben and Katie, have reached their thirties yet still live with parents or have boomeranged from private rental back to the family home on a number of occasions.

The absence of an ethical responsibility to the Other is the key causative absence outlined by an ultra-realist harm perspective and indicates the positive motivation to harm others. Motivation lies at the heart of the subject; the search for satisfaction is central to the capitalist project. Capitalism requires that the subject remains libidinally or emotionally invested in the values, norms and practices of contemporary society; the active solicitation of neoliberalism's invocation of self-interest, human capital, social mobility and competition is reflected in the practices of some employees, employers and customers within the service economy. The ethical void has expanded beyond the former bulwarks of social democracy and civil society to erode a sense of obligation, responsibility or duty towards the Other (Smith and Raymen, 2016; Whitehead, 2018). This absence allows some to wantonly inflict emotional harm on others, either through customer or co-worker abuse, or through the enactment of 'special liberty'.

The entitled workplace bailiff takes away from others in order to gain personally. The negative ideology of neoliberalism entails a negative solidarity among individuals who fail to identify with the Other and instead see co-workers, employees, and customers as either competition or an impediment to their personal satisfaction or success. The reality behind the harms of neoliberal capitalism is not just the structural violence which leaves many in precarious conditions; the emotional investment in the Symbolic Order creates harmful subjectivities which reflect the dominant values of the hegemonic ideology.

The absence of protection, manifested in the evisceration of employment protections and regulations, leaves the service economy worker with few rights and safeguards. These absences leave some, like Jason and Lee, vulnerable to unscrupulous employers who, driven by the same competitive forces as their rivals, circumvent both the spirit of the law and its inadequate enforcement through a deliberate failure to pay the national minimum or living wage. The illegal extension of an entirely legal set of competitive practices and processes also encourages unpaid or under-paid 'work trials' which exploit employees yet simultaneously maximise profitability. The just-in-time method of organisational practice and absence of employee protection creates physical and emotional harms for workers injured through work routines that maximise efficiency, speed and targets. When employees are timed for stock picking, exemplified by Sports Direct and Amazon and outlined in Chapter Six by Daniel, some workers cut corners which result in physical injury. Daniel's physical injuries were exacerbated by his lack of employment protection. Market forces celebrate the 'creative destruction' of 'economic Darwinism' whereby the weak are culled and the strong survive. Redundancies become a fact of life and an existential threat which hangs over service economy employees who work in a sector dependent on consumer spending in a depressed economy. The absence of employment protection often results in loss of jobs and periods of unemployment, but also, crucially, redundancy payouts underrepresentative of one's actual contribution to the company, the result of consistent management use of overtime to supplement minimal contracted hours. Redundancy payments cover contracted hours and fail to reflect the hours actually contributed by the employee. Finally, the absence of protection within the service economy leaves one vulnerable to mental ill health. There is a mental health crisis in the UK and US. For those in low-paid, insecure and flexible jobs where stability and protection are absent, customer abuse is common, management practice embodies 'just-in-time' provision, and minimal employment protections, insecurity, precarity and bullying can lead to an overall decline in levels of mental well-being.

These absences can be contextualised in relation to the political will to fix the harms of work. The symbolic violence of capitalist ideology prevents an encounter with an alternative ideology which leaves those on the bottom slopes of the labour market in continuous precarity. Politicians often appear unwilling to step beyond the confines of 'capitalist realism' and seek alternatives to the market. Reform agendas are doomed to fail as incremental change cannot address the logic of capitalism, competition and the market. Attempts to overlay the market mechanism with piecemeal reform and collaborative projects will not do the job. This reflects the limits of liberalism, which seeks equality through legal means but ultimately accepts freedom and individualism as 'natural' and 'good'. The spirit of individuality at the heart of the Enlightenment project, coupled with the capitalist demand for growth, profit and competition, engenders a valorisation of individual rights and freedoms but largely through the negative ideology of *freedom from*; the individual is free from persecution, free from the shackles of oppression, free from the confines of history, class and background. Individual freedom manifests as social mobility, self-interest and competition within a capitalist market in which success is merited and failure a personal responsibility.

Efforts at reform only ever tinker around the edges because both right and left liberalism fail to offer a positive ideology of recognition or flourishing beyond the confines of the market. The limits of a deaptive ideology are visible in the communities and workplaces where the shadow of the Real colours daily life. The impact of change at the level of depth structures, the political-economic logic of society, is evident in low-paid labour markets, unstable and precarious living and working arrangements and the harmful subjectivities which emerge from the Symbolic Order of neoliberal consumer capitalism. Increasingly, neoliberalism fails to provide coherence and meaning for a large number of people who have begun to turn to political extremes of right and left for an alternative to 'capitalist realism'. The transcendental materialist subject is plastic and flexible; the most coherent Symbolic Order will determine the future direction of Western capitalism.

To fix the harms of work, politicians and social scientists must identify a new set of concrete universals. Workplace security and protection is a start. An agreement on the harms associated with zero-hour contracts and insufficient pay is another. Ultimately, we must break with the preferred tendency to stop at the water's edge and instead get our feet wet. Many suggest that capitalism has begun a downward spiral towards its demise (Mason, 2015; Streeck, 2016). A failure to regard the challenge of alternatives as a positive opportunity is not only short-sighted but also represents a collective disavowal where those in positions to advocate powerfully for change can identify the challenges but *act as if they don't*. Climate change, automation, information technology, and migration will all have a significant impact on the labour markets of the very near future; it is up to scholars and politicians to address this. Piecemeal reform will no longer cut it yet the violence of ideology hampers our attempts to think beyond existing horizons.

Returning to harm

This book set out to investigate the service economy from within the analytical framework of social harm. In order to do so, a synthesis of social harm perspectives and ultra-realist criminology presented a rounded conceptual base from which to explore the harms inflicted on employees through the normal functioning of neoliberal capitalism, termed here the *negative motivation to harm*, and the subjective willingness to inflict harm on others or, the *positive motivation to harm*. The social harm perspectives of Hillyard and Tombs (2004), Pemberton (2016), Scott (2017) and others elucidate the myriad harmful effects of growing inequality associated with neoliberal restructure at the level of political economy and public policy. The theory of subjective motivation and relationship between ideology, symbolic efficiency and subjectivity posed by ultra-realist thinkers (Hall and Winlow, 2015; Smith and Raymen, 2016) and transcendental materialist philosophers (Johnston, 2008) accounts for the subject's libidinal attachment to neoliberal consumer capitalism and the willingness to harm others in pursuit of personal ends rather than desire to change the existing status quo. The subject's libidinal investment in a capitalist economy and neoliberal ideology ties subjective desire to the attendant Symbolic Order.

This is an important advance in social harm theory. The evidence presented here demonstrates that harm is intersubjective and dynamic. For example, Pemberton (2016) acknowledges autonomy harms (the loss of personal freedom) and relational harms. Harm reduction should increase personal freedom and autonomy yet in Chapter Five, Jade outlines an experience of belittlement at the hands of a customer who demonstrates the positive freedom and autonomy to make demands and behave as she wishes. This subsequently constitutes a relational harm in her treatment of Jade. This reflects a bigger question about resolving harms of constrained autonomy while not encouraging the exercise of autonomy in a way that negatively affects our relations with others. By identifying the motivation to act and grounding harm as the absence of positive rights *and* intersubjective recognition, an ultra-realist harm perspective accounts for the dynamic tension between individuals. This is the true value in incorporating ultra-realist theory into a social harm perspective; harms do not just happen *to* us, they are also inflicted *by* us.

Collective ethics and morality become an important factor in this equation yet the competitive individualism that characterises the current Symbolic Order of neoliberalism presents a significant challenge to the call for positive intersubjective relations. In the context of the service economy, the absence of stability and protection clearly creates structural impediments to positive human freedoms, recognition and flourishing, which negatively impinge upon the subject. However, it is also clear that the solicitation of a Symbolic Order, the neoliberal values of competitive individualism, self-interest and social mobility, creates problematic and harmful subjectivities that display negative solidarity towards others and maximise their market shares through harmful acts. Not all co-workers attempt to 'screw over' their colleagues. However, *some* do and explaining this motivation is crucial in understanding how to address the harmful consequences of neoliberalism. An appreciation of the relationship between the subject, motivation, and the emotional attachment to the Symbolic Order of consumer capitalism, has significant implications for reform and transformation of current conditions. If people are neither essentially 'good' nor 'evil' but instead have the capacity for both in any given social order, it allows us to ask questions about the sorts of values, norms and ethics we wish to see in the world – and how we bring those into being.

If inequality is not directly harmful, it creates the conditions within which harms can occur. The deep restructure of political economy and ideology has created conditions within which a number of absences appear; these absences create conditions wherein unintentional and intentional willingness to harm frequently occurs. This approach to social harm removes intention from a theory of violence to provide a continuum of systemic, symbolic and subjective violence which spans the divide between legal and illegal activity while showing its shared origin: the ethical void at the heart of capitalism.

The violence of capitalism inflicts harms, all too clearly exemplified in human subjectivities and organisational functions, especially in the pseudo-work of the service economy. The systemic violence produced by the normal functioning of capitalism, the subjective violence of individuals often motivated by self-interest and competitive behaviour, and the symbolic violence of language which foreclose the possibility of an alternative, symbolically efficient, ideological vision for social relations and organisation. The systemic violence of consumer capitalism generates a set of processes that spawn both legal and illegal practices yet are all embedded within the same ideological circuits. The competitive individualism which encourages the subject to maximise one's human capital and succeed in the dog-eat-dog world of work is entirely legal; the competitive individual who employs 'special liberty' to inflict emotional violence on others to maximise market shares traverses the boundaries of legality. The profit motive within tight labour markets encourages flexible forms of insecure and low-paid labour which are entirely legal; the same imperatives also encourage some employers to underpay workers, keep employees 'off the books' to avoid tax and national insurance contributions, and engage in 'work trials' which fail to pay the mandated minimum wage – all of which are entirely illegal. The continuum of legal and illegal activity stems from a singular imperative of a capitalist mode of production bolstered by a neoliberal ideology which has uncoupled the generative core of capital from its ethico-social restraints. This continuum of activity makes it imperative to consider the workplace from a harm perspective. To foreground profit and growth ahead of well-being, security and intersubjective recognition is also indicative of harm which emanates from within the anti-ethical heart of capitalism.

Some may question whether my respondents and contacts are cognisant of harms, see themselves as victims or experience events as harmful. In some instances, Katie's experience as a driving instructor, Sam's acknowledgment of racist customers, Daniel's bullying at work, Martin's disproportionately low redundancy settlement, my contacts identified explicit harms related to specific events and experiences. On another level, however, the answer is no. The reality of life in the low-paid service economy has reached the level of practical knowledge; this is simply how things are. For many, the insecure, low-paid, flexible forms of often temporary and 'non-standard' forms of work reflect the only work experience they have known. The shift from security to flexibility took place before they entered the labour market and has been steadily embedded throughout their working lives. The objective conditions of their working lives are not experienced as harmful because they know no different. Many also fail to recognise the need for an alternative. When pressed on practical measures to make things better, most responded with suggestions related to management practice and more pay. A comprehensively different set of social relations or alternative labour market composition was not articulated. The route to recognition and flourishing is difficult in a system which binds the subject emotionally; capitalism thrives on the psychic investment of the individual, compelled to act and function in a way that seeks satisfaction through the circuits of consumer capitalism. The absence of a coherent alternative to the status quo and a clear and practical programme which outlines the shift from here to there leaves most to seek refuge in the safety of the familiar or channel their energy in less productive outlets.

Aspects of social life not usually associated with studies of crime or deviance have become subject to analysis through social harm perspectives. This is an important step as it reframes the debate around issues such as low-paid work. A 'parallax view' is a shift in perspective which provides an opportunity to see an object in a different light and reveal new details. The investigation of the low-paid service economy from a harm perspective offers a new way to think about some of the most visible examples of contemporary labour markets in the UK and elsewhere. If we frame the service economy from a harm perspective, it raises significant questions about the processes which drive consumer capitalism in its neoliberal phase to reconfigure labour markets and organisational practice. It also allows for practices which follow the logic of competition, profitability and efficiency yet straddle the line between legal and illicit. Finally, the use of a harm perspective raises an ethical question in terms of our willingness to continue such practices.

These pages tell a story which is yet to be finished. What will happen to those individuals who illustrate the points made within this book? It does not have to be this way. The harms of work are surmountable. It will not be easy but it is possible. Social harm perspectives must not stop short but instead engage in a critique of the status quo which looks beyond the horizons of capitalist realism, particularly in the search for answers. Pemberton (2016) acknowledges that all forms of capitalism generate harms, some more than others, but Streeck (2016) goes further: capitalism is harmful and potentially in its death throes. Beyond capitalism is a return to the 'dark ages', a post-social set of arrangements where institutions fail in their obligation to citizens and the subject retreats into harmful protectionism (Winlow and Hall, 2013; Winlow et al, 2015). If all forms of capitalism are harmful then we should discuss alternatives. If capitalism is ready to utter its death rattle, we should seize the moment and seek a positive set of social relations, based on an ethical obligation towards the Other and an equitable distribution of resources. The transcendental materialist subject at the heart of an ultra-realist schema possesses the necessary plasticity at a material level to adapt to a new set of ethico-social relations and a positive symbolically efficient ideology.

Before we can consider an alternative set of ethico-social relations that challenge the negative ideology of neoliberalism and capitalist relations, we must face the present reality. If we ask about the nature of life and existence in the low-paid reality of the service economy, then answers lie in these pages. Answers also lie in the deliberate shift from security to flexibility in order to stimulate shareholder value, profit and economic growth. In the absence of stable employment conditions. In the growth of a culture of competitive individualism, driven by status and envy. In the harsh realities of workplaces preoccupied with targets, staffed by precarious workers on low-pay and zero-hour contracts. In the predominance of service industries catering to a ubiquitous consumer capitalism. In the growth of a rentier society which extracts value from those who earn the least. In the austerity and deficit reduction measures that penalise the poorest whilst the elites enjoy tax breaks. In a culture that promotes social mobility as a reward for hard work and places responsibility for failure to achieve upward mobility on the shoulders of the individual. And, in a society where the horizons dim to within the confines of the status quo; reform agendas tinker at the edges, and material conditions never really improve as low-paid workers continue to labour in the shadow of capitalism's Real. This is the reality of capitalist labour markets. This is the reality of neoliberal ideology. This is the reality of the harms of work.

References

Adorno, T.W. (1973) *Negative Dialectics*, London: Routledge.

Agerholm, H. (2016) 'Female suicide rate in the UK highest it has been for a decade – for second year in a row', *The Independent*, Friday 2 December, www.independent.co.uk/news/uk/home-news/female-women-suicide-decade-mental-health-killing-themselves-highest-level-a7452491.html

Ahmad, A.N. (2008) 'Dead men working: Time and space in London's (illegal) migrant economy', *Work, Employment and Society*, 22(2), 301-18.

Akerlof, G.A. and Shiller, R.J. (2009) *Animal Spirits: How Human Psychology Drives the Economy, and Why it Matters for Global Capitalism*, Oxford: Princeton University Press.

Althusser, L. (2014) *On the Reproduction of Capitalism: Ideology and Ideological State Apparatuses*, London: Verso.

Antonakakis, N. and Collins, A. (2014) 'The impact of fiscal austerity on suicide: On the empirics of a modern Greek tragedy', *Social Science and Medicine*, 112, 39-50.

Applebaum, E. (2012) 'Reducing inequality and insecurity: Rethinking labor and employment policy for the 21st century', *Work & Occupations*, 39(4), 311-20.

Arnett, J.J. (2000) 'Emerging adulthood: A theory of development from the late teens through the twenties', *American Psychologist*, 55, 469-80.

Arrighi, G. (2010) *The Long Twentieth Century*, London: Verso.

Armstrong, A. (2016a) 'Sports Direct board agrees to external review in wake of working practices row', *The Telegraph*, 18 August, www.telegraph.co.uk/business/2016/08/18/sports-direct-board-agrees-to-external-review-in-wake-of-working/

Armstrong, A. (2016b) 'MPs' surprise visit to Mike Ashley's Sports Direct turns to farce amid spy claims', *The Telegraph*, 7 November, www.telegraph.co.uk/business/2016/11/07/mps-surprise-mike-ashleys-sports-direct-with-unannounced-warehou/

Atkinson, R. (2016) 'Limited exposure: Social concealment, mobility and engagement with public space by the super-rich in London', *Environment and Planning A*, 48(7), 1302-17.

Auer, P. (2007) *Security in Labour Markets: Combining Flexibility with Security for Decent Work*, Employment Analysis and Research Unit Report, Geneva: ILO.

Badiou, A. (2007) *Being and Event*, London: Bloomsbury.

Badiou, A. (2009) *The Century*, Cambridge: Polity.

Barber, B. (2007) *Consumed*, London: W.W. Norton & Co.

Barber, M. (2008) *Instruction to Deliver: Tony Blair, Public Services and the Challenge of Achieving Targets*, London: Politico.

Bauman, Z. (2004) *Wasted Lives: Modernity and its Outcasts*, Cambridge: Polity.

Baudrillard, J. (1981) *Simulacra and Simulation*, Michigan: University of Michigan Press.

Baudrillard, J. (1993) *The Transparency of Evil*, London: Verso.

Baudrillard, J. (2007) *In the Shadow of the Silent Majorities*, Los Angeles: Semiotext(e).

BBC (2013) 'Amazon workers face 'increased risk of mental illness'', 25 November, www.bbc.co.uk/news/business-25034598

BBC (2017) 'Sports Direct calls executive pay report "fake news"', 15 March, www.bbc.co.uk/news/business-39277699

Beirne, P. (2009) *Confronting Animal Abuse: Law, Criminology and Human–Animal Relationships*, New York: Rowman and Littlefield.

Bell, L. (1985) *At the Works: A Study of a Manufacturing Town*, London: Virago.

Berardi, F. (2009) *The Soul at Work: From Alienation to Autonomy*, Los Angeles: Semiotext(e).

Berg, J. (2016) 'Income security in the on–demand economy: Findings and policy lessons from a survey of crowdworkers', *Comparative Labor Law and Policy Journal*, 37(3), https://papers.ssrn.com/sol3/papers.cfm?abstract_id=2740940.

Berlin, I. (1969) *Four Essays on Liberty*, Oxford: University Press.

Berlingieri, A. (2015) 'Workplace bullying: Exploring an emerging framework', *Work, Employment and Society*, 29(2), 342-53.

Bew, J. (2016) *Citizen Clem: A Biography of Attlee*, London: riverrun.

Beynon, H. (1973) *Working for Ford*, London: Penguin.

Beynon, H., Hudson, R. and Sadler, D. (1994) *A Place Called Teesside: A Locality in a Global Economy*, Edinburgh: University Press.

Bhaskar, R. (2010) *Reclaiming Reality*, London: Routledge.

Blumenthal, E. (2016) 'Looking for a job? Amazon's hiring 120,000 holiday workers', *USA Today*, 13 October, www.usatoday.com/story/money/2016/10/13/looking-job-amazons-hiring-120000-holiday-workers/91992248/

Boltanski, L. and Chiapello, E. (2005) *The New Spirit of Capitalism*, London: Verso.

Bourdieu, P. (1989) 'Social space and symbolic power', *Sociological Theory*, 7(1), 14-25.

Brannen, J. and Nilsen, A. (2002) 'Young people's time perspectives: From youth to adulthood', *Sociology*, 36(3), 517-33.

Braverman, H. (1974) *Labor Monopoly and Capital: The Degradation of Work in the Twentieth Century*, New York: Monthly Review Press.

Briggs, D. and Monge Gamero, R. (2017) *Dead End Lives*, Bristol: Policy Press.

Brown, P. and Hesketh, A. (2004) *The Mismanagement of Talent: Employability and Jobs in the Knowledge Economy*, Oxford: University Press.

Bureau of Labor Statistics (2018) 'The Employment Situation – December 2017', 5 January, www.employnm.com/content/files/010518_bls.pdf

Butler, J. (2006) *Gender Trouble*, London: Routledge.

Butler, J. (2011) *Bodies that Matter: On the Discursive Limits of Sex*, London: Routledge.

Butler, P. (2015) 'Thousands have died after being found fit for work, DWP figures show', *The Guardian*, Thursday 27 August, www.theguardian.com/society/2015/aug/27/thousands-died-after-fit-for-work-assessment-dwp-figures

Butler, S. (2018) 'Number of UK restaurants going bust up by a fifth in 2017', *The Guardian*, Monday 19 February, www.theguardian.com/business/2018/feb/19/number-of-uk-restaurants-going-bust-up-by-a-fifth-in-2017

Byrne, D. (1989) *Beyond the Inner City*, Milton Keynes: Open University Press.

Cadwalladr, C. (2013) 'My week as an Amazon insider', *The Observer*, 1 December, www.theguardian.com/technology/2013/dec/01/week-amazon-insider-feature-treatment-employees-work

Caldwell, A.A. (2015) 'Heroin, prescription pain pills top drug threat in the US', www.businessinsider.com/ap-heroin-prescription-pain-pills-top-drug-threat-in-the-us-2015-11?IR=T

Callaghan, G. and Thompson, P. (2002) ''We recruit attitude': The selection and shaping of routine call centre labour', *Journal of Management Studies*, 39(2), 233-54.

Campbell, D. (2016) 'NHS child mental health services are failing the next generation, say GPs', *The Guardian*, Monday 4 July, www.theguardian.com/society/2016/jul/04/nhs-child-mental-health-services-anxiety-depression

Carr, N. (2011) *The Shallows: What the Internet is Doing to Our Brains*, London: W.W. Norton & Company.

Carter, P. (2016) *Operational Productivity and Performance in English NHS Acute Hospitals: Unwarranted Variations*, Independent Report for the Department of Health.

Cederstrom, C. and Spicer, A. (2015) *The Wellness Syndrome*, Cambridge: Polity.

Chakrabortty, A. (2012) 'Economics has failed us: but where are the fresh voices?', *The Guardian*, Monday 16 April, www.theguardian.com/commentisfree/2012/apr/16/economics-has-failed-us-alternative-voices

Chakrabortty, A. and Weale, S. (2016) 'Universities accused of "importing Sports Direct model" for lecturers' pay', *The Guardian*, 16 November, www.theguardian.com/uk-news/2016/nov/16/universities-accused-of-importing-sports-direct-model-for-lecturers-pay

Chamberlain, L.J. and Hodson, R. (2010) 'Toxic work environments: What helps and what hurts', *Sociological Perspectives*, 53(4), 455-77.

Chan, S. and Tweedie, D. (2016) 'Understanding contemporary employment insecurity: Beck's legacy', *Work, Employment and Society*, 30(5), 896-98.

Charlesworth, S.J. (2000) *A Phenomenology of Working Class Experience*, Cambridge: University Press.

Chugh, S. and Hancock, P. (2009) 'Networks of aestheticization: The architecture, artefacts and embodiment of hairdressing salons', *Work, Employment and Society*, 23(3), 460-76.

Collier, A. (1994) *Critical Realism: An Introduction to Roy Bhaskar's Philosophy*, London: Verso.

Conkin, P.K. (1967) *The New Deal*, New York: Thomas Y. Crowell Company.

Cook, P.J. and Frank, R.H. (2010) *The Winner Take-All Society*, New York: Virgin Books.

Cooper, C. (2015) 'Iain Duncan Smith's tougher fit-to-work tests "coincide with 590 additional suicides"', *The Independent*, Tuesday 17 November, www.independent.co.uk/news/uk/politics/iain-duncan-smiths-tougher-fit-to-work-tests-coincide-with-590-additional-suicides-a6737136.html

Copson, L. (2013) 'Towards a utopian criminology' in Malloch, M. and Munro, B. (Eds) *Crime, Critique and Utopia*, London: Palgrave Macmillan.

Copson, L. (2014) 'Penal populism and the problem of mass incarceration: The promise of utopian thinking', *The Good Society*, 23(1), 55-72.

Copson, L. (2016) 'Realistic utopianism and alternatives to imprisonment: The ideology of crime and the utopia of harm', *Justice, Power and Resistance*, Foundation Volume, September, 73-96.

Coté, J. (2014) *Youth Studies: Fundamental Issues and Debates*, Basingstoke: Palgrave.

Crary, J. (2013) *24/7: Late Capitalism and the Ends of Sleep*, London: Verso.

Crisp, J. (2018) 'Finland ends universal basic income experiment', *The Telegraph*, 24 April 2018, https://www.telegraph.co.uk/news/2018/04/23/finland-ends-universal-basic-income-experiment/

Cross, G. (2002) *An All-Consuming Century*, New York: Columbia University Press.

Cross, C., Barry, G. and Garavan, T.N. (2008) 'The psychological contract in call centres', *Journal of Industrial Relations*, 50(2), 229-42.

Davies, P., Francis, P. and Wyatt, T. (2014) 'Taking invisible crimes and social harms seriously' in Davies, P., Francis, P. and Wyatt, T. (Eds) *Invisible Crimes and Social Harms*, Basingstoke: Palgrave Macmillan.

Davis, J., Lister, J. and Wrigley, D. (2015) *NHS For Sale: Myths, Lies and Deception*, London: Merlin Press.

Dean, J. (2009) *Democracy and Other Neoliberal Fantasies: Communicative Capitalism and Left Politics*, London: Duke University Press.

Deery, S., Iverson, R. and Walsh, J. (2002) 'Work relationships in telephone call centres: Understanding emotional exhaustion and employee withdrawal', *Journal of Management Studies*, 39(4), 471-96.

Denham, J. and McDonald, P. (1996) 'Unemployment statistics from 1881 to the present day', *Labour Market Trends*, January, 5-18.

Desmond, M. (2017) *Evicted: Poverty and Profit in the American City*, London: Penguin.

Dorling, D. (2004) 'Prime suspect: Murder in Britain' in Hillyard, P., Pantazis, C., Tombs, S. and Gordon, D. (Eds) *Beyond Criminology: Taking Harm Seriously*, London: Pluto Press.

Dorling, D. (2015a) *Inequality and the 1%*, London: Verso.

Dorling, D. (2015b) *Injustice: Why Social Inequality Still Persists*, Revised Edition, Bristol: Policy Press.

Doyal, L. and Gough, I. (1991) *A Theory of Human Need*, London: Macmillan.

Dumenil, G. and Levy, D. (2011) *The Crisis of Neoliberalism*, London: Harvard University Press.

Dupuy, J.P. (2013) *The Mark of the Sacred*, Stanford: University Press.

Durkheim, E. (2006 [1897]) *On Suicide*, London: Penguin.

Durkheim, E. (2012 [1893]) *The Division of Labor in Society*, Connecticut: Martino Publishing.

Dworkin, D. (1997) *Cultural Marxism in Post-War Britain*, Durham, NC: Duke University Press.

Einarsen, S., Hoel, H., Zapf, D. and Cooper, C. (2011) 'The concept of bullying and harassment at work: The European tradition' in Einarsen, S., Hoel, H., Zapf, D. and Cooper, C. (Eds) *Bullying and Harassment in the Workplace: Developments in Theory, Research, and Practice* (2nd Edn) Boca Raton: CRC Press.

Elchardus, M. and Smits, W. (2008) 'The vanishing flexible: Ambition, self-realisation and flexibility in the career perspectives of young Belgian adults', *Work, Employment and Society*, 22(2), 243-62.

El Gingihy, Y. (2015) *How to Dismantle the NHS in 10 Easy Steps*, Winchester: Zero.

Ellis, A. (2016) *Men, Masculinities and Violence: An Ethnographic Study*, London: Routledge.

Elms, J., de Kervenoael, R. and Hallsworth, A. (2016) 'Internet or store? An ethnographic study of consumers' internet and store-based grocery shopping practices', *Journal of Retailing and Consumer Services*, 32, 234-43.

Eurofound (2015) *New Forms of Employment*, Luxembourg: Publications Office for the European Union.

Fenton, S. and Dermott, E. (2006) 'Fragmented careers? Winners and losers in young adult labour markets', *Work, Employment and Society*, 20(2), 205–21.

Ferguson, C. (2012) *Inside Job: The Financiers Who Pulled Off the Heist of the Century*. Oxford: Oneworld.

Fink, B. (1995) *The Lacanian Subject: Between Language and Jouissance*, Princeton: University Press.

Fisher, M. (2009) *Capitalist Realism*, Winchester: Zero.

Fleming, P. (2015) *The Mythology of Work: How Capitalism Persists Despite Itself*, London: Pluto Press.

Fleming, P. and Sturdy, A. (2011) '"Being yourself" in the electronic sweatshop: New forms of normative control', *Human Relations*, 64(2), 177-200.

Fletcher, D. and Wright, S. (2017) 'A hand up or a slap down? Criminalising benefit claimants in Britain via strategies of surveillance, sanctions and deterrence', *Critical Social Policy*, 38(2) 323-44.

Ford, M. (2016) *The Rise of the Robots*, London: Oneworld.

Frank, T. (2016) *Listen, Liberal: Or, Whatever Happened to the Party of the People?*, London: Scribe.

Fraser, N. (2017) 'The end of progressive neoliberalism', *Dissent*, 2 January.

Freud, S. (2002 [1929]) *Civilization and Its Discontents*, London: Penguin.

Freud, S. (2003 [1920]) *Beyond the Pleasure Principle*, London: Penguin.

Friedman, G. (2014) 'Workers without employers: Shadow corporations and the rise of the gig economy', *Review of Keynesian Economics*, 2(2), 171-88.

Fukuyama, F. (1992) *The End of History and the Last Man*, London: Penguin.

Furlong, A. and Cartmel, P. (2007) *Young People and Social Change: New Perspectives* (2nd Edn) Maidenhead: Open University Press.

Gane, N. (2015) 'Trajectories of liberalism and neoliberalism', *Theory, Culture and Society*, 32(1), 133-44.

Garrahan, P. and Stewart, P. (1992) *The Nissan Enigma: Flexibility at Work in a Local Economy*, London: Mansell.

Garside, R. (2013) 'Addressing social harm: Better regulation versus social transformation', *Revista Critica Penal y Poder*, 5, 247-65.

Garthwaite, K. (2016) *Hunger Pains: Life Inside Foodbank Britain*, Bristol: Policy Press.

Glavin, P. (2013) 'The impact of job insecurity and job degradation on the sense of personal control', *Work and Occupations*, 40(2), 115-42.

Glyn, A. (2006) *Capitalism Unleashed: Finance, Globalization and Welfare*, Oxford: University Press.

Goodley, S. and Ashby, J. (2015) 'A day at "the gulag": what it's like to work at Sports Direct's warehouse', *The Guardian*, 9 December, www.theguardian.com/business/2015/dec/09/sports-direct-warehouse-work-conditions

Gordon, D. (2004) 'Poverty, death and disease' in Hillyard, P. Pantazis, C., Tombs, S. and Gordon, D. (Eds) *Beyond Criminology: Taking Harm Seriously*, London: Pluto Press.

Gould, A.M. (2010) 'Working at McDonalds: Some redeeming features of McJobs', *Work, Employment and Society*, 24(4), 780-802.

Graeber, D. (2013) 'On the phenomenon of bullshit jobs': A work rant', *Strike!*, 17 August, http://strikemag.org/bullshit-jobs/

Gramsci, A. (2000) *The Gramsci Reader: Selected Writings 1916-1935*, Edited by David Forgacs, New York: New York University Press.

Gregg, M. (2011) *Work's Intimacy*, Cambridge: Polity.

Gumbrell-McCormick, R. (2011) 'European trade unions and "atypical" workers', *Industrial Relations Journal*, 42(3), 293-310.

Hall, A. and Antonopoulos, G.A. (2016) *Fake Meds Online: The Internet and the Transnational Market in Illicit Pharmaceuticals*, Basingstoke: Palgrave Pivot.

Hall, G. (2016) *The Uberification of the University*, Minnesota: University of Minnesota Press.

Hall, P.A. and Soskice, D. (2001) *Varieties of Capitalism: The Institutional Foundations of Comparative Advantage*, Oxford: University Press.

Hall, S. (2012a) *Theorizing Crime and Deviance: A New Perspective*, London: Sage.

Hall, S. (2012b) 'The solicitation of the trap: On transcendence and transcendental materialism in advanced consumer-capitalism', *Human Studies*, 35(3), 365-81.

Hall, S. (2012c) 'Don't look up, don't look down: Liberal criminology's fear of the supreme and the subterranean', *Crime, Media, Culture*, 8(2), 197-212.

Hall, S. and Winlow, S. (2015) *Revitalizing Criminological Theory: Towards a New Ultra-Realism*, London: Routledge.

Hall, S., Winlow, S. and Ancrum, C. (2008) *Criminal Identities and Consumer Culture*, Oxford: Willan.

Harvey, D. (1989) *The Condition of Postmodernity*, Oxford: Blackwell.

Harvey, D. (2005) *A Brief History of Neoliberalism*, Oxford: University Press.

Harvey, D. (2010) *The Enigma of Capital*, London: Profile.

Harvey, D. (2014) *Seventeen Contradictions and the End of Capitalism*, London: Profile.

Harvey, G., Rhodes, C., Vachhani, S.J. and Williams, K. (2017) 'Neo-villeiny and the service sector: The case of hyper flexible and precarious work in fitness centres', *Work, Employment and Society*, 31(1), 19-35.

Hatton, E.E. (2011) *The Temp Economy*, Philadelphia: Temple University Press.

Hayek, F.A. (1945) 'The use of knowledge in society', *American Economic Review*, 35(4), 519-30.

Hayek, F.A. (2001) *The Road to Serfdom*, London: Routledge.

Hayward, K. (2013) '"Life stage dissolution" in Anglo-American advertising and popular culture: Kidults, Lil' Britneys and Middle Youths', *The Sociological Review*, 61, 525-48.

Hemmings, C. (2016) 'Male suicide: It's time to face the stark truth about a growing crisis', *The Independent*, Saturday 10 September, www.independent.co.uk/voices/world-suicide-prevention-day-men-emotions-childhood-biggest-killer-in-uk-under-45-a7235766.html

Heyes, J. (2011) 'Flexicurity, employment protection and the jobs crisis', *Work, Employment and Society*, 25(4), 642-57.

High, S. (2003) *Industrial Sunset: The Making of North America's Rust Belt, 1969-1984*, London: University of Toronto Press.

Hill, D. (2015) *The Pathology of Communicative Capitalism*, Basingstoke: Palgrave Pivot.

Hillyard, P. and Tombs, S. (2004) 'Beyond criminology?' in Hillyard, P., Pantazis, C., Tombs, S. and Gordon, D. (Eds) *Beyond Criminology: Taking Harm Seriously*, London: Pluto Press.

Hillyard, P. and Tombs, S. (2017) 'Social harm and zemiology' in Liebling, A., Maruna, S. and McAra, L. (Eds) *The Oxford Handbook of Criminology* (6th Edn) Oxford: University Press.

Hochschild, A.R. (2003) *The Managed Heart*, London: University of California Press.

Hochschild, A.R. (2016) *Strangers in Their Own Land: Anger and Mourning on the American Right*, London: The New Press.

Hoel, H. and Salin, D. (2003) 'Organizational antecedents of workplace bullying' in Einarsen, S., Hoel, H., Zapf, D. and Cooper, C. (Eds) *Bullying and Emotional Abuse in the Workplace: International Perspectives in Research and Practice*, London: Taylor & Francis.

Honneth, A. (1996) *The Struggle for Recognition*, Cambridge: Polity.

Horsley, M. (2015) *The Dark Side of Prosperity*, Farnham: Ashgate.

Hsu, T. (2013) 'Amazon to hire 70,000 seasonal workers, 40% more than 2012', *Los Angeles Times*, 1 October, http://articles.latimes.com/2013/oct/01/business/la-fi-mo-amazon-holiday-hiring-20131001

Hunter, D. (2008) *The Health Debate*, Bristol: Policy Press.

Hutchison, C. (2016) 'Sports Direct: My glimpse inside Mike Ashley's Shirebrook gulag', *The Independent*, 7 September, www.independent.co.uk/news/business/news/sports-direct-my-glimpse-inside-mike-ashleys-shirebrook-gulag-a7230696.html

Johnston, A. (2008) *Žižek's Ontology: A Transcendental Materialist Theory of Subjectivity*, Evanston, IL: Northwestern University Press.

Johnston, A. and Malabou, C. (2013) *Self and Emotional Life: Philosophy, Psychoanalysis and Neuroscience*, New York: Columbia University Press.

Johnston, L., MacDonald, R., Mason, P., Ridley, L. and Webster, C. (2000) *Snakes and Ladders: Young People, Transitions and Social Exclusion*, York: Joseph Rowntree Foundation.

Judt, T. (2010)) *Ill Fares the Land*, London: Allen Lane.

Kalleberg, A.L. (2011) *Good Jobs, Bad Jobs*, New York: Russell Sage.

Keynes, J.M. (2008 [1936]) *The General Theory of Employment, Interest and Money*, Milton Keynes: BN Publishing.

Klein, N. (2014) *This Changes Everything: Capitalism vs the Climate*, London: Allen Lane.

Knox, A. (2010) "Lost in translation': An analysis of temporary work agency employment in hotels', *Work, Employment and Society*, 24(3), 449-67.

Korczynski, M. and Evans, C. (2013) 'Customer abuse to service workers: An analysis of its social creation within the service economy', *Work, Employment and Society*, 27(5), 768-84.

Kotzé, J. (2016) 'Analysing the 'crime decline': Change and continuity in crime and harm', PhD Thesis, Middlesbrough: Teesside University.

Kotzé, J. (2019 forthcoming) *The Myth of the 'Crime Decline': Exploring Change and Continuity in Crime and Harm*, London: Routledge.

Lacan, J. (2007) *Ecrits*, London: W.W. Norton & Company.

Large, J. (2018) 'Spot the fashion victim(s): The importance of rethinking harm within the context of fashion counterfeiting' in Boukli, P. and Kotzé, J. (Eds) *Zemiology: Reconnecting Crime and Social Harm*, Basingstoke: Palgrave Macmillan.

Lasslett, K. (2010) 'Crime or social harm? A dialectical perspective', *Crime, Law and Social Change*, 54(1), 1-19.

Leader, D. (2012) *What is Madness?*, London: Penguin.

Lee, C.K. and Kofman, Y. (2012) 'The politics of precarity: Views beyond the United States', *Work and Occupations*, 39(4), 388-408.

Leidner, R. (1993) *Fast Food, Fast Talk: Service Work and the Routinization of Everyday Life*, London: University of California Press.

Lewchuk, W., Clarke, M. and Wolff, A. (2008) 'Working without commitments: Precarious employment and health', *Work, Employment and Society*, 22(3), 387-406.

Lewis, M. (2010) *The Big Short*, London: Penguin.

Lewis, M. (2014) *Flash Boys: Cracking the Money Code*, London: Penguin.

Lillie, W. (1968) *The History of Middlesbrough: An Illustration of the Evolution of English Industry*, Portsmouth: Grosvenor Press.

Lindsay, C. (2003) 'A century of labour market trends: 1900-2000', *Labour Market Trends*, March, 133-44.

Lloyd, A. (2012) 'Working to Live, Not Living to Work: Work, leisure and youth identity among call centre workers in North East England', *Current Sociology*, 60(5), 619-35.

Lloyd, A. (2013) *Labour Markets and Identity on the Post-Industrial Assembly Line*, Farnham: Ashgate.

Lloyd, A. (2016) 'Understanding the Post-Industrial Assembly Line: A Critical Appraisal of the Call Centre', *Sociology Compass*, 10(4), 284-93.

Lloyd, A. (2017) 'Ideology at Work: Reconsidering ideology, the labour process and workplace resistance', *International Journal of Sociology and Social Policy*, 37(5/6), 266-79.

Lloyd, A. (2018) 'Serving up harm: Systemic violence, transitions to adulthood and the service economy', in Boukli, P. and Kotzé, J. (Eds) *Zemiology: Reconnecting Crime and Social Harm* , Basingstoke: Palgrave Macmillan.

Lloyd, A. (forthcoming) 'Efficiency, productivity and targets: The gap between rhetoric and reality in the call centre', *Critical Sociology* (in production).

Lyotard, F. (1974) *The Postmodern Condition: A Report on Knowledge*, Manchester: University Press.

MacDonald, R. and Marsh, J. (2005) *Disconnected Youth? Growing Up in Britain's Poor Neighbourhoods*, Basingstoke: Palgrave.

MacIntyre, A. (2011) *After Virtue: A Study in Moral Theory*, London: Bloomsbury.

Madrick, J. (2012) 'The deliberate low-wage, high-insecurity economic model', *Work and Occupations*, 39(4), 321-30.

Martin, I. (2017) *Crash Bang Wallop: The Inside Story of London's Big Bang and a Financial Revolution that Changed the World*, London: Sceptre.

Marx, K. (1990 [1867]) *Capital. Vol. 1*, Oxford: University Press.

Marx, K. and Engels, F. (1998 [1845]) *The German Ideology*, New York: Prometheus Books.

Marx, K. and Engels, F. (2011 [1932]) *Economic and Philosophical Manuscripts of 1844*, New York: Dover Publications.

Mason, P. (2015) *Postcapitalism: A Guide to our Future*, London: Penguin.

Maxwell, J.C. (2011) 'The prescription drug epidemic in the United States: A perfect storm', *Drug and Alcohol Review*, 30, 264-70.

McDowell, L. (2009) *Working Bodies: Interactive Service Employment and Workplace Identities*, Oxford: Wiley-Blackwell.

McGowan, T. (2016) *Capitalism and Desire: The Psychic Cost of Free Markets*, New York: Columbia University Press.

McKenzie, L. (2015) *Getting By: Estates, Class and Culture in Austerity Britain*, Bristol: Policy Press.

Meloni, M. (2014) 'How biology became social, and what it means for social theory', *The Sociological Review*, 62(3) 593-614.

Messner, S. and Rosenfeld, R. (2001) *Crime and the American Dream* (3rd Edn) London: Wadsworth.

Mill, J.S. (2002 [1862]) *Utilitarianism*, Indianapolis: Hackett Publishing.

Mills, C.W. (2002) *White Collar*, Oxford: University Press.

Mirowski, P. (2013) *Never Let a Serious Crisis Go To Waste*, London: Verso.

Misra, J. and Walters, K. (2016) 'All fun and cool clothes? Youth workers' consumer identity in clothing retail', *Work and Occupations*, 43(3), 294-325.

Mitchell, B.R. (1998) *International Historical Statistics: Europe 1750-1993*, (4th edn), New York: Stockton Press.

Mitchell, W. and Fazi, T. (2017) *Reclaiming the State*, London: Pluto Press.

Mulholland, K. (2002) 'Gender, emotional labour and teamworking in a call centre', *Personnel Review*, 31(3), 283-303.

Nargiso, J.E., Ballard, E.L. and Skeer, M.R. (2015) 'A systematic review of risk and protective factors associated with non-medical use of prescription drugs among youth in the United States: A social ecological perspective', *Journal of Studies on Alcohol and Drugs*, 76(1), 5-20.

Neill, C. (2014) *Without Ground: Lacanian Ethics and the Assumption of Subjectivity*, Basingstoke: Palgrave.

NHS Digital (2015) *Psychological Therapies: Annual Report on the Use of IAPT Services: England 2014-15*, Leeds: NHS Digital, http://webarchive.nationalarchives.gov.uk/20171102141250/https://digital.nhs.uk/catalogue/PUB19098

NHS Digital (2016) 'Antidepressants show greatest increase in number of prescription items dispensed', 5 July, News archive, http://content.digital.nhs.uk/article/7159/Antidepressants-show-greatest-increase-in-number-of-prescription-items-dispensed

NHS Digital (2017) 'Mental Health Bulletin: 2016-17 Annual Report', https://digital.nhs.uk/data-and-information/publications/statistical/mental-health-bulletin/mental-health-bulletin-2016-17-annual-report

Noys, B. (2014) *Malign Velocities: Accelerationism and Capitalism*, Winchester: Zero.

Nurse, A. (2016) *An Introduction to Green Criminology and Environmental Justice*, London: Sage.

OECD (Organisation for Economic Co-operation and Development) (2015) *In it Together: Why Less Inequality Benefits All*, Paris: OECD Publishing.

O'Hara, M. (2014) *Austerity Bites: A Journey to the Sharp End of Cuts in the UK*, Bristol: Policy Press.

ONS (Office for National Statistics) (2018) 'Statistical bulletin: UK labour market: April 2018', 17 April, www.ons.gov.uk/employmentandlabourmarket/peopleinwork/employmentandemployeetypes/bulletins/uklabourmarket/april2018

Paoli, L. and Greenfield, V.A. (2018) 'Harm: A substitute for crime or central to it?' in Boukli, P. and Kotzé, J. (Eds) *Zemiology: Reconnecting Crime and Social Harm*, Basingstoke: Palgrave Macmillan.

Parenti, C. (2011) *Tropic of Chaos: Climate Change and the New Geography of Violence*, New York: Nation Books.

Pemberton, S. (2007) 'Social harm future(s): Exploring the potential of the social harm approach', *Crime Law and Social Change*, 48(1-2), 27-41.

Pemberton, S. (2016) *Harmful Societies: Understanding Social Harm*, Bristol: Policy Press.

Phillips, J.A. and Nugent, C.N. (2014) 'Suicide and the Great Recession of 2007-2009: The role of economic factors in the 50 US states', *Social Science and Medicine*, 116, 22-31.

Piketty, T. (2014) *Capital in the Twenty-First Century*, London: Belknap.

Polanyi, K. (2002 [1944]) *The Great Transformation*, Boston: Beacon Press.

Pollock, A.M. (2004) *NHS plc: The Privatisation of Our Health Care*, London: Verso.

Power, M. (1999) *The Audit Society: Rituals of Verification*, Oxford: University Press.

Price, R. (2016) 'Controlling routine front-line service workers: An Australian retail supermarket case', *Work, Employment and Society*, 30(6), 915-31.

Quinones, S. (2015) *Dreamland: The True Tale of America's Opiate Epidemic*, London: Bloomsbury.

Ranciere, J. (2007) *On the Shores of Politics*, London; Verso.

Ray, L. (2011) *Violence and Society*, London: Sage Publications.

Raymen, T. (2016) 'Designing-in crime by designing-out the social? Situational crime prevention and the intensification of harmful subjectivities', *The British Journal of Criminology*, 56(3), 497-514.

Raymen, T. (2017) 'Living in the end times through popular culture: An ultra-realist analysis of *The Walking Dead* as popular criminology', *Crime, Media, Culture*, 26 July, http://journals.sagepub.com/doi/abs/10.1177/1741659017721277

Raymen, T. and Smith, O. (2016) 'What's deviance got to do with it? Black Friday sales, violence and hyper-conformity', *The British Journal of Criminology*, 56(2), 389-405.

Raymen, T. and Smith, O. (2017) 'Lifestyle gambling, indebtedness and anxiety: A deviant leisure perspective', *Journal of Consumer Culture*, 26 July, http://journals.sagepub.com/doi/pdf/10.1177/1469540517736559

Reiner, R. (2016) *Crime: The Mystery of the Common Sense Concept*, Cambridge: Polity.

Rousseau, J.J. (1998) [1762]) *The Social Contract*, London: Wordsworth.

Scholz, T. (2017) *Uberworked and Underpaid: How workers are disrupting the digital economy*, Cambridge: Polity.

Schor, J. (2014) 'Debating the sharing economy', *Great Transition Initiative*, October, http://greattransition.org/publication/debating-the-sharing-economy

Scott, S. (2017) *Labour Exploitation and Work-Based Harm*, Bristol: Policy Press.

Sedgwick, P. (1982) *Psycho Politics*, London: Pluto Press.

Senior, P., Crowther-Dowey, C. and Long, M. (2007) *Understanding Modernisation in Criminal Justice*, Maidenhead: Open University Press.

Sennett, R. (1999) *The Corrosion of Character*, London: W.W. Norton & Company.

Sherman, R. (2007) *Class Acts: Service and Inequality in Luxury Hotels*, London: University of California Press.

Shildrick, T., MacDonald, R., Webster, C. and Garthwaite, K. (2012) *Poverty and Insecurity: Life in Low-Pay, No-Pay Britain*, Bristol: Policy Press.

Silva, J.M. (2014) *Coming Up Short: Working Class Adulthood in an Age of Uncertainty*, Oxford: University Press.

Slapper, G. and Tombs, S. (1999) *Corporate Crime*, Harlow: Longman.

Sloan, M.M. (2012) 'Unfair treatment in the workplace and worker well-being: The role of co-worker support in a service work environment', *Work and Occupations*, 39(1), 3-34.

Sloterdijk, P. (2010) *Rage and Time*, New York: Columbia University Press.

Smart, B. (2010) *Consumer Society*, London: Sage.

Smith, A. (2003 [1776]) *The Wealth of Nations*, New York: Bantam.

Smith, O. (2014) *Contemporary Adulthood and the Night-Time Leisure Economy*, Basingstoke: Palgrave Macmillan.

Smith, O. and Raymen, T. (2015) 'Shopping with violence: Black Friday sales in the British context', *Journal of Consumer Culture*, 21 October, http://journals.sagepub.com/doi/pdf/10.1177/1469540515611204

Smith, O. and Raymen, T. (2016) 'Deviant leisure: A criminological perspective', *Theoretical Criminology*, 11 August, http://journals.sagepub.com/doi/full/10.1177/1362480616660188

Soper, S. (2011) 'Workers complain about Amazon warehouse jobs', *The Seattle Times*, 1 October 2011, https://www.seattletimes.com/business/workers-complain-about-amazon-warehouse-jobs/

Southwood, I. (2011) *Non-Stop Inertia*, Winchester: Zero.

Srnicek, N. and Williams, A. (2016) *Inventing the Future*, London: Verso.

Standing, G. (2011) *The Precariat: The New Dangerous Class*, London: Bloomsbury.

Stewart, H. (2015) 'Robot revolution: Rise of "thinking" machines could exacerbate inequality', *The Guardian*, Thursday 5 November, www.theguardian.com/technology/2015/nov/05/robot-revolution-rise-machines-could-displace-third-of-uk-jobs?CMP=share_btn_tw

Stiegler, B. (2013) *Uncontrollable Societies of Disaffected Individuals*, Cambridge: Polity.

Stiglitz, J. (2010) *Freefall: Free Markets and the Sinking of the Global Economy*, London: Allen Lane.

Strangleman, T. and Warren, T. (2008) *Work and Society: Sociological Approaches, Themes and Methods*, London: Routledge.

Streeck, W. (2014) *Buying Time: The Delayed Crisis of Democratic Capitalism*, London: Verso.

Streeck, W. (2016) *How Will Capitalism End?*, London: Verso.

Stuckler, D. and Basu, S. (2013) *The Body Economic: Why Austerity Kills*, London: Allen Lane.

Sutherland, E.H. (1940) *White-collar Crime*, New York: Holt Rinehart and Winston.

Tappan, G. (1947) 'Who is the criminal?', *American Sociological Review*, 12, 96–102.

Tarnas, R. (2010) *The Passion of the Western Mind: Understanding the Ideas That Have Shaped Our World View*, London: Pimlico.

Taylor, P. and Bain, P. (1999) "An assembly line in the head': work and employee relations in the call centre', *Industrial Relations Journal*, 30(2), 101–17.

Thompson, P. and Smith, C. (2009) 'Labour power and labour process: Contesting the marginality of the sociology of work', *Sociology*, 43(5), 913–30.

Tomaszewski, W. and Cebulla, A. (2014) 'Jumping off the track: Comparing the experiences of first jobs of young people living in disadvantaged and non-disadvantaged neighbourhoods in Britain', *Journal of Youth Studies*, 17(8), 1029–45.

Tombs, S. (2004) 'Workplace injury and death: Social harm and the illusions of law', in Hillyard, P., Pantazis, C., Tombs, S. and Gordon, D. (Eds) *Beyond Criminology: Taking Harm Seriously*, London: Pluto Press.

Tombs, S. and Hillyard, P. (2004) 'Towards a political economy of harm: States, corporations and the production of inequality', in in Hillyard, P. Pantazis, C., Tombs, S. and Gordon, D. (Eds) *Beyond Criminology: Taking Harm Seriously*, London: Pluto Press.

Tombs, S. and Whyte, D. (2007) *Safety Crimes*, Cullompton: Willan.

Tombs, S. and Whyte, D. (2011) *The Corporate Criminal*, London: Routledge.

Townsend, K. (2005) 'Electronic surveillance and cohesive teams: Room for resistance in an Australian call centre?', *New Technology, Work and Employment*, 20(1), 47–59.

Traverso, E. (2016) *Left-Wing Melancholia: Marxism, History, and Memory*, New York: Columbia University Press.

Ugwudike, P. (2015) *An Introduction to Critical Criminology*, Bristol: Policy Press.

US Census Bureau (1999) '20th Century Statistics', *US Census Bureau: Statistical Abstract of the United States, 1999*, www.census.gov/prod/99pubs/99statab/sec31.pdf

Vance, J.D. (2016) *Hillbilly Elegy: A Memoir of a Family and Culture in Crisis*, London: William Collins.

Varoufakis, Y. (2013) *The Global Minotaur: America, Europe and the Future of the Global Economy*, London: Zed Books.

Varoufakis, Y. (2016) *And the Weak Suffer What They Must? Europe, Austerity and the Threat to Global Stability*, London: Vintage.

Varoufakis, Y. (2017) *Adults in the Room: My Battle with Europe's Deep Establishment*, London: The Bodley Head.

Wacquant, L. (2008) *Urban Outcasts: A Comparative Sociology of Advanced Marginality*, Cambridge: Polity.

Wacquant, L. (2009) *Punishing the Poor: The Neoliberal Government of Social Insecurity*, Duke: University Press.

Wakeman, S. (2017) 'The one who knocks and the one who waits: Gendered violence in *Breaking Bad*', *Crime, Media, Culture*, 3 January, http://journals.sagepub.com/doi/abs/10.1177/1741659016684897

Wallace, C.M., Eagleson, G. and Waldersee, R. (2000) 'The sacrificial HR strategy in call centers', *International Journal of Service Industry Management*, 11(2), 174–84.

Walther, A. (2006) 'Regimes of youth transitions: Choice, flexibility and security in young people's experiences across different European contexts', *Young: Nordic Journal of Youth Research*, 14(2), 119–39.

Warhurst, C. and Nickson, D. (2007) 'A new labour aristocracy? Aesthetic labour and routine interactive service work', *Work, Employment and Society*, 21(4), 785–98.

Weber, M. (2012 [1905]) *The Protestant Ethic and the Spirit of Capitalism*, London: Dover.

Webster, C, Simpson, D., MacDonald, R., Abbas, A., Cieslik, M., Shildrick, T. and Simpson, M. (2004) *Poor Transitions: Social Exclusion and Young Adults*, Bristol: Policy Press.

Wheatley, D. (2016) 'Employee satisfaction and use of flexible working arrangements', *Work, Employment and Society*, 1 April, http://journals.sagepub.com/doi/full/10.1177/0950017016631447

White, R.D. and Heckenberg, D. (2014) *Green Criminology: An Introduction to the Study of Environmental Harm*, London: Routledge.

Whitehead, P. (2015) *Reconceptualising the Moral Economy of Criminal Justice*, Basingstoke: Palgrave Pivot.

Whitehead, P. (2016) *Transforming Probation: Social Theories and the Criminal Justice System*, Bristol: Policy Press.

Whitehead, P. (2018) *Demonising the Other: Urgent Responses to a Moral Horror Show*, Bristol: Policy Press.

Whitehead, P. and Hall, S. (forthcoming) 'How the generative core overpowered the regulatory sleeve: The fate of public institutions from the Keynesian settlement to the neoliberal order' (in production).

Whyte, W.H. (1956) *The Organization Man*, Pennsylvania: University of Pennsylvania Press.

Wilkinson, R. and Pickett, K. (2009) *The Spirit Level: Why Equality is Better for Everyone*, London: Penguin.

Williams, C.L. (2006) *Inside Toyland: Working, Shopping and Social Inequality*, London: University of California Press.

Wilson, W.J. (1997) *When Work Disappears*, New York: Vintage.

Winlow, S. (2001) *Badfellas: Crime, Tradition and New Masculinities*, Oxford: Berg.

Winlow, S. (2017) 'The uses of catastrophism' in Atkinson, R., McKenzie, L. and Winlow, S. (Eds) *Building Better Societies: Promoting Social Justice in a World Falling Apart*, Bristol: Policy Press.

Winlow, S. and Hall, S. (2006) *Violent Night: Urban Leisure and Contemporary Culture*, Oxford: Berg.

Winlow, S. and Hall, S. (2013) *Rethinking Social Exclusion: The End of the Social?*, London: Sage.

Winlow, S. and Hall, S. (2016) 'Realist criminology and its discontents', *International Journal for Crime, Justice and Social Democracy*, 5(3), 80-94.

Winlow, S., Hall, S. and Treadwell, J. (2017) *The Rise of the Right: English Nationalism and the Transformation of Working-Class Politics*, Bristol: Policy Press.

Winlow, S., Hall, S., Treadwell, J. and Briggs, D. (2015) *Riots and Political Protest: Notes from the Post-Political Present*, London: Routledge.

Withagen, T. and Tros, F. (2004) 'The concept of 'flexicurity': A new approach to regulating employment and labour markets', *Transfer: European Review of Labour and Research*, 10(2), 166-86.

Woodcock, J. (2016) *Working the Phones: Control and Resistance in Call Centres*, London: Pluto Press.

Yar, M. (2012) 'Critical criminology, critical theory and social harm', in Hall, S. and Winlow, S. (Eds) *New Directions in Criminological Theory*, London: Routledge.

Žižek, S. (1989) *The Sublime Object of Ideology*, London: Verso.

Žižek, S. (2000) *The Ticklish Subject: The Absent Centre of Political Ontology*, London: Verso.

Žižek, S. (2006) *How to Read Lacan*, London: Granta Books.

Žižek, S. (2008) *Violence: Six Sideways Reflections*, London: Profile Books.

Index

Lightning Source UK Ltd.
Milton Keynes UK
UKHW041122101019
351350UK00003B/74/P